# SUSPECTED *of* INDEPENDENCE

ALSO BY DAVID MCKEAN

*Tommy the Cork: Washington's Ultimate
Insider from Roosevelt to Reagan*

*Friends in High Places: The Rise and Fall of
Clark Clifford* (with Douglas Frantz)

*The Great Decision: Jefferson, Adams, Marshall,
and the Battle for the Supreme Court* (with Cliff Sloan)

# SUSPECTED *of* INDEPENDENCE

## THE LIFE OF THOMAS MCKEAN, AMERICA'S FIRST POWER BROKER

### David McKean

PUBLICAFFAIRS
NEW YORK

PublicAffairs books are available at special discounts for bulk purchases in the U.S. by corporations, institutions, and other organizations. For more information, please contact the Special Markets Department at the Perseus Books Group, 2300 Chestnut Street, Suite 200, Philadelphia, PA 19103, call (800) 810-4145, ext. 5000, or e-mail special.markets@perseusbooks.com.

*Book design by Linda Mark*

Library of Congress Cataloging-in-Publication Data
Names: McKean, David (Director of policy planning)
Title: Suspected of independence : the life of Thomas McKean. America's first power broker /
David McKean.
Description: First edition. | New York : PublicAffairs, A Member of the Perseus Books Group, 2016. | Includes bibliographical references and index.
Identifiers: LCCN 2016005686| ISBN 9781610392211 (hardcover) | ISBN 9781610392228 (ebook)
Subjects: LCSH: McKean, Thomas, 1734–1817. | Statesmen—United States—Biography. | United States. Declaration of Independence—Signers—Biography. | United States. Continental Congress—Biography. | Governors—Pennsylvania—Biography. | United States—History—Revolution, 1775–1783—Biography.
Classification: LCC E302.6.M13 M35 2016 | DDC 973.3092—dc23
LC record available at http://lccn.loc.gov/2016005686

First Edition

10 9 8 7 6 5 4 3 2 1

*To the next generation:*
*Shaw, Christian, Kaye, Adam, Matthew,*
*Ben, Bobby, Sarah, and John*

# Contents

## PART III: THE POLITICIAN

*Illustrations follow page 126*

# Chronology

| | |
|---|---|
| *1734 (March)* | Thomas McKean born in New London, Pennsylvania, to William and Letitia Finney McKean. |
| *1742* | Letitia Finney dies. McKean enters Dr. Alison's Academy. |
| *1750* | McKean studies law in the office of David Finney, New Castle, Delaware. |
| *1754–1763* | French and Indian War. |
| *1762* | McKean elected to the Delaware of House of Assembly. He is reelected for the next seventeen years until he declines reelection. |
| *1763 (July)* | McKean marries Mary Borden of Bordentown, New Jersey. |
| *1765 (March)* | The Stamp Act, designed to raise £60 annually in the colonies, calls for a tax in the form of stamps affixed to newspapers, legal documents, and other papers. |
| *1765 (July)* | James Otis of Boston argues that there can be no colonial taxation without representation. |
| *1765 (summer)* | Sons of Liberty groups are formed in Boston, New York, and other colonies to oppose the Stamp Act. |
| *1765 (October)* | Stamp Act Congress meets in New York City with representatives from nine colonies. McKean and Caesar Rodney are delegates. |
| *1766 (March)* | Parliament repeals the Stamp Act but passes the Declaratory Act, stating it has the right to make laws for the colonies "in all cases whatsoever." |

| | |
|---|---|
| *1770 (March)* | British soldiers kill four Massachusetts protesters in an incident known as the Boston Massacre. |
| *1772* | McKean is unanimously elected Speaker of the Delaware Assembly. |
| *1773 (March)* | Mary Borden McKean dies at New Castle, leaving six children. |
| *1773 (May)* | Parliament passes the Tea Act to save the East India Company from bankruptcy. |
| *1773 (December)* | Known as "the Boston Tea Party," a band of men disguised as Indians and led by Samuel Adams board ships and throw 342 chests of tea into Boston Harbor. |
| *1774 (September)* | McKean marries Sarah Armitage at New Castle. |
| *1774 (fall)* | First Continental Congress meets in Philadelphia with fifty-five delegates, including McKean. All the colonies are represented except Georgia. |
| *1775 (April)* | Battles of Lexington and Concord in which Paul Revere and William Dawes summon Minutemen, who inflict heavy casualties on the British. |
| *1775 (May)* | Second Continental Congress convenes in Philadelphia with McKean in attendance. Congress votes to raise an army, and George Washington is named commander in chief. |
| *1775 (July)* | General Washington takes command of an army of fifteen thousand men in Cambridge, Massachusetts. |
| *1776 (June)* | Richard Henry Lee proposes a resolution in Congress calling for independence from Great Britain. Days later, Congress authorizes a committee to draft a formal declaration. |
| *1776 (July)* | Congress votes—McKean votes aye—to approve the Declaration of Independence, with New York abstaining. |
| *1776 (summer, fall)* | Americans suffer heavy losses in New York and are pushed south through New Jersey. Colonel McKean, commanding the Fourth Battalion of the "Associators," marches to Perth Amboy, New Jersey, and returns to Delaware in August. |
| *1776 (December)* | Washington with his army crosses the Delaware into Pennsylvania, and the British retire for the winter. |

| | |
|---|---|
| *1777 (July)* | McKean becomes the first chief justice of Pennsylvania under the first Pennsylvania state convention of 1776 and serves for the next twenty-two years. |
| *1777 (October)* | General John Burgoyne captures Ticonderoga in a stunning victory for the Continental Army. |
| *1777 (August–October)* | British General Howe defeats General Washington at Brandywine, and later at Germantown. The British occupy Philadelphia. |
| *1778 (February)* | France, which had recognized American independence the previous December, joins the United States in its war against Great Britain. |
| *1780* | British rout the Americans in South Carolina. |
| *1781 (July)* | McKean is elected president of Congress under the Articles of Confederation. |
| *1781 (August)* | Cornwallis establishes a base at Yorktown, Virginia. |
| *1781 (October)* | After a three-week siege at Yorktown by General Washington and French commander Comte de Rochambeau, Lord Cornwallis surrenders his force of nearly nine thousand men. |
| *1783* | The Peace of Paris between the United States and Britain establishes the independence of the United States. |
| *1787 (May)* | The Constitutional Convention convenes in the Pennsylvania State House, and fifty-five delegates meet over the course of the summer. |
| *1787* | McKean is elected chairman of the Pennsylvania Constitutional Convention. |
| *1789 (April)* | In New York City, George Washington is inaugurated as the first president of the United States. |
| *1789 (July)* | A Parisian mob storms the Bastille during the French Revolution. |
| *1789 (September)* | Federal Judiciary Act establishes a Supreme Court with a chief justice and five associates. |
| *1793 (January)* | The Reign of Terror follows the execution of Louis XVI in France, and conservatives in America increasingly turn against the French Revolution. |

| | |
|---|---|
| *1794 (July)* | The "Whiskey Rebellion" in western Pennsylvania occurs in which farmers protest against a tax on spirits. |
| *1794 (November)* | The Jay Treaty provides that the United States can negotiate with the British on a most favored nation basis. There is significant opposition in the United States, especially among Republicans. |
| *1796 (September)* | President Washington delivers his Farewell Address and cautions against political parties and "permanent alliances." |
| *1798 (June–July)* | The Alien and Sedition Acts are passed, providing for deportation of aliens and severe punishment for statements made against the government. |
| *1799* | McKean is elected second governor of Pennsylvania under the new constitution and the first Republican governor in the nation. He is reelected twice, in 1802 and again in 1806. |
| *1800 (December)* | Thomas Jefferson is elected third president of the United States. |
| *1802 (December)* | McKean is reelected governor of Pennsylvania. |
| *1803 (April)* | The Louisiana Purchase doubles the territory of the United States. |
| *1803 (June)* | President Jefferson gives instructions to Meriwether Lewis for an expedition to the West. |
| *1805 (December)* | McKean elected governor on the "Quid" ticket in his third and final campaign. |
| *1817 (June)* | McKean dies in Philadelphia, survived by his wife, five children, and thirty-four grandchildren. |

# Preface

I HAVE A GOLD RING GIVEN TO ME BY MY LATE FATHER THAT THOMAS McKean, a signer of the Declaration of Independence, allegedly gave to his son. It has been handed down through generations over two hundred years. At one time it held a stone carved with the family crest, but the stone was lost, and I have since had the empty setting filled with gold and etched with the family crest, an eagle clutching a serpent. For many years, the ring has been the only connection I had to the enigmatic signer. The truth is that, although I have enjoyed the ring, I never really gave my ancestor a lot of thought.

But a few years ago, I became more interested in Thomas McKean. As America, a diverse nation of 350 million people, entered the twenty-first century, I marveled at the facts that my grandfather was born during the Civil War and that only five generations separate me from the Thomas McKean who lived during an era when the population soared from five million to fifteen million. The relative generational proximity intrigued me. Who was this man born in the first half of the eighteenth century, before the United States became a sovereign nation?

I also began to notice references to him in a number of books about the Revolutionary era. He tends to make fleeting appearances but always at significant historical events. He is not trapped in one narrative: he is a soldier, yet not a career soldier or general like Washington or Nathanael

Greene; he is a politician, present from the First Continental Congress, yet free of any one affiliation or group; he is a jurist of distinction and importance, a landowner, and even an intelligence coordinator. Because of his several roles, he does not dominate in books that focus solely on one facet of Revolutionary America. He perhaps uniquely crosses over the many centers of power in the still-formative country during its most vulnerable years, and he shows the degree of flux and uncertainty that was a feature of newly independent America, at war, unsure of its future or its identity. In short, he is everywhere that is most vital. Although he had a very different temperament, he reminded me of another character I had already written about: Tommy Corcoran—a political fixer whose career spanned the Roosevelt to the Reagan eras. Corcoran was one of the most interesting American political figures of the twentieth century—a zelig, widely underestimated. I wondered whether history had accorded to McKean a similar fate, and whether his story was equally fascinating. After significant research, I decided his life was indeed a compelling one.

And there was another reason. These days, politicians like to refer to the Founders as a monolithic group, often proclaiming that they had a unified vision for the nation. Besides irritating me because it so obviously panders to a false patriotism, this claim has never struck me as being historically accurate. I at least wanted to know to what extent my ancestor had views in common with Washington, Adams, Jefferson, and Franklin, who, of course, were at odds with one another from time to time. As I began to research McKean's life, I discovered that he interacted not only with all of the most prominent men of his day but also with many of the lesser known characters—fascinating men such as Caesar Rodney, Francis Hopkinson, and Alexander Dallas—all of whom were important to the era. Their stories deserve to be told in greater detail as well.

Notwithstanding the many references to McKean in a number of sources, this has not been an easy book to research or to write. A deeply private man, McKean did not keep a diary like George Washington nor was he a prolific letter writer like John Adams or Thomas Jefferson. His story can only be pieced together through the events of his time and the observations of his illustrious contemporaries. He did write a short, self-serving monograph late in life, which is largely self-congratulatory about the mark he made on the emergence of the nation. But it doesn't come close to telling his life story. A couple of academic biographies have also tried, but despite the prodigious research, they failed because, in my opinion, they never placed McKean in the context of the times.

Thomas McKean was a patriot, a jurist, and a politician who had an impact on the rule of law in America, the politics of the new nation, and the emergence of the Republic itself. He was in every sense present at the creation. This book tells his story and, I hope, provides some insight into the turbulent times in which he lived.

# Introduction:
# The Grand Procession

IN JULY **1788,** PHILADELPHIA HELD AN ENORMOUS PARADE TO MARK another seminal event: the ratification of a new constitution. The greatly anticipated occasion celebrated not only the signing of the document but also what nationhood would mean to the daily lives of all Americans.

The path to a national constitution had not been easy. Nine of the thirteen states were needed to ratify, and there was opposition in all but a few. Delaware had been the first to ratify, on December 7, 1787, only three months after receiving the proposed document. Pennsylvania followed on December 12, and New Jersey on December 19. In the new year, Georgia ratified on January 2, Connecticut on January 9, Massachusetts on February 6, Maryland on April 28, and South Carolina, on May 23, joined in. That made eight states, with only one more needed. Three states—New Hampshire, Virginia, and New York—had scheduled state conventions to meet in June, and though opposition to the constitution was strong in each state, it was assumed that soon at least one would ratify by the early summer. Francis Hopkinson, a signer of the Declaration of Independence, hoped to make the most of this fortuitous timing by planning a July Fourth celebration. When New Hampshire tipped the balance on June 21, followed closely by Virginia on June 25, the Constitution went into effect. Hopkinson was ready to launch the "Grand Federal Procession," a huge parade through the heart of the capital of the new nation. Historian David McCullough has characterized the day "as striking as any sign of the country's energy and productivity."[1]

At dawn on July 4, on Second Street in Philadelphia, the bells of Christ Church, the first Episcopal Church in America, rang out. Shortly thereafter, the *Rising Sun,* a ship decorated with the flags of America's international allies and anchored in the harbor off Market Street, discharged its cannons. The combination of bells and blasts could be heard for miles, and Philadelphians began pouring into the streets. At eight o'clock in the morning on a cool and cloudy summer day, those marching in the parade assembled at South and Third Streets.

By nine o'clock, nearly five thousand Philadelphians had lined the streets to watch the elaborate floats, crafted and sponsored by Philadelphia's artisans, be pulled down Chestnut Street by draft horses. Representatives from forty-four trades and professions had taken the day off from their labor to march in the parade with the floats, or with bands, or simply with each other. The renowned physician and statesman Benjamin Rush observed that

> . . . every countenance wore an air of dignity as well as pleasure. Every tradesman's boy in the procession seemed to consider himself as a principal in the business. Rank for a while forgot all its claims, and Agriculture, Commerce and Manufactures, together with the learned and mechanical professions, seemed to acknowledge, by their harmony and respect for each other, that they were all necessary to each other, and all useful in cultivated society.[2]

In the harbor, ten ships anchored side by side each flew a white flag with gold letters identifying the name of a state that had ratified the Constitution, beginning with the northernmost and progressing to the southernmost. The other ships in the harbor were also decorated with brightly colored flags and pennants that billowed in a strong southern breeze.

Leading the parade, according to Hopkinson, who later memorialized the procession, were "twelve axe-men, dressed in white frocks with girdles around their waists, and wearing ornamental caps, and headed by Major Phillip Pancake." Next followed the First City Troop of Light Dragoons, wearing blue coats with red trim and riding horses outfitted with white saddlecloth trimmed in blue. Thomas Fitzsimmons, a member of Congress and delegate to the Constitutional Convention, rode the steed of Revolutionary ally Count Rochambeau and carried a standard with the date of the Franco-American alliance emblazoned on it in bold numbers. Another horseman bore a staff of laurel and olive to celebrate the Peace Treaty of 1783 and was followed by a herald with a trumpet and, finally, war hero Peter Muhlenberg riding a high-stepping gray stallion.

The biggest float of all was the Grand Federal Edifice, which featured a thirty-six-foot-high dome supported by thirteen Corinthian columns. The float was pulled by ten white horses. Not far behind was another of the largest and most festive floats, fashioned as a giant eagle painted bright blue and pulled by six horses. Atop the moving platform there sat Chief Justice Thomas McKean dressed in the scarlet robes of the judiciary, holding a staff and carrying a framed copy of the Constitution. The staff was emblazoned with gold letters that read simply "the people." McKean waved to the crowds as the float moved through the streets. Rush observed, "The Constitution was carried by a great law officer to denote the elevation of the law and justice above everything else."[3]

⊷⊷

ALTHOUGH LESSER KNOWN TODAY THAN MANY OF HIS PEERS IN THE STRUGGLE for independence, McKean was among the most prominent of the Founding Fathers during the Revolutionary era. For more than forty years, he worked in the public arena and played an important role in the early Republic's defining moments. He served in the Continental Congress longer than any other member and was the only founder who served, virtually without interruption, in the Stamp Act Congress, in the First Continental Congress, and in the Second Continental Congress. Only a few of his countrymen held as many public offices; McKean served in the legislative branch and in the judicial branch, and even assumed quasi-executive powers as president of Delaware and later as president of the Continental Congress at the time of Lord Charles Cornwallis's surrender in Yorktown. He was an early ally of John Adams and signed—was the last to sign—the Declaration of Independence. Moreover, he was the only member of Congress present on July 4, 1776, who supported independence and then followed through by turning words into action by serving in the military. As the only soldier-statesmen to sign the Declaration of Independence, McKean joined a handful of others to inject a more muscular revolutionary spirit into the early continental congresses. Without it, other influential if now forgotten signers of the Declaration who wanted reconciliation with Great Britain might well have prevailed.

McKean never lost his distaste for the British, and he never abandoned his faith in the rule of law. Perhaps no one other than Chief Justice John Marshall did more than McKean to establish an independent judiciary. As chief justice of the Pennsylvania Supreme Court, which for most of the latter half of the eighteenth century was arguably the most powerful court in America, McKean developed a body of law that was memorialized in the Dallas' Reports, the touchstone for American common law.

McKean achieved this extraordinary career by being an astute lawyer and, notwithstanding occasional arrogance, an unusually nimble and pragmatic politician. As political parties emerged in the United States, he straddled both federalism and republicanism. As the first Republican governor in the United States, McKean paved the way for the election of Thomas Jefferson and, along the way, helped establish the two-party system, including—for better or worse—the spoils system. Yet, he embraced the Federalist philosophy on many levels, especially during his time as chief justice of Pennsylvania and with his support for the federal constitution.

He held a fundamentally conservative view of the world, but he supported change at critical junctures and had an intuitive sense of both how and when to build alliances in his up-and-down relationships with Washington, Adams, Jefferson, Franklin, and other founders.

Although accused by antagonists during his time, and later by some historians, of being a political opportunist, McKean can also be viewed as the only founder, other than George Washington, who was actually bipartisan. Whereas Washington, wearing the mantle of military hero of the Revolution, remained above the political fray throughout most of his public career, McKean lived much of his revolutionary life in the thick of it. He was a Founding Father with a skill set instantly recognizable in modern political times, a wily, determined political operative who never seemed to doubt his own centrality to the major events of the day. And, in fairness, perhaps he had a point: he was present at many of them, played a vital role, and rarely lived on the sidelines during the formative decades of the world's newest republic.

# SUSPECTED *of* INDEPENDENCE

# PART I
# THE PATRIOT

# 1

## The Early Years

O N MAY 3, 1679, AS THE MIDDAY SUN EMERGED FROM BEHIND WHITE clouds over Magus Muir, near St. Andrews, Scotland, Archbishop James Sharpe and his eldest daughter, Isabelle, were riding in his horse-drawn carriage when it was intercepted by a band of "Covenanters," God-fearing Scottish nationalists. After shooting the coachmen, nine assassins drew their swords and repeatedly stabbed the archbishop as Isabelle looked on in horror.

James Sharpe, a Presbyterian minister, had been a political moderate during the decades following the English Civil War, but the English king, Charles II, nevertheless imprisoned him. Rather than spend the rest of his life in a dungeon, Sharpe converted to the Anglican Church and swore allegiance to the Crown. In return, Charles made Sharpe archbishop of St. Andrews and chief prelate of all of Scotland. Sharpe thereupon embarked on a strategy of repressing the religious practices and teachings of Covenanters—devout Presbyterians—whom he had formerly represented. The archbishop brutally enforced the Act of Supremacy, which gave the king complete authority over the church. Viewed as a traitor, Sharpe was widely despised throughout Scotland and news of his death was greeted with jubilation.

The king ordered a military tribunal to investigate the crime. John Graham Claverhouse, the viscount of Dundee, who had earned the nickname "Bloody Clavers" for his brutal repression of religious dissent, headed the tribunal. Claverhouse ordered the constable to round up dozens of Covenanters, including a well-known sympathizer, William McKean. Descended from the McDonald clan, the McKeans were highlanders from the rugged west coast of Scotland who made their living as farmers.

Standing before Claverhouse, McKean denied complicity in the murder of the archbishop but defiantly declared the killing "a wonderful deed." Claverhouse, who ironically would marry into a Covenanter family a decade later, reprimanded McKean but ultimately released him. Although a free man, McKean feared retribution and, with his wife, Susannah, fled Scotland for the north of Ireland, where many Presbyterians had already relocated. While there, Susannah gave birth to a son who they named William. Notwithstanding their Scottish heritage, from this point forward the McKeans identified themselves as Irish.

But their stay in Ireland was brief; learning of opportunities in the New World, the McKeans packed up their belongings once again. They set sail for America, leaving behind a hardscrabble, often poverty-stricken, existence for the promise of a better life. They were part of a wave of Ulster-Scots, immigrants who were traditional Presbyterians and who had battled against both their Catholic neighbors and the English overlords.[1]

The McKeans settled in Chester County, Pennsylvania, an Irish American enclave ruled by William Penn, a Quaker and wealthy member of the English aristocracy. Charles II had granted to Penn a charter for land between the 40th and 43rd latitudes totaling twenty-nine million acres. Even though he was ultimately responsible to English law and to the Crown, Penn's promise of religious freedom proved a magnet for thousands of settlers.

In the early seventeenth century, Chester County offered ideal conditions for farming. Pennsylvania and the Delaware Valley had been the ancestral homeland of Iroquois, Shawnee, and Susquehanna Native Americans. Conflict with the new European colonists eventually drove the Indians out of their coastal homes to new settlements beyond the Allegheny Mountains. They left behind lush meadows, bountiful hardwood forests, and pristine rivers and streams.

By the time the McKeans arrived, Penn had established a representative government with a governor, a council, and an assembly elected by freeholders. He granted a Charter of Privileges, which weakened but nevertheless continued proprietary rule. Governing the vast territory of Pennsylvania became increasingly unwieldy, so Penn granted the three lower counties of his colony, an area that he christened Delaware, a separate government, but one that shared a governor with Pennsylvania.[2] It was in the small hamlet of New London, Delaware, that Thomas McKean was born on March 19, 1734.

━┼━┼━

THOMAS NEVER KNEW HIS SCOTTISH GRANDPARENTS, WHO HAD DIED decades earlier. When his mother Letitia died in the fall of 1742, Thomas, only eight years old, his older brother Robert, and the two toddlers, William and Dorothea, might as well have been orphans. Their father was a failed innkeeper and likely an alcoholic, totally incapable of providing for his family.[3]

Thomas's younger brother and sister went to live with their aunt and uncle. With prodding from Letitia's parents, William sent eight-year-old Thomas and ten-year-old Robert to the Reverend Francis Alison, Presbyterian minister of the New London rectory who had recently established a boarding school for young boys. The school had only a dozen students, and Thomas and Robert were among the first. They would remain at the school for nearly a decade.[4]

In the early eighteenth century in colonial America, access to primary school education varied widely. Customarily, a parent or relative home-schooled children, although in New England a fledgling public school system was developing as was a strong private and higher education system. In most cases, social and family status determined how much education a child received. The three "Rs" were widely available, especially to whites and boys residing in the northern and middle colonies.[5]

The Reverend Francis Alison was in his mid-thirties when he took over the New London rectory. He had immigrated to America in 1743 after studying at Edinburgh University during the Scottish Enlightenment, when scholars such as David Hume, among the most brilliant in Europe, were at the height of their prominence. Well versed in Latin, Greek, and Hebrew, Alison was a serious-minded intellectual and counted among his friends Reverend Ezra Stiles, the president of Yale College. Rather than teach the elite and well connected, Alison hoped to prove that theology and science, combined with classical scholarship, could transform the raw wilderness of the New World into the base for a civilized, enlightened society. He wanted his young students to learn to think and to reason, and to become disciplined through study and careful observation. The school curriculum concentrated on Latin, English composition, and natural and moral philosophy. He also taught mathematics, which he applied to practical skills such as navigation and accounting.

The education that McKean received was based entirely on the European Enlightenment model—there was no American model. After all, McKean and the other boys were English subjects, and with 90 percent of the population living on farms there was little contact among citizens in the American colonies, and trade was largely conducted with the mother country and European capitals. There was no body of American scientific research, no American literature, and no American culture to speak of. Alison may have made the children aware of fast-growing cities such as Boston, New York, Baltimore, Charleston, and, of course, nearby Philadelphia. But these cities were dwarfed by London, capital of a faraway kingdom they could only imagine. The king of England must have seemed like some distant god.

Alison was a prolific writer, and his published essays provide insight into the philosophical perspective that he likely imparted to his students. One essay, "On the Rights of Supreme Power and the Methods of Acquiring It," is particularly revealing. Alison declared, "A good subject should bear many private injuries rather than take arms against a prince, who was in the main good and useful to the state, but if an attempt is made against him for a precedent to hurt the community, the prince evidences his disregard for the public welfare and forfeits the power committed to him." A decade later, Thomas McKean would use similar logic in opposing British rule.

Alison envisioned his students graduating to careers in ministry, education, and law. One student later recalled, "We were taught to speak and write correct English." Every morning, Alison reviewed the students' homework, or as another student put it, "we received the greatest advantage of his critical examination." Although he provided his pupils with a rigorous education, he did little to nurture their emotional well-being, preferring instead the dictum of "spare the rod and spoil the child." Charles Thomson, a classmate of the McKeans, recounted in a letter decades later that in his four years at the academy, he "never saw him [Alison] smile, nor in a good humor during that time." Another student's recollection of Dr. Alison was that he was "prone to anger."[6]

The living conditions at the rectory were spartan. The boys' lives were reduced to two rooms attached to the rectory. They slept on thin mattresses on wooden bed frames lined up one after another in one large room. They took classes and meals in a second room where a long wooden table and chairs stood. Alison led the boys in daily prayer, and they were expected to help with chores around the rectory.

Young Thomas seems to have had few boyhood pursuits beyond his studies, although by the time he was a teenager he had learned how to ride a horse and shoot a gun. Besides his brother Robert, McKean's classmates included a number of boys who would later achieve prominence and, in one case, notoriety. Jacob Duche, like Robert, would become a clergyman and give the convocation at the first Continental Congress. Charles Thomson would become the secretary of the Continental Congress and sign the Declaration of Independence, and George Read, with whom McKean shared his early years at the academy, would sign the Declaration as well. The school was just for boys; the only females McKean encountered were the Reverend Alison's young wife, Hannah Armitage, and her toddler half-sister, Sarah. Sarah was so much younger than Thomas that in all likelihood he paid her little attention, but they would cross paths again as adults.

After a decade at Dr. Alison's academy, Thomas's brother Robert, then eighteen, left for London to study medicine. It was the first time the older McKean boys had been separated, and Thomas must have felt as though he had lost his best friend.

A YEAR LATER, THOMAS MCKEAN COMPLETED HIS STUDIES WITH DR. ALI-
son and obtained a legal clerkship with his cousin David Finney, an attorney
in New Castle, who was ten years older than he and whom he barely knew.

New Castle, the capital of the lower counties of Pennsylvania and
located twenty miles from rural New London, was a bustling metropolis
of a thousand or so residents. Built on the banks of the Delaware River,
the city was a center for local commerce, mostly on the river, and boasted
ocean trade with Britain, Europe, and the West Indies. Farmers from
the countryside brought wagonloads of fresh produce to the market, and
wealthy merchants and lawyers built stately brick residences set back from
the cobblestoned streets.

One of the grandest residences in the city belonged to John Finney,
David Finney's uncle, who was among the largest landowners in the county
and one of the richest men in Delaware. David also had substantial wealth
and practiced law only because he enjoyed the intellectual stimulation.
For Thomas, the Finneys' lifestyle was unlike anything he had ever experienced. It was more than mere wealth: his cousins were educated, well
respected, and formed a close-knit family. In contrast, although Thomas
adored his brother Robert, he barely knew his younger siblings. He was
ashamed of his father, who by this time had remarried and who contacted
Thomas only when he needed help, usually to keep out of jail.

The practice of law was a fledgling profession in Delaware during the
first half of the eighteenth century. There were no law schools, and lawyers were either self-taught or spent time apprenticed to more experienced,
practicing lawyers. There were no law books, and courts did not retain
trial records. As a result, there was no indigenous American law—only a
body of law that was largely imitative of what English-trained lawyers had
bequeathed to their colonial brethren. The Finneys had acquired a large
law library, including leather-bound volumes imported from England that
provided Thomas with access to some of the most important and widely
read treatises of the era.

It was as good a start as could be had for a young lawyer in 1750.

DELAWARE'S SMALL POPULATION INHERENTLY LIMITED THE NUMBER OF legal transactions and cases; no more than a dozen formally trained trial lawyers served the lower counties. The majority of Delaware's prominent lawyers lived in New Castle because, as one lawyer observed, "the county was poor," populated by farmers who owned small properties in the countryside surrounding the city.[7]

David Finney did not know his younger cousin particularly well when the teenager arrived in New Castle, but he was happy to teach him everything he knew about the law. Finney was immediately struck by Thomas McKean's acumen and work ethic. McKean would saddle his horse and follow the circuit judges from New Castle to Lewes and then to Dover, where they presided and heard cases. By listening and observing attentively, McKean became well versed in both the language and customs of the court. Finney had more work than he could handle and directed the overflow to his protégé. Soon, McKean began to develop his own clientele; his legal business ranged from the collection of debts to contesting wills to acting as the agent for the recovery of a runaway slave. But his bread-and-butter specialty was providing legal advice to the many Irish immigrants settling in the lower counties who were unfamiliar with the common law. After only a few months, McKean was arguing cases in court by himself.[8]

By the time he was twenty, Thomas McKean had a reputation as one of the hardest-working and most effective lawyers in New Castle. His nephew Thomas McKean Thompson later wrote that he was "remarkable for his industry and preciseness." One story, perhaps apocryphal, recounted how he defended a local scalawag, a certain Mr. Buncom, who had slandered a neighbor. Represented by a prominent Philadelphia lawyer, Miers Fisher, the aggrieved neighbor filed a civil suit in neighboring Chester County. Fisher presented an ironclad case that Buncom had defamed his client. When it was McKean's turn to present his defense, he called numerous witnesses who never disputed the slander but insisted one after the other that McKean's client Buncom was a notorious liar. Because no one in the county believed a word that Buncom ever said, McKean argued, the plaintiff could not possibly have incurred any damages. The jury agreed, and Buncom was released with only a reprimand.[9]

In 1754, McKean, at only twenty years old, earned 400 pounds sterling, four times as much as the average lawyer and a staggering sum for someone of his age and experience. Later in his life he remembered that his rapid rise had elicited a great deal of envy "not only among the Juniors but also . . . some of the seniors of the profession." Though technically still a legal apprentice, McKean believed he was capable of bigger things and decided to run for election as sheriff of New Castle. Candidates for public office in larger cities such as Philadelphia often campaigned personally, but in smaller communities like New Castle, they generally allowed others, usually friends, family, and like-minded supporters, to press their case for election. McKean, however, signaling his ambition, solicited votes through placing advertisements in the *Pennsylvania Gazette*, noting that he was doing so "pursuant to a practice in a neighboring province." His brash self-promotion, advertising his ambition in the pages of the press as part of his campaign, did not win over the hearts of the voters of New Castle. Big-city political tactics lost him the election.[10]

Nonetheless this first foray into elective politics brought McKean to the attention of some of Pennsylvania's top lawyers and political figures, including the attorney general John Ross, who also served as the chief law enforcement officer for the lower counties. Two years after McKean's defeat, Ross named him a deputy prosecutor for the Crown, instructing him to "sign all indictments in and with my name." At the time, no law barred a lawyer from serving as both a prosecutor and a defense attorney, except in the same case. The deputy prosecutor position not only was prestigious but also allowed Thomas to supplement his income from private practice.[11]

❦

WITH HIS REPUTATION GROWING, MCKEAN SET HIS SIGHTS ON A LARGER stage and expanded his practice to the courts of Philadelphia, including its supreme court. At the time, Philadelphia, the largest city in the colonies and the preeminent city in America, boasted a population of thirty thousand. The steeples of the statehouse and the Christ Church punctuated the city's skyline. Its many shops offered the finest in European clothing—colorful hoopskirts from France and finely woven waistcoats and knee-length breeches from England. Import houses sold luxury items from London, such as silver and porcelain. Increasingly, local artisans, such as John Gillingham, began to produce mahogany furniture in the Chippendale style that rivaled the best in Europe. Elegant horse-drawn carriages paraded up and down wide, cobblestone streets lined with imposing red brick Georgian-style residences.

Reverend Andrew Burnaby, an Anglican clergyman from England who had traveled from Virginia to Massachusetts in 1759 and stopped over in Philadelphia on the way, vividly described the city in a travel log as "the object of everyone's wonder and admiration." Burnaby noted that "the streets are laid out in great regularity in parallel lines, intersected by others at right angles, and are handsomely built. On each side there is a pavement of broad stones for foot passengers, and in most of them a causeway in the middle for carriages."[12]

The city had evolved into a vital center of foreign trade. Its merchants shipped a wide variety of goods to inland farms and towns. Burnaby recorded that "the city is in a very flourishing state" and "inhabited by merchants, artists, tradesmen and persons of all occupations." He was greatly impressed by "the public market held twice a week, upon Wednesday and Saturday, and almost equal to that of Leadenhall" in London. Additionally, Philadelphia was a religiously diverse city with "eight or ten places of religious worship," including "three Quaker meeting houses, two Presbyterian ditto, one Lutheran church, one Calvinist ditto, one Romish [Catholic] chapel, one Ana-baptist meeting house, one Moravian ditto." The arts, education, and sciences all flourished in the "city of brotherly love"; several newspapers and magazines were in circulation; and America's first hospital had been built there, which Burnaby described as tending to "lunatics and other sick persons."[13]

Each of the thirteen colonies was separate and distinct, and Philadelphia was in many ways the most influential colonial city in terms of culture, economics, and politics; it offered numerous opportunities for an ambitious

young lawyer like Thomas McKean. He enjoyed expanding his social net-
work by spending evenings at one of the city's nearly one hundred taverns.
They were more than mere drinking establishments where patrons could
drink beer and sip Madeira. They also served as meetinghouses where clubs
and organizations gathered to carry out their business, gossip, and hatch
schemes. In some, such as City Tavern, patrons could listen to classical
music in one room, eat dinner in another, and debate politics or talk business over a whiskey in a third.

McKean's visits to Philadelphia permitted him to spend time with a
new friend, John Dickinson, a young lawyer who had first been introduced
to McKean by his older brother, Robert. Robert McKean, pursuing his medical studies in London, met Dickinson, who was studying at Middle Temple at the Inns of Court. As two young students away from home, both
of whom hailed from the middle colonies, they established an immediate
connection. They discovered that, coincidentally, Reverend Francis Alison, prior to opening his academy, had tutored Dickinson as a young boy.
Robert suggested that Dickinson meet his brother when he returned to
Philadelphia.[14]

Thomas McKean and Dickinson formed an instant and lasting friendship. Thomas saw in Dickinson, as he did in David Finney, the kind of man
he aspired to become. Dickinson, a Quaker, was a third-generation American. He had been born to wealth on his family's tobacco plantation, Crois-
adore, in Talbot County, Maryland. His father was the first judge of the
Court of Common Pleas in Delaware. Well educated and rich, Dickinson
carried himself with an air of refinement and confidence. He was tall and
thin with a long nose, taut smile, and bright blue eyes. But from the time
he was boy, Dickinson was often dogged by illness and fatigue. When, years
later, John Adams first met him at the Continental Congress, he described
him as "a Shadow—tall, but slender as a Reed—pale as ashes. One would
think at first sight that he could not live a month."[15]

For his part, Dickinson admired Thomas's earnestness, intellectual curi-
osity, and great energy. Soon after they met, Dickinson wrote Thomas that
he hoped they would be "friends to each other throughout life." In 1757, Dickinson recommended Thomas to the Inns at Court in London, considered a

prestigious capstone of a legal education after a stint in a lawyer's office. At the Middle Temple, as it was commonly known, the finest English lawyers studied to become barristers and solicitors, and each year a handful of Americans were admitted for matriculation. As Benjamin Chew, one of the most powerful lawyers in Pennsylvania and a future state supreme court justice, put it, the experience of studying in London offered "polish" as well as "the address and manner of speaking gracefully, and with proper elocution."[16]

In anticipation of his travels abroad, McKean went so far as to purchase, at great expense, English law books, one of which he inscribed, prematurely, "Thomas McKean of the Middle Temple." Though he would have undoubtedly benefited from studying English common law, he neither traveled to London nor explained why he passed up the opportunity. He was already making a substantial amount of money and may have decided that he didn't want to forgo the economic opportunity. Or he may have found himself increasingly preoccupied with sorting out his father's never-ending legal problems.

After the death of Thomas's mother, William McKean had remarried but continued to prove himself a poor businessman. He gave up farming and opened a drinking establishment in the small town of Londongrove, but the townspeople complained that he "hath for some time past kept or permitted a very ill conduct and practice . . . in permitting or suffering people to swear, curse, fight, or to be drunk." William wound up the defendant in several lawsuits involving property or contract disputes as well as actions filed by his creditors. Thomas loyally represented his father over a period of several years. However, he never wrote about William in letters or suggested that his support of his father stemmed from anything but a sense of filial duty. He seemingly considered his elder an embarrassment. When it came time for Thomas to name his own sons he would choose the names of his father-in-law, his brother, and himself—but not of his father.[17]

By the 1750s, whether defending his father or pressing the claim of a client, Thomas could be found most often in the courtrooms of the lower counties and Philadelphia pleading a case before a judge. He had developed a confident speaking style, and other lawyers marveled at his eloquence and ability to formulate a persuasive argument. Perhaps his greatest admirer was

John Dickinson, who acknowledged that he didn't like to work as hard as his more ambitious colleague. Dickinson once teased McKean that he needed to enjoy life more: "Moderation in everything is the source of happiness— too much writing—too much reading—too much idleness—too much loving—too much continence—too much law—physics or religion—all equally throw us from the balance of real pleasure." Dickinson encouraged McKean to visit Philadelphia even more frequently, writing him in flowery prose typical of the day, "if you have as much pleasure in being with me, as I have in being with you, you will come up sooner than you mentioned."[18]

In the fall of 1757, Benjamin Chew, then Speaker of the Delaware Assembly, appointed McKean clerk of the assembly, where the young lawyer acted as legal counsel for all of the legislation the legislature considered. This position not only added to McKean's soaring reputation and to his thriving legal business but also introduced him to public service. When the assembly was in session, McKean heard the issues of the day deliberated and debated. He quickly learned that the citizens of the lower counties had very little real influence and that power resided in the Penn family and the English Parliament.

Four years after his first attempt to run for elective office, McKean was ready, as he put it, to cast himself once again "on the stormy seas of politics."[19] He didn't campaign this time—there were no self-promoting ads in newspapers. He was by this point well known from both his legal and public activities, and he easily won election as a representative from New Castle, one of eleven lawyers in the eighteen-person assembly. He made the empowerment of the local judiciary his signature issue. As a practicing attorney, he had seen firsthand the disconnect between English law and its applicability to the local population. He argued that the Crown-appointed governor had too much authority over the implementation and interpretation of the colony's laws.

He served in the assembly for the next seventeen years, and for the duration of his public life he remained focused on strengthening the judiciary and rule of law.

# 2

## The Stamp Act Congress

O N A BRISK DAY IN THE FALL OF 1765, WEARING A BLACK COCKADED hat and bracing himself against the chill, Thomas McKean bounded up the marble steps of City Hall. Thirty-one years old, he was tall by the standards of the era—over six feet—with a hawk-like nose, a rigid jaw, and piercing blue eyes. McKean had arrived in New York to attend the Stamp Act Congress.[1]

Passed by the British Parliament in the spring of 1765, the Stamp Act was due to take effect just one month later, on November 1. As a result of England's Seven Years' War with France, the British national debt had nearly doubled. And with nearly ten thousand troops based in America, the Crown's expenses were expected to remain high. Parliament decided not to raise taxes in Britain, where there had been intense opposition to a tax on cider just a few years earlier, and instead to place the burden on the colonies. The Stamp Act required a revenue stamp on every legal document, newspaper, and book—even a deck of playing cards. But, more importantly, it represented the first time the British Parliament and King George III, who had ascended to the throne four years earlier, had imposed a direct tax on the colonies.[2]

Months before McKean arrived in New York to attend the congress, James Otis, a mercurial lawyer in Boston, published a radical pamphlet entitled "Rights of British Subjects Asserted and Proved." Otis joined forces with Samuel Adams, a Boston brewer, who the previous year had argued before the Boston Town Committee that Britain did not have the right to place a tax on sugar sold to the colonies. Otis railed against what he viewed as the unjust taxation of Americans, and in the summer of 1765, he and Adams stood before the Massachusetts Assembly and called on all the colonies to oppose implementation of the Stamp Act.[3]

Opposition to the act spread throughout the colonies and poured out in newspapers and pamphlets. One of the most widely read and admired polemicists of the day, Maryland lawyer Daniel Dulany, wrote a treatise with the somewhat stilted title "Consideration on the Propriety of Imposing Taxes in the British Colonies, for the Purpose of Raising a Revenue, by Act of Parliament." In his piece Dulany opined, "No Parliament can alter the Nature of Things, or make that good which is really evil. . . . There is certainly some bounds to their power, and tis pity they were not more certainly known."[4] Even though the colonists were British subjects, they had no voice in Parliament and were governed by appointed governors. Dulany conceded that the colonial assemblies had the right to tax them, but in his view, Parliament did not. Dulany's view resonated with a wide swath of the American public. In Pennsylvania, Charles Thomson, McKean's boyhood friend and now a leader of Philadelphia's resistance, summed up the reaction of colonists as willing to launch against "the works of darkness." An assemblyman in New York wrote a friend in England, "This single stroke has lost Great Britain the affection of all her colonies."[5]

On June 8, the Massachusetts House of Representatives sent a circular to the other colonial assemblies inviting them to send delegates to New York in October to "consider of a general and united, dutiful, humble Representation of their condition to his majesty and the Parliament, and to implore relief." Nine assemblies responded to the invitation. New Hampshire declined (although later approved of the proceedings). The colonial governors of Virginia, North Carolina, and Georgia refused to convene the assemblies to elect delegates. The governor of Delaware also refused to convene the assembly, but assemblymen from each of three counties met anyway and chose McKean and Caesar Rodney to represent them. McKean had recently been appointed a judge of the Court of Common Pleas in New Castle, Delaware. Unlike some judges, who pledged to close their courts rather than pay for the hated stamps, McKean went a step further. He promised to keep his court open, but in defiance of the act, he used unstamped documents. He could have been tried by a British admiralty court and, if convicted, sent to jail. Because he was a prominent lawyer and a judge who vowed so boldly to defy the British, McKean was an obvious choice to represent Delaware.[6]

Over the summer, before the congress convened, opposition to the act turned violent—first in Massachusetts, where a mob calling themselves the "Sons of Liberty" attacked the homes of Daniel Oliver, the Massachusetts tax commissioner, and Thomas Hutchinson, the lieutenant governor. Only weeks later, a mob in Newport, Rhode Island, attacked the homes of government officials responsible for enforcement of the Stamp Act. In Connecticut, the stamp master, charged with implementing the act, was confronted by a mob that threatened to lynch him. In New York City, a mob of two thousand marched through the city to the governor's mansion, where they broke into the carriage house, stole the governor's gilded carriage, and then burned it with his effigy in the driver's seat.[7] And in September, in Philadelphia, angry demonstrators gathered to burn down the home of Benjamin Franklin, the colonial representative who was in England at the time. The mob accused Franklin of having advocated the Stamp Act in London and dispersed only when Franklin's wife and several neighbors united to protect the house.[8]

◆—◁ ▷—◆

UPON ENTERING THE GREAT ROOM IN NEW YORK'S CITY HALL, MCKEAN scanned the room, searching for his colleagues, John Dickinson and Caesar Rodney. It was in the Delaware Assembly where McKean first met Caesar Rodney, a wealthy and civic-minded lawyer who became not only a trusted political ally but a good friend as well. Rodney, a landowner and politician from Kent County, was six years older than McKean. It would have been easy for McKean to spot him in the crowd of legislators that day because of his distinctive appearance. John Adams once described him as "the oddest looking man in the world; he is tall, thin and slender as a reed; his face is not bigger than a large apple, yet there is a sense of fire, wit and spit and humor in his countenance."[9]

McKean also likely surveyed the great room in City Hall searching for Joseph Borden, a delegate representing New Jersey. He had met Borden two years earlier through his brother, Robert, who had left the clergy to become the first president of the Medical Society of New Jersey. Borden was the owner of a stage line connecting Philadelphia with New York, and his family had been politically active in colonial affairs for decades. He served as a member of the New Jersey Assembly. Unlike the McKeans of Delaware, the Bordens of New Jersey were wealthy, politically connected, and socially prominent.[10] McKean and Borden were politically aligned, but it was not politics that had brought them closer together.

—+—+—

MARY BORDEN, A VERY PRETTY, QUIET, AND DELICATE YOUNG WOMAN, MET Thomas McKean in 1762. She was immediately taken with the tall, polite, ambitious lawyer. Although the Borden family was Anglican and McKean was a Presbyterian, Joseph Borden approved of Thomas and gave his blessing for marriage. On July 21, 1763, Mary Borden's nineteenth birthday, she and Thomas wed in a small ceremony at her father's home in Bordentown, New Jersey. During the candlelit ceremony, Mary's younger sister Ann stood at her side while Thomas's older brother Robert acted as his best man.[11]

In America, more than in England, the acquisition of wealth largely defined social status. Marriage to the right person, however, often offered both. As one modern observer noted, "Newspapers, with no thought of impropriety would describe a bride as 'a most amicable young lady with a handsome fortune.'"[12] Soon after their wedding, Thomas and Mary settled in New Castle, where they bought a house on one of the finest streets in the city.

Almost a year after they were married, Mary gave birth to their first child, Joseph, who they nicknamed "Josie." Thomas continued to practice law, and following in the footsteps of his Finney cousins, he invested his growing wealth in real estate. He put down roots, purchasing parcels of land in West Fallowfield, in Cumberland County, and in Chatham County. These were among the first of several tracts of land that he would acquire during his lifetime. At his death, he would own in excess of ten thousand acres.[13]

━━━

AS A CONSEQUENCE OF HIS MARRIAGE, HIS PROFESSIONAL SUCCESS, AND HIS political prospects, by the time he arrived at the Stamp Act Congress, McKean had risen far above his humble economic beginnings and seemed destined to play a role in shaping the future of the colonies in America. Although he knew Dickinson, Rodney, and Borden and had heard of men such as Otis and Adams, he personally knew none of the other delegates. In fact, most of the twenty-seven delegates to the Stamp Act Congress had never met one another. They represented different colonies with different social mores and economic bases, but the delegates were united in their desire to voice their grievances about British rule and eager to share views about the future.

They met for twelve consecutive days, including Sundays. The meetings were not open to the public, and no information about the deliberations was released. Accounts written by delegates after the congress describe the debate in Federal Hall over the abuse of power by Parliament. Many delegates adopted the argument of James Otis that Parliament could not tax citizens if it did not give them a political voice. Members of six of the nine delegations, including McKean and the Delaware delegation, wanted to take the bold step of signing some form of a petition addressed to Parliament and King George III objecting to the act's provisions. Other delegates recoiled from such direct expression of opposition to the king.

As the debates in the congress dragged on into the second week, McKean grew increasingly frustrated by the reluctance of some representatives to take a firm stand. He later recalled, "Some of the members seemed as timid as if engaged in a traitorous conspiracy."[14]

McKean's close friend, John Dickinson of Pennsylvania, drafted a proposed document, called "The Declaration of Rights and Grievances," which raised fourteen points of colonial dissent. In addition to protesting the Stamp Act, the declaration asserted that colonists possessed all the rights of Englishmen, and yet they had no voting rights. Dickinson argued that given such a contradiction, Parliament could neither adequately represent them nor directly impose any taxes upon them. It became the rallying cry for protest against the Crown: "No taxation without representation."

The congress finally agreed to vote and approved the declaration, but even after the declaration was adopted by the delegates, some refused to sign it, most notably the congress's president, Timothy Ruggles, a portly, six-foot-tall, Harvard-educated lawyer with dark eyes and a permanent scowl. Ruggles, chief justice of the Court of Common Pleas and a former Speaker of the Massachusetts House of Representatives, rose from his seat to argue that the document should be sent back to the individual colonies for their consideration. As soon as Ruggles finished speaking, McKean bolted from his chair. He strongly disagreed, arguing that the colonies had appointed the delegates to represent their interests and that they were expected to do something beyond debating and deferring decisions to their assemblies back home. Ruggles equivocated and filibustered, but McKean, like a good prosecutor, would not relent. He pressed Ruggles on whether or not he believed there was anything either treasonous or offensive in the declaration. Soon the great hall echoed with their shouts as the other delegates watched the tension turn to anger. Ruggles, twenty years older than McKean, became visibly flustered to the point that he challenged his younger and vastly more articulate colleague to a duel the next day. McKean accepted and was prepared to meet the challenge at dawn. But during the night Ruggles had a change of heart, and very early that morning he fled New York and rode back to Massachusetts. There, the Massachusetts Assembly publicly rebuked him for not signing the petition. A decade later, Ruggles would flee another encounter, this time accompanying the British army when they withdrew from Boston to Nova Scotia.[15]

After the Stamp Act Congress, as word spread of his altercation with Ruggles, McKean returned to New Castle with enhanced stature among the city's legal and political elite. He was appointed a justice of the peace in 1765 and, three years later, a collector of customs and commissioner of revenue—a powerful and extremely lucrative position. It meant, of course, that he was working for the British Crown, but he seems to have decided at that point in his career that meeting his financial goals took precedence over his political views. McKean was ambitious but also pragmatic. He objected to taxation without representation, but unlike his Stamp Act congressional colleague Sam Adams, he was not yet committed to a different arrangement with Britain.

Charged with overseeing the Port of Wilmington, McKean not only received a generous salary as commissioner but also was permitted to supplement his government salary by extracting local fees. Only nine months later he yielded the position to his wife's brother-in-law, Francis Hopkinson. It is unclear whether McKean decided that imposing fees was not so different from levying taxes and therefore resigned on principle or whether he simply wanted to help out his brother-in-law, who needed employment.

Thomas and Mary were part of the wedding party for Mary's younger sister Ann when she married the multitalented Hopkinson, who was a lawyer as well as an amateur poet, satirist, songwriter, and musician. The only thing Hopkinson did not seem to know how to do was make money. He was not a wealthy man and had five children to support. He previously had asked McKean to lend him two hundred dollars "paid in any way you may please."[16] McKean was happy to help. The two brothers-in-law started out as close friends—Hopkinson later wrote that at the time he was struck "with a certain awe" of McKean. Hopkinson would later sign the Declaration of Independence, but he and McKean would eventually part ways as the politics of Pennsylvania became increasingly partisan and bitter in the aftermath of independence.

⊶⊹⊷

THE EXTRALEGAL NATURE OF THE STAMP ACT CONGRESS WAS VIEWED IN Parliament as a challenge to its authority, but those worries were superseded by protests from British merchants whose business with the colonies suffered as a consequence of the boycott. Parliament repealed the Stamp Act on March 18, 1766, but passed the Declaratory Act on the same day, asserting expressly that it could make laws binding the American colonies "in all cases whatsoever." Even with the assertion of British hegemony, the events proved to be a humiliating defeat for the leader of the Whig party in England, Lord Grenville.[17]

That same month, as the relationship between Britain and its American colonists spiraled downward, McKean's second child, Robert, was born. The boy was named after McKean's older brother Robert, who had fallen ill months before his nephew was born. Robert had written to a friend that he "was seized with a very tedious and dangerous sickness that rendered him incapable of any business for about three months."

After completing several years as a pastor at Saint Peter's church in Amboy, on July 14, 1765, Robert both organized and presided over the first meeting of the New Jersey Medical Society. The meeting was held at Duff's Tavern in New Brunswick, New Jersey, and was attended by seventeen doctors who shared McKean's vision for the "mutual improvement [and] the advancement of the profession." The society was the first institution of its kind in the American colonies and, under Robert McKean's leadership, produced a kind of Hippocratic oath as well as a table of fees and rates, ranging from the extraction of a tooth for one shilling to the amputation of a leg for three English pounds.[18]

As it turned out, only two years later, in the summer of 1767, Robert needed to call on his medical connections when he became virtually incapacitated by illness. He consulted Dr. John Morgan of Philadelphia, who had recently married Mary Hopkinson, Francis Hopkinson's sister. Morgan's diagnosis was phthisis pulmonalis, or as he explained in a letter to Robert, "That these are Tubercles in the Lungs is highly probable from that constant irritation to cough." He prescribed "Tinctures of bark to begin with, then bitters and Elixir may come in. . . . But above all a free and temperate air is necessary throughout the whole of the disease, therefore get out as often as you can."[19]

Dr. Morgan's prescription did little good. On October 17, 1767, Robert McKean died at the age of thirty-five at Raritan Landing near New

Brunswick. To the end he had remained his younger brother's best friend. The loss of his older brother devastated Thomas, who erected a granite monument at Raritan in Robert's honor with an inscription that read in part: "An unshakable friend, An agreeable companion, A rational Devine, A skillful Physician, And in every Relation of Life A truly Benevolent and Honest Man. Fraternal Love hath erected This monument." Thirty years later, in a letter to John Dickinson, McKean remembered his "brother so long deceased" and in a moment of genuine humility and self-knowledge added, "May I die as good a man." His brother's example lived with Thomas for the rest of his life.

# 3

## A New City

B Y THE DAWN OF 1773, McKEAN WAS NOT ONLY EXTREMELY SUCCESS-
ful but appeared supremely happy as well. He had been unanimously
reelected a member of the assembly of the lower counties. He had amassed
a small fortune, largely in real estate. He had professional stature as a prominent attorney. And he had married above his social rank a wealthy wife
who had by then borne him five beautiful children. On February 25, Mary
gave birth to their sixth child, a healthy baby girl they named Ann after
Mary's sister. But in the age before painkillers, the delivery was a difficult
one, and Mary, exhausted and dehydrated, suffered from a high fever. Three
weeks later, at the age of only twenty-eight, Mary Borden McKean died.

Thomas was too devastated to speak at the funeral, so his brother-
in-law Francis Hopkinson delivered the eulogy. He described Mary: "Fair
her form, serene her mind / Her heart and hopes were fixed on high." He
went on to deliver several florid verses and concluded, "Love, peace and joy,
her soul possest." Mary was buried in the cemetery in Emanuel Episcopal
Church in New Castle.[1]

At thirty-nine years of age, McKean was suddenly the single parent of
six young children. As he labored to figure out how best to raise them, his
friend Caesar Rodney quietly stepped in to take over his day-to-day responsibilities as the Speaker of the Delaware Assembly. Thomas and Mary's

oldest child, Josie, was only nine years old, approximately the same age as Thomas when his own mother had died. Instead of sending the boy off to boarding school or having him raised by servants, McKean arranged for Josie, Josie's little brother, and the two oldest girls to go and live in Wilmington with his sister, Dorothea McKean Thompson. He was not especially close with his only sister—he hadn't grown up with her—but he believed she and her husband could provide his children with a loving and secure family environment. McKean asked Mary's parents to raise the two youngest girls. The Bordens, grieving over the loss of Mary, were only too happy to welcome the infant girls to their large home in New Jersey.

The personal tragedy of Mary's death and the dispersal of their children left McKean distraught, and he wore a black armband for many months to signify his grieving.[2] He was still a relatively young man and, as he slowly emerged from the loss, found himself strangely free to focus on something else—the politics that would thrust him into the forefront of the coming Revolution and the beginnings of the new country. He maintained the house in New Castle, but without his family to surround him, he grew increasingly lonely. He began to spend more and more time in Philadelphia, where he had many friends and where the debate over the American colonies' future with England was the essential topic of discussion. McKean stayed at an inn on High Street in the center of the city, and with introductions from John Dickinson and others, he soon found himself socializing regularly with some of the city's most politically active and connected elite citizens such as Benjamin Rush, David Rittenhouse, and Edward Shippen. He took pains to dress in fine attire, and because he was articulate, well read, and opinionated, he quickly gained a reputation as a young man on the rise.[3]

Like many of his political contemporaries, McKean was incensed when Parliament passed the Tea Act in May 1773. The act was designed primarily to shore up the fortunes of the East India Company, which was struggling under the burden of eighteen million pounds of unsold tea and competition from black market tea that was being sold by smugglers. Though the East India tea was to be shipped to the colonies and sold at below the smugglers' prices, Parliament had imposed a "tea tax" that made it competitive. Americans were outraged, and a boycott of tea spread from colony to colony. McKean was asked to join the Philadelphia City Committee, a merchants group dedicated to maintaining order as well as enforcing a boycott of English tea. As part of the boycott, the committee prohibited any ships that brought tea up the Delaware River from docking in Philadelphia. When a British ship, the *Polly*, tried, a group of angry Philadelphia merchants confronted the captain and ordered him to depart without unloading his cargo. This coterie of Philadelphia merchants, who increasingly identified themselves as "Whigs," named after the opposition party in the British Parliament, was generally committed to individual liberty and political representation. Even though American Whigs were not a political party—they had no formal organization, no hierarchical leadership, and no ideology—they vowed to boycott English goods such as tea, paint, paper, and glass unless the Tea Act was repealed.[4]

Another element within the city organizing in opposition to British rule wanted something more than political rights. In June 1774, twelve hundred Philadelphia artisans joined together to march on the State House where the City Committee was meeting. They interrupted the meeting, demanding to be heard. They made it clear that Philadelphia's working class not only wanted to participate in the political process but also wanted social equality.

The political elite of Philadelphia considered these men radicals. Even though America's colonies comprised immigrants from Britain and Europe, they had adopted a class system—albeit one somewhat different from that in England where family lineage defined status. In America, social status often accompanied wealth, and wealth was derived from the learned professions such as medicine and law. Significant wealth was usually accompanied by property, but religion also played a role in social mobility. Because America was a British colony, Anglicans were considered to be higher class than Catholics or Presbyterians. The radicals who descended on the State House were tradesmen and laborers, mostly uneducated and with little or no property. They were also primarily Presbyterians, like McKean, or Quakers, like Dickinson. And yet they wanted the same rights and privileges as the wealthier and more educated Anglican elite.

McKEAN FULLY SHARED THE RADICALS' CONTEMPT FOR THE BRITISH—BUT the unsettled question was about the appropriate alternative to British rule. He had developed a view of how society should be ordered that had been informed by his own experience. He believed that if one had natural ability, and received sufficient education, hard work would then produce great benefit, including wealth and significant influence in political affairs. McKean didn't believe that just any citizen, particularly an uneducated one, should have a voice in the affairs of state. He did not want equal rights for all citizens. He eyed the radicals warily but nevertheless agreed to work with them because he quickly understood that they could be a potent, if potentially unpredictable and dangerous, force for change. McKean's willingness to work with the radicals, coupled with his commitment to the rule of law, allowed radicals and moderates alike to trust him. This combination of political pragmatism and revolutionary zeal made him one of the most skilled politicians of his day, someone who would not only survive but also help navigate the twists and turns of an emerging American identity.

IN EARLY 1774, THE *PHILADELPHIA PACKET* AND OTHER LEADING PHILA-delphia newspapers reported that weeks earlier the *Dartmouth*, a British ship carrying 114 chests of tea, had arrived in Boston. According to the *Packet*, "the inhabitants informed the captain that they would not offer him to land or enter his cargo to the customs house." The *Packet* described how Bostonians dressed as Mohawk warriors dumped chests of tea into Boston harbor, noting, "The tea thrown into the sea at Boston is valued at 18,000 pounds sterling."[5] For Americans, the Tea Party represented an act of courageous defiance of Britain's Parliament.

Parliament responded by passing what later became known in America as the Intolerable Acts, a series of punitive measures that closed off the port of Boston, provided for the prosecution and trial of colonists in England, and authorized quartering of British troops in private homes in

Boston. The royal governor had the power to act essentially like a dictator. The Intolerable Acts sparked outrage among the colonists and a collective call for resistance to England from leaders in a number of colonies. Acting as a catalyst for action, the Virginia House of Burgess called for a new continental congress to convene in Philadelphia. Like the Stamp Act Congress before it, this new congress would comprise delegates from each of the colonies.

In August 1774, the Delaware Assembly appointed McKean along with Caesar Rodney and George Read, McKean's former classmate at Alison's Academy and now the attorney general of Delaware, as delegates to the First Continental Congress in Philadelphia. The assembly directed the delegates to maintain their allegiance to the Crown with the goal that Great Britain and the colonies should "remain bound together by mutual respect forever."[6] Although he publicly supported reconciliation, McKean was already privately flirting with the idea that the colonies should separate from the Crown. In a speech before a packed courthouse in Lewes, he inveighed against the erosion of colonial rights, accusing the "British ministry" and "a majority of Parliament" of pursuing "a plan to rob us of our dearest liberties."[7]

In the meantime, he had already made an extremely important personal decision. In early 1774, he began spending time with Sarah Armitage, also from New Castle, whom he had first met when they were children. She was the younger half-sister of the wife of his former teacher and mentor, Francis Alison. Like Mary, McKean's first wife, she was beautiful, wealthy, and socially prominent. But unlike Mary, who was only a teenager when she married him, Sarah, twenty-eight years old, was a mature, self-confident, if somewhat spoiled woman. She was not delicate and reserved but rather tall, shapely, outgoing, and independent. Her father, James Armitage, the youngest of nine children, born in Yorkshire, England, had immigrated to America as a young man. He had died when Sarah was only seven years old. He had been a judge in New Castle County and had acquired a number of real estate holdings.

Little is known of the courtship between Thomas and Sarah, except that they took long walks or carriage rides in the Delaware countryside.

That summer the romance blossomed, and only two days before McKean attended the opening of the Congress, the Reverend Joseph Montgomery married the couple in the Presbyterian church in New Castle. McKean already had six children from his first marriage, yet given both the high mortality rate of women during childbirth and the patriarchal nature of society at the time, it was not unusual for a prominent man to remarry and start a second family. He and Sarah would have five children of their own.[8]

⇥⇤

McKEAN TRAVELED TO PHILADELPHIA ON AUGUST 28 TO WELCOME THE arriving delegates. Fifty-six delegates from all of the colonies except Georgia journeyed to Philadelphia over the course of several weeks. Most had never met one another, although they were aware of the leadership roles many had played in their respective colonies. They dressed differently, spoke different dialects, and came from a variety of backgrounds and professions. Yet they had been thrown together to decide America's future with England. Many were initially overwhelmed by Philadelphia, with its large population, busy port, and broad avenues.[9]

Among the many distinguished delegates: John Jay and James Duane came from New York; George Washington and Patrick Henry represented Virginia; Samuel Chase and Matthew Tilghman arrived from Maryland; John Rutledge and Edward Rutledge made the journey from South Carolina; and Roger Sherman came from Connecticut. The Pennsylvania delegation included Benjamin Rush and John Dickinson. John Penn, Pennsylvania's deputy governor, described the group as "the ablest and wealthiest men in America."[10] Although McKean had earned substantial wealth, he was still not as rich as most of the other delegates. Nonetheless, as a result of his participation in the Stamp Act Congress a decade earlier, he had instant stature among his peers.

John Adams and John Hancock, delegates from Massachusetts, arrived on August 29 "dirty, dusty and fatigued" after a long journey. They signed for lodgings at Sarah Yard's boardinghouse on the corner of Second and Market Streets, and that evening they dined with McKean and others at the City Tavern, where, according to Adams, they enjoyed "a Supper . . . as elegant as was ever had upon a table."[11]

Thirty-eight years old, John Adams was short, stout, and balding, but what he lacked in physical stature, he compensated for with passion, blunt speech, and clear-eyed determination. McKean paid great attention to his own appearance and likely noticed that Adams dressed plainly, in contrast to Hancock, who always appeared elegantly attired. Notwithstanding their sartorial differences, Adams and Hancock were close friends; they shared a passion for independence, underscored by the fact that the British had offered £1,500—a significant sum—for the capture of each man. Adams didn't want war with Britain, but he believed it was inevitable. Only months later he would write of relations with England, "I am as fond of Reconciliation as any, [but] the cancer is too deeply rooted, and too far spread to be cured of anything short of cutting it out entirely."[12]

Adams sized up other men quickly. Deeply insecure, he was also highly ambitious and contemptuous of those he regarded as his intellectual or moral inferiors. Weeks before arriving in Philadelphia, he had written his wife Abigail, "I will not see blockheads, when I have a right to disagree, elevated above me."[13] He was impressed by McKean's long history of opposition to British rule and during dinner that first night in Philadelphia peppered him with questions about his experience as a delegate to the Stamp Act Congress. McKean recounted the contentious debate in City Hall and his heated confrontation with Timothy Ruggles, whom Adams knew from Massachusetts political circles. Adams recorded in his diary later that evening how McKean had been "treated pretty cavalierly" by Ruggles.[14]

Adams and McKean were both members of the bar, and McKean estimated that of the fifty-five total delegates, twenty-two were lawyers. They agreed that the prominence of lawyers in the Congress would contribute to an orderly debate and decision-making process and be essential to establishing the future governance framework for the colonies.[15]

Beyond the stories and the cheerful banter, Adams would later write that he was immediately struck by McKean's passion and his vision for the colonies—which at the time likely meant nothing more than creating a loose affiliation. Of McKean, along with Caesar Rodney and Patrick Henry, the young, eloquent firebrand from Virginia, Adams concluded, "Those three appeared to me to see more clearly to the end of the business than any others of the whole body."[16]

The delegates had considered meeting at the Pennsylvania State House but decided against it because Tory sympathizers dominated the state assembly. Instead, on September 5, 1774, they convened in Carpenters' Hall, a two-story, Georgian-style brick building set back from Chestnut Street that had been constructed by the Carpenters' Company. Peyton Randolph of Virginia gaveled the First Continental Congress to order, and the delegates, organized by delegation, including the newly married McKean representing Delaware, took their seats at tables in the great room on the first floor as sunshine streamed through the large Palladian windows.[17] There, for the next two months, they debated the relationship of the colonies to the Crown. At one point Adams told Henry, "I expect no redress, but, on the contrary, increased resentment and double vengeance." Henry said simply, "We must fight."[18]

⟞⟞ ⟝⟞

ONE OF THE LEADERS OF THE PENNSYLVANIA DELEGATION WAS JOSEPH Galloway, a contemporary of Benjamin Franklin's son William. Galloway, Speaker of the state assembly, opposed the status of Pennsylvania as a proprietary colony of the Penn family, and in the First Continental Congress he laid out a bold plan to unite the colonies. On September 28, 1774, Galloway proposed to the delegates assembled in the State House a "Plan of Union" that would have created a continental legislature to deal with internal problems but would have left external relations to the Parliament and King. The plan held little appeal for McKean because Galloway proposed that the colonies be governed by an American president—appointed by the king. Congress narrowly defeated Galloway's plan.

Another of Galloway's colleagues in the delegation was John Dickinson, who was elected a delegate in October 1774. To celebrate his election, the Pennsylvania Assembly invited foreign dignitaries, as well as every member of Congress, to the City Tavern on Walnut Street, the favorite meeting place for many of the Founding Fathers. McKean was there, dressed in a dark red velvet jacket and seated alongside his friend and colleague Caesar Rodney. Although McKean and Dickinson had remained fast friends since their youth, at this time their views of the future relationship between the colonies and the Crown differed significantly. In Congress the Quaker lawyer had emerged as the leading voice for reconciliation with Britain, while McKean was more skeptical, favoring a boycott of British imports.

McKean was always respectful and friendly to Dickinson, but John Adams had less patience with him. In late June, after Dickinson drafted a petition asking the king to intervene on behalf of reconciliation, Adams wrote a letter to a friend in Boston, James Warren, in which he referred to Dickinson as a "piddling genius" who gave "a silly cast to the whole proceedings."[19] The British intercepted the letter and released it to a number of Tory newspapers. The day after the letter was published, Adams arrived at the State House and sheepishly bowed to Dickinson as he entered the chamber. Dickinson turned his back and continued to ignore him for weeks afterward.

The First Continental Congress adjourned on October 26, 1774, after adopting a statement of general principles outlining their grievances with the Crown as well as a pact for nonimportation of English goods. They also agreed to work together and communicate with one another in resisting the Intolerable Acts imposed by Great Britain. Finally, they moved to convene a Second Continental Congress the following year if the Crown did not adequately address their concerns.

Once Congress adjourned, Thomas McKean returned to New Castle, to Sarah, and to the practice of law. Since the opening of Congress had taken place only two days after his wedding, his first months of marriage to Sarah had effectively been deferred. They looked forward to living together as husband and wife. However, their honeymoon would not last for long.

# 4

## Soldiers and Statesmen

O N APRIL 19, 1775, EVERYTHING CHANGED.
In Massachusetts, Lieutenant Francis Smith and seven hundred British troops set out from Boston to seize a store of weapons they suspected the patriots were hoarding in Concord, about twenty miles away. After a silversmith, Paul Revere, and a tanner, William Dawes, sounded the alarm and alerted militia in neighboring towns, Minutemen gathered at the Concord Bridge and the Lexington Green to intercept the British infantry. The hastily assembled militia killed eight British Redcoats, forcing Smith to order his troops to retreat. As the British fought a rearguard action back to Boston, militia continued to pour in from surrounding towns, killing or wounding another 247 soldiers. The Americans suffered 95 casualties, but they scored an astonishing victory over an army that to most colonists had once seemed invincible.[1]

Within days, the Massachusetts Committee on Safety published a handbill with a description of the attack and a characterization of the Redcoats as "Barbarous Murderers." By week's end the story was recounted in every major paper in New England and shortly thereafter in New York and Philadelphia as well. The *New York Journal* described Britain as "a vile impostor—an old abandoned prostitute—crimsoned o'er with every abominable crime, shocking to humanity."[2]

Three weeks after the battle, the British Parliament approved the Restraining Act, proclaiming that all the colonies except New York, North Carolina, Georgia, and Delaware should confine their commerce to British ports. Though he represented one of the excepted colonies, McKean increasingly questioned whether any meaningful reconciliation was still possible.

As news of the conflict spread to the other colonies, revolutionary passions were stirred and colonists began to organize themselves to defend their families, their homes, and their towns. In Pennsylvania, members of militia gathered to drill in preparation for a potential conflict with the British. There were thirty-one designated companies of Philadelphia militia, and ad hoc militia, known as "Associators." The Associators had formed three decades earlier in the backcountry of Pennsylvania and represented the state's de facto armed force. Though they formed an all-volunteer military force, every Associator was required to arm himself with a good flintlock, a bayonet, a steel ramrod, twenty-three cartridges, twelve flints, a knapsack, a powder horn, and a pouch that would hold four rounds of lead balls.

Unlike most of their fellow patriots in the Congress, Thomas McKean and John Dickinson were soldiers as well as statesmen. Within days of learning of the events at Concord and Lexington, McKean enlisted as a private in Captain John Little's company of the Second Battalion of Philadelphia Associators. McKean knew how to ride a horse and how to shoot a gun, but he had never led men into a battle, much less fought in one himself. Nevertheless, Pennsylvania's militia began forming into battalions, fifty-three in all, and McKean was commissioned a colonel after only one month of training.[3]

Dickinson, a colonel in the First Battalion, was an anomaly in the Quaker community because the overwhelming majority of male Philadelphia Quakers had petitioned the Pennsylvania Assembly to be exempted from military service. A wedge could have developed between McKean and Dickinson because McKean resented the Quakers' request and helped draft a response to the petition claiming that conscientious objectors bore "an aspect unfriendly to the liberties of America and . . . principles destructive to society and government." But, like McKean, Dickinson was determined to defend his family and his colony against British aggression, though he still hoped for reconciliation with the Crown.

For the moment, however, military duty for men like McKean and Dickinson was secondary to their political obligations as members of the Congress. On May 10, 1775, the Second Continental Congress convened at the Pennsylvania State House.[4]

━╬╬━

THE STATE HOUSE WAS AN ELEGANT, TWO-STORY COLONIAL BRICK BUILD-ing near Chestnut Street between Fifth and Sixth Streets. With arcades connecting two 50-foot wings, it was set back about a hundred feet from the street. The steeple of the main structure contained a giant iron bell with an inscription from Leviticus: "Proclaim liberty through all the land unto all the inhabitants thereof." The large room on the first floor of the State House had been the meeting room for the Pennsylvania State Assembly and served as the chamber for the Continental Congress. The room had blue-gray paneled walls, wide oak plank floors, and wooden desks covered with olive green felt cloths with high-backed Windsor chairs pulled under them. At the center of the west wall of the chamber were two large fireplaces and between them a dais with the president's desk and chair. Across the hallway from the assembly chamber was another grand room where the Pennsylvania Supreme Court convened to hear cases. With the arrival of members of the Congress, the Pennsylvania State Assembly retired to the second floor of the building, a long, rectangular room with pumpkin-colored walls. Over the course of the next several months, depending on which political hat he was wearing, Thomas McKean sat in all three chambers.[5]

The First Continental Congress, and the Stamp Act Congress before it, had been convened primarily to set out a list of colonial grievances and to seek redress from the British crown. After the events in Concord and Lexington, the Second Continental Congress had the far more grave responsibility of managing both the economic and military components of an escalating war. On June 15, the Congress named George Washington the commanding general of the Continental Army. Washington had served in the British military during the French and Indian War and, afterward, rose to the rank of colonel in charge of the Virginia regiment. Besides his significant military experience, he was known as a patriot who had spoken out against British rule after Lexington and Concord. Standing six feet two inches, he arrived in Congress wearing his military uniform. On July 3, 1775, he took command of nearly fifteen thousand men whom he described as "a mixed multitude of people under very little discipline, order or government."[6]

⊷⊶

BECAUSE OF ITS POLITICAL TRADITIONS, NOTABLY ITS PROPRIETARY government and its Quaker-dominated assembly, the path to independence for Pennsylvania was different—more convoluted—than in the other colonies. No one understood this better than Benjamin Franklin, who had risen to power earlier in the century by confronting two of the most powerful and entrenched interests in the state: the founding Penn family and the conservative yet pacifist Quakers. Franklin had been a member of the Pennsylvania Assembly and had been sent to England as a colonial agent to lobby Parliament against continued control of the colony by the Penn family, who acted as proprietors.

Franklin returned from England in 1762, and McKean likely first met him in May the following year when McKean was honored for his commitment to Dr. Francis Alison's Academy and to public education in Pennsylvania with the presentation of a master's degree from the College of Pennsylvania before a "vast" audience that included Franklin. Afterward, Franklin and McKean crossed paths occasionally, but McKean did not know Franklin especially well.

In December 1764, Franklin left for Europe once again to represent Pennsylvania before Parliament. Franklin's tireless efforts to achieve reconciliation with the British government earned him the respect of colonial leaders across America. In April 1768, Georgia appointed him as its representative before the Crown. New Jersey did the same in November 1769, and Massachusetts followed suit one year later. Including his original job as representative from Pennsylvania, Franklin now oversaw the interests of four colonies. Increasingly, he was the voice of America in Britain and well known throughout America and Europe for his publications, his inventions, and his political views. He would remain in London for another eight years.[7]

When Franklin decided to return to Philadelphia in May 1775, he was not only one of Pennsylvania's most prominent citizens, he was one of America's most powerful leaders. Within twenty-four hours of returning to American soil, the Pennsylvania Assembly overwhelmingly elected him to Congress.

Later that month, Franklin proposed that Congress establish a "confederation of states," an anticolonial union organized for the colonies' "common defense against their enemies." Even though he still favored reconciliation with Britain, Franklin knew that there were pockets of rebellion throughout America, and he believed that Great Britain would fail to differentiate between those who wanted greater independence and those who favored continued relations. Only by banding together could the colonies assert any leverage. Franklin's proposal went nowhere, but years later it would become the blueprint for the Articles of Confederation.

McKean agreed with Franklin that the Crown's strategy was to divide the colonies. According to John Adams, who made notes on the debate in Congress, McKean declared, "Their design is insidious," because no one colony "had less virtue than others." He proposed that all the colonies should unite and close off their ports to British ships.[8]

Also joining Franklin in the Pennsylvania congressional delegation was one of the richest men in America, Robert Morris. Born in Liverpool, England, in 1734, Morris immigrated to Oxford, Maryland, when he was thirteen years old. At age twenty he joined a shipping company, quickly rose to the status of partner in the enterprise, and soon thereafter gained a reputation as one of the smartest investors in America. He was a large man, tall and stout, and had little time for those he considered his intellectual or social inferior whom he routinely referred to as "vulgar souls." He favored reconciliation with Britain—not for any ideological or political reasons, but rather because he believed that war would negatively affect trade and therefore his profits.

⊷⊱⊰⊶

ALTHOUGH McKEAN ADVOCATED AN ECONOMIC BOYCOTT OF BRITAIN, THE fact that he was also assuming an increasingly active role in the military affairs of the Congress was a clear indication that his confidence in possible reconciliation with Britain was waning. He chaired five committees and was secretary of the prestigious Secret Committee, created on September 18, 1775, which acted as a war council with the immense responsibility of obtaining the necessary weapons, supplies, and men to defend against the vastly more powerful, better-equipped, and wealthy motherland. In the fall of 1775, the committee made a bold decision and began quietly working to raise men and resources for an armed force that would launch a surprise attack on the British in Quebec, Canada.

The plan to invade Canada had been hatched in the spring of 1775 by Ethan Allen and General Benedict Arnold, who had led the attack and successful capture of Fort Ticonderoga weeks earlier. They argued that the rebels needed to inflict a serious blow against the British before they could reinforce the Canadian border. Given the increasing level of British militarization in the colonies—Washington estimated that there were at least five thousand British troops in Boston alone—Congress approved the expedition during the summer. On New Year's Eve 1775, Allen and Arnold led four hundred troops during a blinding snowstorm in an attack on Quebec City. They met stiff resistance from the Redcoats. Arnold was badly wounded, three hundred men were captured, and another hundred were killed in battle. The Canadian expedition, the first organized military campaign by the Continental Army, had failed miserably.

For many in Congress, the defeat only confirmed that the colonies should cut their losses and seek reconciliation with Britain. But McKean became even more determined. In early 1776, Edward Tilghman, a prominent Philadelphia lawyer, confided in John Dickinson that McKean leaned too far toward independence and away from the reconciliation with Britain that he and Dickinson favored. The colonies were engaged in armed conflict with Britain, but for men like Tilghman and Dickinson, the purpose was to convince Parliament that the colonies deserved a greater degree of autonomy, but not a separation. "McKean," Tilghman wrote somewhat conspiratorially, is "suspected of independence."[9]

# 5

## The Fight for Independence

J ANUARY 17, 1776, WAS BITTERLY COLD. A HEAVY SNOW WAS FALLING
when the dispatch rider arrived at the headquarters of General Washington in Cambridge, Massachusetts, with the news of the Continental Army's defeat at Quebec. Washington immediately called a meeting of his war council for the following morning to review their military strategy. The cold weather made it virtually impossible to launch an attack against the British, who were ensconced in nearby Boston, and the "feeble state" of his army prevented him from sending any reinforcements to Canada. Making matters more complicated, Washington had received intelligence that British soldiers, led by General Howe, were preparing to sail from Boston south to Staten Island, where they could potentially launch an attack on New York City through its exposed harbor and with the support of its significant Loyalist population. If the British captured New York, Washington knew Pennsylvania would be next.[1]

No colony had been more committed to the mending of relations with England than Pennsylvania. Because of its large population and economic power, it dominated its neighbors in the mid-Atlantic; Delaware, New Jersey, and Maryland regularly followed its lead. The "Keystone State," as it was commonly referred to after independence, divided the north from the south. Philadelphia's port was the busiest and most important in America and served as economic gateway between the two regions. Not surprisingly, the British considered Pennsylvania along with New York as the two most strategically important colonies.[2]

While British generals plotted, Pennsylvania's politicians squabbled over the nature of the relationship they wanted with Great Britain. There was a byzantine quality to Pennsylvania's politics: the assembly, controlled by men such as John Dickinson, favored reconciliation, while the Philadelphia City Committee, controlled by radicals and chaired by McKean, increasingly favored independence. Complicating matters, the assembly appointed the delegates who represented Pennsylvania in the Congress. McKean, of course, was also a delegate to the Congress—but from neighboring Delaware. Because Congress played an executive role and had no legislative function, the colonial assemblies provided instructions as to how the delegates should vote on key issues. This made for a confusing and often frustrating process whereby delegates claimed they would have to abstain on a vote until they received instructions from their home state. Those delegates who now supported independence—by no means a majority at this juncture—knew independence could not be achieved without the support of the sharply divided Pennsylvania delegation.[3]

Adding to the confusion, during the first half of 1776 members of Congress were gathering conflicting information. In early February, they learned from London newspapers published the previous November that Prime Minister Lord North was sending a large number of reinforcements for a major military campaign later in the year. A month later, the London press reported that King George was sending peace commissioners to negotiate an end to the conflict. Then, in early May, members of Congress learned from an Irish newspaper that the king had hired as many as twelve thousand German mercenaries to come to America to suppress the colonists.[4] This final bit of news, though hinted at previously by the king and therefore known to American colonists, outraged McKean. It was one thing for Parliament to pass laws taxing the colonists but quite another for the king to pay foreign soldiers to enforce English laws. McKean concluded the king had become a despot who ruled capriciously with no respect for the rule of law and with little regard for his subjects.

Though McKean never revealed exactly when he committed himself to independence, news of German mercenaries clearly influenced him; he cast his lot with revolutionaries like Adams. He knew he could work with Caesar Rodney to persuade the Delaware Assembly to permit the delegation to vote their conscience, but McKean worried about his adopted state of Pennsylvania. He would need to find a creative solution to bypass the assembly, and he found it in the Philadelphia City Committee, the quasi-political organization composed of local merchants opposed to British interference in their affairs that he had joined three years earlier.

McKean's position as the chairman of the Philadelphia City Committee meant that he had aligned himself with a group of Pennsylvania farmers, artisans, and working-class activists with whom he actually had very little in common. The committee was led by men such as Timothy Matlack and Dr. Thomas Young, whom McKean, according to the historian William Hogeland, "would have considered, under normal circumstances . . . unfit for his company." Matlack, forty-one years old, was a failed brewer, while Young, forty-four years old, hailed from Massachusetts, where he had been a follower of Sam Adams.[5]

These men were in trade, not members of a learned profession, and they were more radical than McKean, who was a classic liberal. In many respects McKean's political views anticipated the political philosophy of John Stuart Mill a half century later. The chairman of the City Committee embraced the virtues of democracy, but only to a limited extent; he believed that political participation should be based on a stake in society, most clearly represented by property rights. McKean believed, as did many liberals of his day, that the rule of law must be the bedrock of democracy and that an educated elite should lead the rest of society. Knowing the radicals in Pennsylvania favored expanded political participation regardless of property ownership, McKean wisely kept his more elitist views to himself and focused only on deteriorating colonial relations with Britain, on which there was a broad consensus.

The radicals saw in McKean a bundle of contradictions but nevertheless considered him someone who might be useful to their cause. He was a prominent Whig who seemed to value his rising social stature in

Philadelphia, yet he clearly loathed British rule. He was a close friend of John Dickinson, a conservative member of the Pennsylvania Assembly, yet he clearly had aligned himself in the Continental Congress with John Adams, who was known to be a radical on the issue of independence. He could be patient and listen to the arguments on all sides, but he was also a formidable debater who arrogantly dismissed any argument he deemed poorly constructed.

Matlack and Young, alarmed by worsening relations with Britain in early 1776 and by what they perceived as a tepid and dithering Continental Congress, paid a visit to McKean at his lodgings, likely Clarke's Inn, located in a grove of walnut trees opposite the State House. They wanted to know if there was any way to break the logjam in Congress. McKean advised the radicals that the only way to change the dynamic was to change the profile of the Pennsylvania delegation; to that end they needed to actually alter the composition of the Pennsylvania Assembly. Because he was serving as both a delegate to the Congress and a member of the state assembly, Dickinson was in the ironic position of giving himself and the other members of the Pennsylvania congressional delegation their marching orders.[6] Although McKean despaired that Dickinson still believed that conflict with Britain could be avoided and that reconciliation might be possible, he continued to refrain from personally or publicly criticizing his close friend.

With encouragement from John Adams, McKean and the radicals hatched a plan to expand the Pennsylvania Assembly by adding seats from the western part of the state, which they argued was underrepresented and, more importantly, was a hotbed of anti-British sentiment dating from set-tlers' sympathy for the French during the French and Indian War.

When the City Committee formally presented their petition for an expansion to the assembly in early 1776, the legislature balked; Dickinson and other delegates argued that the size and apportionment of seats in the assembly was both adequate and reasonable. The committee refused to back down and threatened to call a provincial convention—a citizen caucus—and simply bypass the assembly. Unwilling to plunge the state politic into turmoil, Dickinson and the assembly agreed to add seventeen seats, and, just as the City Committee had recommended, the new representatives hailed from the western part of the state. McKean, Adams, and the other radicals believed they had reason to celebrate: the additional seats would give the radicals a majority in the assembly and allow for a change in the instructions to Pennsylvania's congressional delegation.

But their euphoria was premature. With the new representatives in their seats, the assembly took a vote on May 1, but to the shock of conservatives and radicals alike, the majority of assemblymen once again voted for reconciliation. McKean was disappointed, but not willing to give up. There was still hope in Congress, where Adams was pressing for a resolution that he and Richard Henry Lee, a delegate from Virginia, had written calling for independence. The word was now out in the open and before Congress. Adams had also introduced a resolution calling on the states to dissolve their governments and form new ones in the hope that new state assemblies would permit their delegations in Congress to vote their conscience. Most of Adams's colleagues ignored him. McKean did not.[7]

⊷⊹⊹⊱

McKEAN COULD BE AS IMPERIOUS AS HIS MASSACHUSETTS COLLEAGUE, BUT unlike Adams, he knew how to charm his adversaries. He cajoled fellow congressional delegates wherever and whenever he could get in a word, buttonholing them outside the State House, and engaging them in the city's coffeehouses and taverns. He urged them to go to their home states and to lobby for new instructions from their legislatures to vote for independence. He summoned the most persuasive arguments, as though he were still a young prosecutor, and impressed on any colleague who would listen the rationale for seeking independence.[8]

The colonies were deeply divided over the question of independence. In many of them the issue pitted town against town, neighborhood against neighborhood, and even family members against one another. Years later McKean would describe this period as one during which Pennsylvania was not part of a "nation at war with another nation, but involved in a civil war." He plotted with his fellow City Committee radicals, Thomas Mifflin and Timothy Matlack, to take another run at the assembly. They prepared pamphlets for distribution and the circulated fliers and bills to be posted around the colony. The pamphlets declared that the City Committee hoped to "prevent your being deceived."

As part of its campaign, the City Committee dispatched its members to every county in the colony to explain to fellow citizens what was at stake and to seek their support. On April 29, McKean rode to Reading, a large town in the middle of Pennsylvania sixty miles from Philadelphia, where the colony's iron industry was located and where armaments were being manufactured for the soldiers. It was also the county seat, home to a large portion of the colony's German population, and considered a gateway to the backcountry. There, McKean held a town meeting, told Reading's citizens about the Continental Congress, and explained it had voted to allow militiamen to participate in local elections, a change that would lead to a much more democratic process and, perhaps, as he and other radicals hoped, a new assembly supportive of an independent United States. Greatly inspired by McKean's indefatigability, Benjamin Rush, the physician and political activist, told his wife that success depended "chiefly upon Colonel McKean and a few more of us for the salvation of the Province."[9]

By the middle of May, McKean seemed to be wearing a different political hat almost every day. On May 15, John Adams presented to Congress the preamble for the Lee resolution on independence that stated the colonies ought to be "free and independent states." Adams felt it was critical to provide the political rationale for the resolution, which, as one historian described it, was "precise and technical."[10] The preamble, in contrast, was replete with Adams's colorful, at times biting, rhetoric that denounced England and the loyalty oaths to the king. According to the Massachusetts patriot, King George "excluded the inhabitants of the United Colonies from the protection of his crown." Standing before fellow delegates, his voice rising, a red-faced Adams pounded the table, declaring the necessity of "the exercise of every kind of authority under the said crown be totally suppressed, and all the powers of government exerted under the authority of the people of the colonies."[11]

As soon as Adams finished his presentation, James Duane from New York asked to be recognized. Duane opposed the preamble and favored reconciliation with Britain, but his rejection of Adams's argument was not based on substance but rather on the by then familiar excuse that, under instructions from the New York State Assembly, he did not have the authority to vote for Adams's resolution. McKean rose to support Adams, but on this occasion his argument was anything but radical. He knew that pro-independence delegates feared the arrival of foreign mercenaries: "I think," he said, "we shall lose our liberties, properties, and lives too, if we do not take this step [to declare independence]." But McKean also recognized that pro-reconciliation delegates might be nervous that Adams's preamble was too radical, so he never mentioned the word "independence"—instead framing his support for both the preamble and the resolution in terms of *security*. McKean maintained that the measure might actually bring the colonies and Great Britain closer together if the king could be convinced that the colonies only wanted to live free without fear and in peace. It was a politically shrewd argument designed to influence the fence-sitters.[12]

Five days later, on May 20, McKean was back among the Pennsylvania radical leaders behind the State House attempting to dissolve the government—not the royal government that ruled the colonies, but the Assembly of Pennsylvania that he and others had tried to reform through elections earlier in the month. In a drenching rain, more than four thousand citizens had gathered within the brick-walled yard. Workmen had constructed a stage on which McKean joined Timothy Matlack and Daniel Roberdeau, a popular militia commander and timber merchant. Roberdeau began the meeting by reading the congressional resolve of May 15 that called for the formation of new state governments and the abandonment of British rule.

According to John Adams, who was in the crowd, Roberdeau spoke "with a loud stentorian voice that might be heard a quarter of a mile." Adams recorded that the crowd responded with "three cheers, hats flying as usual." Next, McKean approached the rostrum wearing his trademark cockaded black hat. He described to the audience how the Philadelphia City Committee had petitioned the assembly to alter the instructions to the congressional delegation. He bemoaned that Pennsylvania's delegates opposed independence; they had been ordered by the assembly to support restoration of "union and harmony between Great Britain and the colonies." The crowd booed the assembly. McKean declared that the bond between Britain and the colonies had been ruptured. He denounced the assembly, and the audience booed even louder. Raising his voice, McKean declared the citizens of Pennsylvania deserved to have their voices heard and that Pennsylvania should inaugurate a new state government through a constitutional convention. The crowd shouted huzzahs and once again tossed hats into the air.[13] William Bradford, the official printer for the Congress, was in the crowd that day and later noted that the meeting marked "a coup de grace to the King's authority."[14]

That evening John Adams wrote to James Warren, Speaker of the Massachusetts Lower House, describing the town meeting that he had witnessed that afternoon in Philadelphia. Adams was impressed by the size of the crowd and greatly encouraged by their spirit and determination. He told Warren the rally for independence had been conducted with "great order, decency and propriety." It also marked McKean as a populist leader who was beginning to hone the political skills that would propel him to the highest echelons of American government.[15]

# 6

## War

On June 7, 1776, Congress passed the Lee-Adams Resolution on independence. Now what was needed was a statement of principle that colonists throughout America could rally around. Four days after passing the Lee-Adams Resolution, Congress appointed a committee of five delegates, consisting of John Adams, Benjamin Franklin, Roger Sherman, Robert Livingston, and Thomas Jefferson, to write a declaration of independence for the consideration of the larger group. Adams suggested, and his colleagues quickly agreed, that Jefferson should prepare the first draft. Tall, taciturn, and elegant, Jefferson was only thirty-three years old, but, as Adams would later write, he had "a reputation for literature, science and a happy talent for composition."[1]

Notwithstanding the charge to conceptualize American independence, Congress remained divided, and nowhere was this more evident than in the middle colonies. On June 13, McKean traveled by coach to New Castle and the following day placed before the Delaware Assembly the May 15 resolve permitting the state congressional delegations to vote their conscience. The word "independence" was absent from the resolution, which instead stressed "promoting the liberty, safety, and interests of America." Joined by Caesar Rodney, his Delaware colleague, McKean pleaded with the assembly to suspend the proprietary government and to issue new instructions to the congressional delegation. In spite of the misgivings of many members of the Delaware Assembly, the resolution was "unanimously" adopted, and McKean returned to Philadelphia, where he reported to John Adams that he and Rodney now had "full powers" to vote for independence. Tiny Delaware had taken a pivotal step in the quest for independence.[2]

On the same day that McKean had placed the May 15 resolve before the Delaware Assembly, the Pennsylvania Assembly adjourned without having taken a position on independence during its three-week session. In response, the City Committee convened its members to decide on a course of action. Benjamin Franklin had been chosen to lead the gathering, but when he became immobilized by an attack of gout, the conference presidency passed to McKean. He was one of the few delegates with any experience in committee-style politics, recognized as someone who could manage an orderly gathering and make sure that all who wanted to speak could have their voices heard.[3] McKean, already driving the political direction of Delaware, now found himself holding the levers of power in Pennsylvania as well.

On June 18, more than a hundred noisy delegates, mostly small farmers and tradesmen, crowded into Philadelphia's Carpenters' Hall. McKean gaveled the meeting to order. As the room quieted, he announced that the purpose of the meeting was to provide a new constitution for the state of Pennsylvania, and he read a resolution calling for the annulment of the existing one. It passed unanimously. Next, he proposed a convention to frame a new state constitution. Again, there was overwhelming approval. Finally, McKean explained that independence could only be realized if the conservatives in Pennsylvania's delegation to Congress were replaced. Again, there was not a single dissenting voice. Afterward, the delegates celebrated with cheers, the ringing of bells, and bonfires. McKean and the City Committee had declared the independence of Pennsylvania from colonial rule. They would write their own constitution, elect their own delegates, and decide their future without Tory interference.

McKean was pleased by the outcome, but not entirely comfortable in his role as a radical leader. He supported independence but continued to be wary of what he viewed as the radicals' vision of a workers' democracy. Democracy, in his view, had to be carefully nurtured and administered by an educated elite—by men like him. Moreover, he recognized that declaring the independence of Pennsylvania did not mean that the congressional delegation would be replaced anytime soon.

This was made clear when, on June 28, Jefferson's declaration, edited by Adams, Franklin, and Jefferson himself, was presented to the Continental Congress. Adams's pro-independence faction had gained momentum, but victory was still far from certain. Each state would cast its ballot yes or no based on a majority vote within the respective delegation. Those delegates favoring independence agreed that simply winning a majority of the states would not be sufficient; independence required unanimity.

Every available vote would be needed, but Pennsylvania was still a problem. The delegation was badly split over independence, with Franklin leading the supporters and Dickinson leading the opponents. Neither could Delaware be considered safely in the independence column: although McKean supported independence, the other delegate from Delaware, George Read, did not. Delaware's deciding vote belonged to the third delegate, Caesar Rodney. And he, crucially, was not in Philadelphia.

Rodney supported independence, but he had returned to his home in Dover to quell an uprising by British loyalists. In Kent County, Delaware, five thousand citizens had signed a petition *denouncing* independence and were threatening violence. In addition to his role as a delegate to the Congress, Rodney served as Speaker of the Delaware Assembly and the de facto county sheriff. He ordered the arrest of the loyalist leader who had organized the demonstration. When a mob assembled to protest the arrest, Rodney summoned the local militia. Calm was restored, but the atmosphere remained tense.[4]

On July 1, members of Congress arrived at the Pennsylvania State House under a cloudless sky. At nine o'clock, President Hancock called the Congress to order and immediately began to read from a pile of papers on his desk that included a letter from George Washington, one from Benedict Arnold, and others from the conventions of New Jersey and New Hampshire—all concerning the flagging military campaign.

The church bells struck noon, and Hancock announced that Congress would "resolve itself into a Committee of the whole in order to take into consideration the resolution concerning independence." Hancock then came down from the podium to take his seat with the other representatives from Massachusetts. The question of independence would finally be put to a vote. John Dickinson rose to his feet, declaring, "My conduct this day I expect will give the finishing blow to my once too great, and my now too diminished popularity. Yet I would rather forfeit popularity forever, than vote away the blood and happiness of my countrymen." Dickinson led the opposition to independence by providing a carefully reasoned and thoughtful argument. Looking tired and sallow, he argued that America was simply not ready to govern itself. He predicted that in the future foreign powers would try to take advantage of American weakness. He observed that many colonies were uncomfortable declaring independence because they had not worked out their own internal politics. No one had a clue as to what institutions would be required for actually governing a nation. Most ominous of all, he predicted that the outcome would ultimately be an American civil war.[5]

John Adams rose to respond. He argued vociferously, but respectfully, that there was no turning back and that it was time for the colonies to unite in opposition to British rule. Others, including McKean, spoke in support of Adams. Late in the afternoon, after the delegates had exhausted the debate for the day, McKean joined John Adams, Samuel Adams, as well as the New Jersey delegation at the Fountain Tavern across the street from Carpenters' Hall. They worried that, notwithstanding the majority they now had in Congress, four states might still dissent, including McKean's own state of Delaware as well as Pennsylvania, New York, and South Carolina. They were a long way from the unanimity they deemed critical. McKean suggested Pennsylvania might be placed in the independence column if Dickinson and Morris stayed away. New York was unpredictable, but McKean relayed that South Carolina would vote "aye." Referring to Edward Rutledge, who at twenty-seven years of age was the youngest delegate in Congress, McKean said, "That young popinjay from South Carolina . . . took me by the coat as I came out [of Carpenters' Hall] and promised as much."[6]

"What about Delaware?" asked one of the New Jersey delegates, who worried that, with Rodney in Delaware, McKean and Read would split Delaware's vote and thereby place it in the undecided column. McKean assured his colleagues that Delaware would vote for independence. He revealed that at his own expense, he had dispatched a rider to Delaware to find Rodney and plead with him to return immediately to Philadelphia. Caesar Rodney was not a well man: he had a cancer that had disfigured one side of his face and had weakened him physically.[7] But McKean assured his colleagues that Rodney was a patriot; he would come.[8]

⟶⟵

ON THE MORNING OF JULY 2, MCKEAN ARRIVED EARLY AT THE STATE House. He paced the hallway, greeted fellow delegates as they arrived, and nervously peered out the hall's tall, stately windows, looking up toward Chestnut Street in the hope that Rodney would arrive before President Hancock gaveled the Congress to order. McKean likely was also keeping an eye out for his friend John Dickinson, who had made it clear that although he could not support independence, he would not act as a spoiler. Dickinson had decided to stay away from Carpenters' Hall that morning, as had Robert Morris, the other Pennsylvania delegate who opposed independence from Britain. With their abstentions, McKean knew that Pennsylvania was now in the independence column, but the final outcome depended on breaking the deadlock in his home state of Delaware. Where was Rodney?[9]

At nine o'clock, Charles Thomson, secretary of the Congress, settled into his chair directly in front of and below the president's chair. President Hancock, nattily attired in tweed and ruffled shirt, stepped onto the dais and took his seat in the red upholstered chair. As the rest of the delegates seated themselves, McKean, gazing intently out of the large windows in the rear of the room, saw the distant image of a rider and horse galloping down Chestnut Street. He turned and walked briskly from the room. Minutes later, McKean made a dramatic entry into the hall beside Rodney, who upon receiving McKean's letter had mounted his horse and ridden through the night the ninety miles to Philadelphia, braving thunder, lightning, and a pelting rain. Rodney was still wearing his spurs and mud-spattered boots and a green silk scarf to cover his disfigured face. Although memories differ, McKean recalled that the proceedings commenced almost immediately after he and Rodney took their seats. The first order of business was the reading of the latest report from General Washington: 110 British ships had moored off Sandy Hook, New Jersey, and more ships and troops were on the way.[10]

At around ten o'clock that morning, a roll call vote on independence was ordered. It had started to rain again. Thomson called the roll of the individual states, and when it was Delaware's turn to vote, Rodney rose to his feet: "As I believe the voice of my constituents and of all sensible and honest men is in favor of independence and my own judgment concurs with them, I vote for independence!" Exhausted, Rodney sank back into his chair.[11]

In the absence of Dickinson and Morris, the Pennsylvania delegation voted 3 to 2, also in favor of independence. Next, South Carolina, which previously had been an outlier, voted for independence. In the end, twelve colonies voted aye; only New York abstained. In the absence of a no vote, the decision was unanimous: independence for America had carried the day.

The next morning, the delegates began the process of final editing of Thomas Jefferson's draft declaration, and the following day, on July 4, 1776, which was unseasonably cool and comfortable, they completed their work. The delegates then voted that the declaration be authenticated and printed. President Hancock and Secretary Thomson signed the document that day. It would be another month before an embossed copy would be available for the other delegates to sign.[12]

# 7

# "Love Me and Pray for Me"

I T WAS DONE. AMERICA HAD DECLARED ITS INDEPENDENCE FROM
England, and although the founders knew that they had accomplished
something significant—Adams wrote his wife Abigail that he believed the
event "will be celebrated by succeeding Generations . . . from one end of
the Continent to the other from this Time forward forever more"—few
completely grasped the significance of the document and what it meant
for the future.[1] Benjamin Franklin remained one of the few who had vision
that the colonies would need some governance structure to bind them
together. Most of the delegates, including McKean, simply wanted to live in
peace in their respective colonies. The thirteen colonies, after all, had been
in existence for several decades, and though they shared a common language and an expanding middle class, residents otherwise had very little in
common. Massachusetts was in many ways the most English of the group;
Pennsylvania was the most diverse with a citizenry comprising German,
Irish, Dutch, Swedish, and Scottish immigrants; South Carolina already
had a large African slave population. At the time no one was seriously contemplating a strong national government. Instead, they were focused on
winning a war.

On July 9, 1776, George Washington, commander of the Continental
forces in New York, received a copy of the Declaration. With hundreds

of British naval ships occupying New York Harbor, revolutionary spirit and military tensions were running high. Standing before a raucous crowd numbering in the hundreds, Washington read the document aloud in front of City Hall. Later that day a number of patriots toppled a nearby statue of George III. The statue was subsequently melted down and used to mold more than forty thousand musket balls for the fledgling American army.[2]

Washington had previously conveyed to Congress his belief that the British strategy was to break America in half by invading the middle colonies. The general had proposed the formation of a strategic mobile military reserve, a "flying camp," to be made up of 10,000 men—6,000 from Pennsylvania, 3,400 from Maryland, and 600 from the lower counties of Delaware.[3] He envisioned that the new recruits would eventually join with other, more seasoned troops from New Jersey, Virginia, Massachusetts, and Connecticut.

There was no time to lose: Congress needed to act immediately. Though he had stayed away from the vote on independence, John Dickinson was back at work on July 5. Dickinson served on the Committee on Safety with fellow delegates Benjamin Franklin, Robert Livingston, and McKean's first wife's brother-in-law, Francis Hopkinson. For his part, McKean chaired the Committee on Inspection and spent the afternoon of July 4 conferring with field officers. Later that afternoon, Congress ratified letters proposed by the Committees on Safety and Inspection to the Lancaster militia and ordered that they be printed as a single document that read:

> Gentlemen, the Congress . . . directed us . . . to form a flying camp, to cover Pennsylvania and New Jersey, from the attacks of the enemy who have landed on Staten Island, and will probably direct their march this way, if they imagine the attacks on New York too hazardous.[4]

After the vote for independence, McKean's work intensified. He had been appointed to four standing committees of the Second Continental Congress, including the highly influential Secret Committee that had planned the Canadian expedition. Besides McKean, it included some of the Congress's most prominent members: Benjamin Franklin, Robert Morris, Robert Livingston, and John Dickinson. The Secret Committee gathered intelligence about Tory ammunition stores and authorized missions to seize enemy supplies in the southern states. It also arranged for the purchase of military equipment in Europe through intermediaries to conceal the fact that Congress was the true purchaser, and then used foreign flags to attempt to protect the vessels from the British fleet. The committee also took over and administered secret contracts for arms and gunpowder that had been previously negotiated by members of the Congress on an ad hoc basis. Finally, the committee ran a rudimentary espionage service by employing agents overseas to gather intelligence about Tory ammunition stores. Living up to its name, the committee regularly destroyed its records to ensure the confidentiality of its work.[5]

As they prepared for war, McKean must have known and been deeply concerned that the American army would be vastly outnumbered and would have nothing comparable to the training and equipment of the British army. But McKean and the other members of the Continental Congress were committed to the fight because they had something that the British didn't have: a cause.

⊷⊹⊹⊷

ON JULY 23, 1776, COLONEL MCKEAN, RESPLENDENT IN HIS BLUE AND white uniform, a gleaming silver sword at his side, marched his battalion of 360 men from the outskirts of Philadelphia to Perth Amboy. There, he reported to General Hugh Mercer, who had been elevated by the Continental Congress the previous month to the rank of brigadier general and who had been in command at Perth Amboy for only three days.[6]

One hundred miles from Philadelphia, Perth Amboy was the capital of East Jersey from 1684 until the union of East Jersey and West Jersey in 1702, and it remained one of the two capitals, with Burlington, until 1790. Situated on a bluff, the city dominated the mouth of the bay where the Raritan River emptied into New York Bay just inside Sandy Hook. This created a channel around Staten Island, the peninsula where the British army led by

Sir William Howe had been encamped since June. By July 1776, Admiral Richard Howe, William's brother, had landed more troops, bringing the total British force to approximately forty thousand. Just as General Washington had anticipated, the Howe brothers had developed a plan to subdue Perth Amboy, make it their base, and ultimately conquer New York, New Jersey, and—the real prize—Pennsylvania.

For the next several weeks, British ships ferried men and supplies to Staten Island. There was a violent thunderstorm on McKean's first day in camp. As he stood next to his artillery and gazed across the rain-swept bay, he saw a British ship sailing close to the shore and ordered it fired upon. The command, as he wrote his wife Sarah, marked "the first guns I ever order to be fired against human beings—if the enemy can be called such."[7] On July 25, five more ships came up through the narrows, and the day after, eight more arrived. On July 29, another twenty British ships arrived, carrying men and supplies, followed three days later by a flotilla of forty-five ships, carrying three thousand troops under the command of Generals Henry Clinton and Lord Cornwallis. The British reinforcements had come from South Carolina, and as one British soldier noted, they were both surprised and delighted to discover Staten Island—"the most beautiful island that nature could form, or art improve."[8]

Washington's troops at Perth Amboy were badly outnumbered, but that was the least of his worries. His army suffered from poor morale; they endured oppressively humid weather and squalid conditions. Washington had little communication, no direction, not even a defined mission from the Congress. Nevertheless, the presence of the "flying camp" persuaded Howe to turn his army away from New Jersey and Pennsylvania toward Washington's main force in New York.

The two armies watched each other through spyglasses and occasionally exchanged gun and cannon fire. McKean wrote his wife that British soldiers were within "six hundred yards" and he saw "hundreds of them everyday." General Washington opined that it was "provoking . . . to have them so near without being able to give them any disturbance."[9]

McKean got another taste of war in late July when he espied "five shallops"—large sailboats—sailing along the river and ordered his soldiers to fire their four-pounder cannons at the large boats. The British returned fire with ferocity, bombarding his position for almost an hour. Cannonballs landed all around him, killing a horse barely ten yards from where he was standing. By the time the shelling stopped, one of his soldiers had been killed and two others wounded. It was the first time that he had ever heard a cannonball explode near him, the first time he had seen a man killed in war, and he admitted to Sarah that he was shaken by the carnage he had witnessed. He wrote her, "Love me and Pray for me."[10]

Colonel McKean missed his wife and the children, but he initially wrote Sarah that he had "not a wish to see you . . . in a Camp, which may be drawn into a battle every day, nay every hour." However, as days and weeks of relative calm passed, McKean observed other officers' wives visiting on a regular basis—even arranging formal dinners, which McKean wrote Sarah, "I did not expect when I left Philadelphia." Convinced that it was safe for his wife to make a brief visit, he persuaded her to leave the children with their grandparents in Bordentown and come to Perth Amboy.[11]

Meanwhile, on August 2, the delegates to Congress still in Philadelphia assembled to sign the Declaration of Independence. Standing before the members, John Hancock declared, "There must be no pulling in different directions; we must all hang together." Benjamin Franklin echoed Hancock, noting somewhat mordantly, "Yes, indeed, we must all hang together, or most assuredly we will hang separately."[12] By affixing their names to the document, they were making official—and permanent—the treasonous vote for independence they had orally taken a month earlier. Dr. Benjamin Rush, who didn't join the Pennsylvania delegation until after the July 2 vote, later remembered "the pensive and awful silence which pervaded the house when we were called upon, one after another, to the table of the Congress to subscribe what was believed by many at the time to be our own death warrant."[13]

Even John Dickinson and Robert Morris signed the document, although they were no supporters of independence personally. The two delegates from Pennsylvania had purposely stayed away from Congress for the final vote, but Dickinson had accepted his defeat and wanted to preserve the unity of the Congress. Morris, who always calculated the economic impact of any action he took, now decided that an independent America offered a potentially robust trade with other nations and inscribed his name boldly at the top of the list of Pennsylvania's delegates. Richard Henry Lee, George Wythe, and Elbridge Gerry were absent but would sign later. Although they would eventually sign as well, McKean and Oliver Wolcott, a delegate from Connecticut who was not a member of Congress on July 4, were with Washington's army, the only signers to actually serve on active duty in the Continental Army.[14]

In all likelihood, at some point in early 1777, McKean traveled from New Castle to Philadelphia and attached his name to the Declaration of Independence. He did so without any fanfare, applying his signature in the fourth column, near the bottom of the parchment, and under the signatures of his Delaware colleagues, Caesar Rodney and George Read. The widely held belief at the time, as well as today, was that all the delegates had signed their names on July 4. The account was based on what historian Peter de Bolla has characterized as "sketchy" notes that Thomas Jefferson had kept on the meetings in Philadelphia throughout the summer of 1776 and subsequently used to describe the events in his personal journals. Jefferson wrote, "The debates having taken up the better parts of the 2nd, 3rd and 4th days of July, were, in the evening of the last closed," and he then noted, "The declaration was reported by the committee, agreed to by the house; and signed by every member except Mr. Dickinson."[15]

As the principal author of the Declaration of Independence, Jefferson happily perpetuated this myth for many years, and it was not until 1796, twenty years later, that McKean became the first signer to challenge the faulty narrative. In a letter to his close friend Alexander Dallas, he noted that only Hancock and Thomson had signed the document on July 4. The majority of delegates signed on August 2. With the precision of a meticulous lawyer, he also pointed out that six delegates who eventually signed were not even present for the vote on July 4 and another five were not even members of Congress at the time.[16] McKean had certainly understood the great significance of the vote on July 4, 1776, but as the historian John Coleman expressed it, "So far as he was concerned, at the time, it was not a literary occasion but a military crisis."[17]

ALTHOUGH THERE HAD BEEN AN EXCHANGE OF GUNFIRE BETWEEN BRITISH and Continental troops the day before, on Sunday, August 25, all was quiet at the Perth Amboy barracks. Colonel McKean had just completed a morning ride on horseback when a military orderly handed him a letter. He immediately recognized the handwriting of Caesar Rodney. His old friend and colleague wrote to implore him to return immediately to Delaware to help write the state's constitution.

As in other states, Delaware's leaders had welcomed the Declaration of Independence but had little notion of what came next. If the states were to separate from England, they would need to govern themselves and work with each other, but no protocols existed to guide them. The state legislatures could pass laws, but who would interpret the laws and who would enforce them? The Crown had previously appointed the governor, so how would that person now be chosen and what powers would he have? Perhaps the most important unanswered question was: How far did the rights of citizens extend? Rodney acknowledged the value of McKean's military service but also knew McKean as one of the most skilled lawyers in Delaware, someone with an intimate knowledge of the state's politics. He was needed to help organize a government, and just as McKean had once urged Rodney to come quickly, now Rodney begged McKean to return as soon as possible.[18]

McKean didn't hesitate; he informed General Mercer that he was needed in his home state and asked that the general grant him leave, which Mercer promptly did. McKean was not sorry to be leaving the military. Although he had experienced war firsthand and the "flying camp" had achieved its objective of bottling up British forces, most of his time at Perth Amboy had been spent idly and in boredom. Days passed when the only time he encountered the enemy was through the portal of his spyglass, observing the redcoats as they milled about their camp across the river. Moreover, a midsummer drought had descended with stifling heat. One British sailor described "No air, and the thermometer at 94 degrees."[19] McKean wrote Sarah that he had found "a very neat little bath house" and that he bathed "in the evening in the salt water."[20]

But the camps were overcrowded and unsanitary, and more men were falling sick every day; an estimated six thousand American soldiers were ill. One English visitor wrote that soldiers "desert in large numbers, [and] are sickly, filthy, divided and unruly."[21] McKean agreed with this assessment. Even though he had been elected by his troops to lead them, he held them somewhat in contempt. In letters to his Sarah, he empathized with soldiers homesick for their families but described them as "some of the most rude, turbulent, impudent, lazy, dirty fellows that I ever beheld."[22] The truth is McKean was never comfortable in a uniform commanding men in war. The very day he was granted leave by General Mercer, McKean packed his belongings and set off for Delaware. The lawyer-turned-soldier would resign his military commission that autumn.

McKean returned to New Castle and years later recalled that he had paid for a room at an inn, stayed up through the night, and written Delaware's constitution in one sitting. This was an exaggeration. If he did write a constitution, it was not the version finally adopted by Delaware. McKean was not a member of the majority in the assembly, and notwithstanding his reputation as a first-rate lawyer, he had little influence over the backbenchers in the state assembly and played only a marginal role in the final drafting of the state's constitution. The version ultimately adopted was quite different from his. However, McKean may have authored the bill of rights to Delaware's governing document—it is generally ascribed to his pen. Delaware was one of the first states to adopt its own state constitution. Its bill of rights, twenty-three articles specifying individual rights, served as a model for other states and, more importantly, alongside George Mason's 1776 Virginia Declaration of Rights, foreshadowed the federal Bill of Rights to come over a decade later.[23]

McKean was also busy in neighboring Pennsylvania. Delegates to the state constitutional convention had convened only days after the Declaration of Independence, and by early September, they had completed their work. The new state constitution was published in two Philadelphia newspapers and distributed throughout Pennsylvania as a twelve-page folio.[24] McKean had worked hard to promote this new constitution, but when he read the document, his heart sank. Drafted by many of the same

Pennsylvania radicals McKean had worked with during the spring—Thomas Mifflin, Timothy Matlack, Thomas Young, and Benjamin Franklin—the document, in McKean's view, was as flawed, if not more so, than the original constitution that he had sought so vehemently to abrogate. The radicals had set out to create a robust democracy in Pennsylvania, but, ironically, the document was never submitted to the people for a vote. It provided for a unicameral assembly, and instead of a governor, an executive council, chosen and paid by the assembly, would preside over the state. The assembly and the executive council had the right to impeach any executive or judicial officer and to do so without trial or any showing of misbehavior. The proposed constitution provided for no checks and balances.

Most disturbing to McKean, there were few limitations on who could vote; just as the radicals had envisioned, there were no requirements for property holding so that even a common laborer could vote. Many conservative justices and lawyers, members of the old guard, refused to support the new government. Benjamin Rush complained that the new constitution was the work of a "mobracy." Nevertheless, the assembly adopted the state constitution on September 28, leading pundits at the time to call Pennsylvania the most democratic government in the colonies.[25]

In McKean's opinion, the radicals and their constitution made a mockery of the aspect he most valued in a democracy: an independent judiciary. Ironically, he was thrust back into alliance with his close friend John Dickinson, who had remained both a member of the Pennsylvania Assembly and a member of the Continental Congress. Together they organized a debate in Philadelphia at the Philosophical Society, the organization founded by Benjamin Franklin in 1743. McKean was practicing law and living in Delaware at the time, but he traveled back to Philadelphia on October 17 for the meeting, which one participant described as a gathering of "all the rich and wise men, the lawyers and doctors."

Some speakers, including Francis Hopkinson, argued that the new constitution needed to be given a chance. Because of personal jealousy or political differences, Hopkinson increasingly viewed McKean with contempt and criticized him for his abandoning the democratic movement. But the vast majority of participants that evening, including McKean and

Dickinson, argued that the new constitution would inevitably lead to ruin. Dickinson characterized the document as "confused, inconsistent, and dangerous."[26]

McKean's opposition to the Pennsylvania constitution meant that he would be known for the next decade as an "anti-constitutionalist." He had previously worked with the "radicals" during the debate over independence and, before that, been labeled a "Whig" during the First Continental Congress. There were no political parties in America in 1776, and so the labels were largely meaningless in terms of identifying McKean ideologically. What they reveal, however, is that McKean could not be pigeonholed; he was a pragmatist, and depending on the issue, he worked with anyone he believed would advance the interests of the American people. The combination of his pragmatism and political dexterity would become a hallmark of his career.

# PART II
# THE JURIST

# 8

## Chief Justice McKean

AMERICA HAD DECLARED ITS INDEPENDENCE BUT BY THE END OF 1776 was fighting for its survival. The state governments were in disarray. There was no money. And most troubling of all, the war was going badly. After capturing hundreds of Revolutionary soldiers in Manhattan in November, General Howe's army had forced General Washington and the Continental Army to retreat from New York to New Jersey and ultimately to northern Pennsylvania. The Continental Army, approximately five thousand in strength, was in tatters: nearly a third of the soldiers were sick, and the rest were poorly equipped and dispirited.

The number of casualties mounted, and daily essentials became scarce; Americans increasingly were seized by doubt and uncertainty about the future. Yet just as the cause seemed hopeless, General Washington orchestrated a daring nighttime crossing of the Delaware River and launched an assault on British troops in Trenton on December 26. It was an engineering feat ferrying horses, artillery, and twenty-five hundred Revolutionary soldiers across the icy river in the middle of winter and launching a surprise attack that resulted in a rout of the Redcoats. Only a week later, Washington and his troops surprised the British garrison at Princeton and won another battle. These two victories breathed new life and hope—at least temporarily—into the Continental Army.

As the fighting intensified, loyalists to the Crown and anti-independence moderates who controlled the Delaware Assembly passed over McKean and Caesar Rodney as delegates to the Continental Congress. The purge of these two long-serving patriots was evidence that the issue of independence was far from settled in the colonies. In Pennsylvania the controversy over the state constitution likewise highlighted the fact that Americans remained deeply divided over their future. The problem was simple: beyond separation from England, Americans had no clear vision of what united them. Few knew what an American government would look like once the British left. Few could cogently describe an American identity. McKean had a vision of a nation guided by the rule of law, but ironically, for the first time in nearly twenty-five years, he found himself a private citizen with no government position. His absence from public life wouldn't last for long.

By the spring of 1777, the fighting was at Delaware's border, and the assembly was desperate for leadership. The same Delaware Assembly that had rejected McKean's draft of a state constitution and recalled him from the Congress only months earlier now elected him Speaker, a powerful legislative position. McKean devised a plan for the defense of Wilmington and immediately set about working with like-minded legislators to reform the state's militia so that it would be a more effective fighting force. But Governor McKinly failed to act on McKean's plan, a decision that would have dire consequences for the citizens of Delaware.

━┼┼━

WHILE MCKEAN STRUGGLED WITH THE POLITICAL MACHINERY IN DELAWARE, conservatives in neighboring Pennsylvania, in opposition to the constitution, boycotted the courts and effectively shut down the judiciary. James Allen, a Pennsylvania Loyalist, wrote in his diary, "Not one of the laws of the Assembly are regarded. . . . No courts open. No justice administered."[1] Making matters worse, the state supreme court had no leadership. Benjamin Chew, its chief justice for the previous three years, counted both George Washington and John Adams as close friends. Chew had supported additional rights for the colonies, but he had not supported the Declaration of Independence, so in 1777 Pennsylvania's Executive Council removed him from office, accused him of treason, and kept him in preventive detention in New Jersey. With the conservatives in open revolt and the chief justice out of the picture, the judicial system essentially collapsed. Without guidance from an authoritative judicial figure, the lower courts lacked direction, cases piled up, and individuals increasingly settled disputes extrajudicially, often by force.

In Philadelphia the radicals took matters into their own hands and set up ad hoc committees to dispense justice. Trials were held at the Indian Queen Tavern on Fourth Street. Mobs hauled in citizens suspected of disloyalty—which extended to anyone accused of having sung "God Save the King," having raised a toast to the Crown, or having done anything that implied opposition to independence.[2]

Executive Council leaders in Pennsylvania were alarmed by the disintegration of the rule of law and fearful that everything they had fought for might end in anarchy. They offered the position of chief justice to Joseph Reed, who was at the time serving as the adjutant general to General Washington and was integral to the war effort. He turned down the offer. Five days later, on July 28, 1777, the council offered the position to Thomas McKean.

McKean might have seemed a strange choice given his opposition to the new constitution, not to mention that he was at the time serving as the Speaker of another state's assembly. But McKean was respected by radicals in Pennsylvania for having promoted the convention in the first place and for his support of the Declaration of Independence. Moreover, McKean had continued in his role as the chairman of the Philadelphia City Committee and had increasingly been called upon to act as a kind of arbiter in settling disputes. Months earlier, for instance, McKean had chaired a meeting of the committee at the Indian Queen Tavern to consider cases involving alleged Tory sympathizers. The recorded minutes of the meeting indicate that "Mr. Wm Inlay appeared and offered reasons to the Co. why he might not be accused as an enemy to his country."[3] The minutes also recorded that "Mr. Smith attended & Informed that he thinks Joseph Stansbury sang God save the king in his house and a number of persons present bore him chorus."[4] McKean presided over this meeting and others like it with the view that anyone accused deserved a fair hearing. Members of the Pennsylvania Executive Council took note and admired McKean's fidelity to the rule of law, though no one really knew what it meant.

Several of McKean's friends advised him to reject the offer of chief justice because they saw it as a political dead-end and feared he would ultimately meet the same fate as Chief Justice Chew. McKean, however, accepted the position, explaining in a letter to John Dickinson that he agreed to take on the role in order "to prevent the least suspicion that I was against any government but that I framed myself and that I wanted to embroil the state and occasion disaffection to the common cause."[5] McKean went on to declare that he "had nothing in view but to promote the happiness of my country."[6] Committed to the military success in the war against Britain, McKean also understood that no government—no civilized country—could be sustained without the rule of law.

McKean's elevation to chief justice of the highest court in Pennsylvania prompted some to label him a hypocrite, an opportunist, and an unprincipled and unscrupulous political striver. His detractors observed tartly that he had opposed the state constitution and now only embraced it because it suited his political needs. Moreover, McKean, who as Speaker of the Delaware Assembly had voted to reappoint himself to the Congress, was criticized for continuing to represent Delaware in both the assembly and the Congress. One critic, writing in the *Pennsylvania Packet*, complained of the "lamentable situation we are reduced to, when we are obliged to go to another state for a chief justice and when he has bitterly execrated as tyrannical the very Constitution he has since sworn to execute."[7]

It was true that McKean's appointment was replete with contradictions and ironies. Years later he supported a federal constitution with the kinds of checks and balances that were so obviously absent in 1777. But the fledgling legal structures were degenerating in Pennsylvania, and he worried that citizens looked increasingly to extralegal committees, such as the one he served on—the City Committee, to solve disputes and to provide some sense of an orderly society. Thus, when asked to serve as chief justice, he agreed to do so: if he could help establish the rule of law, then perhaps Pennsylvania could serve as a model for other states.

McKean believed that his predecessor, Benjamin Chew, had been "the greatest single person in Pennsylvania before the Revolution." But he was aware that the Chew court had experienced difficulty reconciling draconian English law, which a large segment of the population now rejected, with the customs and evolving political mores of Pennsylvanians. The greatest challenge, McKean believed, was for him and his colleagues on the court to decide which laws had validity, agree how to apply to them, and, ultimately, determine who would enforce them. Though he recoiled from British hegemony, McKean nevertheless viewed the English legal system as his touchstone. A student of English jurisprudence, he told Dickinson that he intended to emulate the great British jurist Lord Hale. Hale, ironically, had been a Royalist during the English Civil War, but he was also known for his integrity and willingness to take on politically unpopular issues in order to uphold the law.

McKean instinctively understood that to augment the power of the court he would need to expand its reach and demonstrate its capacity to dispense justice. He and the other justices moved quickly to broaden the jurisdiction of the court to the northern and western parts of the state where the court was not well known. In the east, where the majority of citizens lived and where political dissatisfaction simmered, he boldly asserted the authority of the court in a number of high-profile cases.

The widening jurisdiction of the court brought greater attention to the chief justice; he understood that both his role and the administration of the law involved a large element of theater. The first oyer and terminer court, a court designated to hear criminal law cases, was in Lancaster, eighty miles west of Philadelphia. McKean rode to the courthouse escorted by "a number of gentlemen of the law, justices of the Peace . . . [and] officers."[8] Astride his steed, upright in the saddle, and flanked by an entourage of law enforcement officials, McKean would have cut an intimidating figure and impressed the inhabitants of any small town. While rejecting

British rule, the chief justice adopted many of the trappings of the English legal system by appearing in court in long scarlet robes and traditional powdered wig.[9]

McKean gained a reputation as fair and judicious, but he was feared as much as respected. From his perch on the bench, he barked orders to attorneys, court officers, and defendants and rarely missed an opportunity to lecture the public on the importance of law in civil society. He commanded respect because he knew the law better than anyone else, or at least he appeared to do so by always speaking in an authoritative tone.

One story about McKean from this time is almost certainly apocryphal but all the more revealing because it reflects his public reputation: facing an unruly mob assembled outside the supreme court, McKean sent for the sheriff and ordered him to disperse the crowd. "I cannot do it," replied the timorous official. McKean leaned forward. "Why do you not summon your posse?" he asked. "I have summoned them but they are ineffectual," replied the sheriff. "Then, Sir," thundered McKean, "why do you not summon me?" The sheriff, stunned for a moment, decided that was a good idea, "I do summon you, Sir." Whereupon the chief justice stood to his full six feet, leaned forward, came down from the dais, and according to one observer, "swooped down on the mob like an eagle on a flock of sheep, and catching two of the ringleaders by the throat, quelled the riot."[10]

In his flowing robes and powdered wig, McKean may have both looked and acted imperiously, but he presided over his court with a view toward helping to build a compassionate society. In an address to the court in early 1778, he acknowledged "to dissolve all connection with Great Britain was like separation of soul and body," but the separation was necessary because "Americans had come to embrace the belief that all men are equal with respect to civil power and civil disobedience; and [that] all authority must be originally derived from the people." And McKean's belief was that they were fundamentally good, and therefore "it was safer to err in acquitting than in punishing." One observer sitting in the court that day, an apothecary, thought McKean had delivered "an elegant and spirited charge" not only to the jury but to the spectators in the court as well.[11]

McKean's charitable view of humanity was at times controversial. On September 9, 1777, Philadelphia authorities arrested and jailed twenty-nine Quakers whom the sheriff deemed "dangerous to the community."[12] They were not charged with anything specific—and were only detained because they were suspected of being sympathizers of the Tory cause, as, indeed, many Quakers were at the time. However, because they had not been charged with any crime, McKean ruled that their continued detention was illegal and granted them a writ of habeas corpus, a fundamental English common law principle, thereby setting them free. The radicals in Pennsylvania, especially those in the assembly, who assumed McKean supported the Revolution in every instance, were outraged. They simply could not understand how he could let reputed British sympathizers go free. The assembly immediately reversed the chief justice's order and the Quakers were arrested once again, and this time they were deported to Virginia. McKean had been overruled, but he had served notice that his court would fight to uphold the rule of law even when it wasn't popular, and, more importantly, even if the legislature overwhelmingly opposed his decision. As the deportation of the Quakers showed, the courts in Pennsylvania and elsewhere were still the weakest link in government, but that would change over time.

# 9

## Occupation of Philadelphia

**W**HILE MCKEAN WORKED TO STRENGTHEN THE RULE OF LAW IN Pennsylvania, the British resolved to break the backbone of the Revolution by capturing Philadelphia. In late August 1777, General Sir William Howe landed 250 ships carrying nineteen thousand troops at the Head of Elk on the north end of Chesapeake Bay, only fifty miles from Philadelphia. Though the Continental Army had acquired intelligence days before that the ships were bound for the Chesapeake, the British encountered no opposition, and three battalions under Howe's command marched north from Delaware into Pennsylvania.

Howe's inner circle included many Tories whom McKean knew well. One of Howe's principal aides was William Allen Jr., who had served alongside McKean on the Philadelphia Committee of Safety and whose father, James Allen, had been a prominent Pennsylvania lawyer. At one time, William had championed American rights, but he always favored reconciliation, and now he served England's military commander in America. Howe's other close American aide was Joseph Galloway, who had served with McKean in the First Continental Congress and who had been a close associate of Benjamin Franklin. These men wanted greater autonomy for America but ultimately yearned to remain Englishmen.

During the early fall of 1777, Howe continued his march to Philadelphia by winning a decisive battle at Brandywine, a small town on the outskirts of the city. In a skirmish that raged the entire day and ended in hand-to-hand combat, Howe's army outmaneuvered the Revolutionaries and forced their retreat. One thousand Americans lost their lives—at the time, the greatest single defeat for the Continental Army.[1] Then, on September 12, the British marched into Wilmington; one Loyalist described his elation at witnessing "a beautiful sight" as British troops advanced "with their scarlet coats, their bright guns and bayonets gleaming in the rays of an early September sun."[2] But pageantry was quickly replaced by rapacity as the Redcoats sacked the capital, seized the state treasury, and plundered whatever valuables they found. They also captured the governor, John McKinly, and threw him into the brig of a man-of-war vessel. McKinly was a tepid Revolutionary, and one Delaware patriot speculated that his capture "had so little the appearance of accident, that many people suspected design."[3]

George Read, McKinly's political ally, as well as McKean's Delaware colleague in the Congress, served as Speaker of the legislative council and was next in the line of succession for governor. But Read was in Philadelphia when the British captured Wilmington. Adding to his ambivalence about returning to his home state was the fact that he had always straddled the independence issue and had no intention of returning to British-occupied Delaware and subjecting himself to possible imprisonment. At the time of Wilmington's fall, McKean was with his family in Chester, Pennsylvania, only fifty miles away. Eight days after McKinly's capture, McKean, as speaker of the lower House, took over as the state's de facto chief executive. The new "president" of Delaware, who continued to serve as both chief justice of Pennsylvania and a member of Congress, wrote to Caesar Rodney that he did not intend to remain in office any longer than necessary but felt obliged to "do all that I can in this most difficult of times."[4]

The situation in Delaware was growing more precarious by the day as citizens loyal to the Crown fought pitched battles against those seeking independence. The state council pleaded with McKean to find a way to disarm any residents "who have taken up arms, much to the terror of the good people . . . and the encouragement of the British forces."[5] McKean had few resources at his disposal, but he nevertheless took charge. He ordered the recruitment of new militia, named his friend Caesar Rodney a major general, and gathered around him a group of colleagues to devise a plan to liberate Delaware. He moved the state government temporarily from Wilmington to Newark, Delaware, out of the reach of British troops. Still worried that his family might not be safe, he moved them to Newark as well.

⊷⊹⊹⊷

WHILE SERVING AS DELAWARE'S ACTING PRESIDENT, MCKEAN OFTEN returned to Philadelphia to hear cases as the chief justice of the Pennsylvania Supreme Court. That changed in late September 1777 when, following their victories at Brandywine and Wilmington, the British army marched to the outskirts of Philadelphia and prepared to occupy it. Writing from Delaware, John Dickinson, concerned about his wife Mary's safety, told her, "Come immediately."[6]

Thousands of residents fled the city before the arrival of the Redcoats. One prominent Philadelphia matron, Sarah Logan Fisher, described the panic that gripped residents as word came that the British were at the gates of the city: "wagons rattling, horses galloping, women running, children crying, delegates flying and altogether the greatest consternation, fright and terror that can be imagined. Some of our neighbors took flight before day, and I believe all Congress moved off before 5:00 a.m."[7]

Still, many sympathizers and Loyalists stayed behind in Philadelphia. As the British moved down Market Street, not only was there no resistance, throngs of citizens welcomed them, as one Loyalist remembered, "by loudest acclamations of joy."[8] Howe's Tory aides, Allen and Galloway, managed to shield from British soldiers some well-to-do radical sympathizers who had remained in the city, but hundreds of others were thrown into city jails. The *Pennsylvania Evening Post*, once a pro-independence newspaper, continued to publish, but now as a pro-Loyalist daily. The *Post* published glowing accounts of British military successes and praised the "good manners" of the occupying force in Philadelphia.[9]

With American cities falling one after another, on October 4, Washington launched a surprise attack on the British garrison in Germantown, Pennsylvania. His army rushed the soldiers' barracks at night, with four columns advancing from different directions. But British and Hessians repelled the Americans and ultimately handed them another defeat, killing more than 150 soldiers. After the Battle of Germantown, British officers in Philadelphia prepared to settle in for the long, cold winter, having moved into some of some of the finest houses in the city. One of the more flamboyant commanders, Major John Andre, occupied Benjamin Franklin's vacant house on Market Street. The Redcoats burned "that damned rebel Dickinson's house," as one British officer reported to General Howe.[10]

With the fighting paused, British soldiers had little to do, so they cast about for distractions by organizing cockfights and boxing matches. They also pursued cultural activities, putting on concerts and plays. The officers mixed with the city's elite families, and both hosted and attended elaborate dinners and dances. One of the most sought after young socialites in Philadelphia during this period was a family friend of the McKeans, Peggy Shippen, a beautiful, wealthy, aristocratic young woman. She would later marry Benedict Arnold, the American general who had fought so bravely and been wounded during the Canadian expedition.

Many residents who opposed the British remained in Philadelphia because they had nowhere to go; others simply felt that a British victory was inevitable and decided to endure the occupation. The Redcoats didn't make it easy, taking whatever they wanted from shopkeepers and merchants and often refusing to pay. Rampant inflation made it expensive to buy basic goods if they were even available. After General Howe opened up the Delaware River to commerce, business improved somewhat as a few new artisans and merchants moved to Philadelphia to seize the opportunities made available by the exodus of revolutionaries. Still, most Philadelphians lived in fear and misery.

McKean tried to keep his family close to him during this perilous period, writing John Adams that he had been "compelled to move my family five times in a few months." Congress reconvened in Lancaster, Pennsylvania. When the British threatened to occupy Lancaster as well, Congress

moved to the city of York, and Thomas and Sarah, now six months preg-
nant with their second child, followed. Worried that his family was still
not safe, McKean once again moved Sarah and the children to "a little
log house on the banks of the Susquehanna" in Paxton, a small farming
community in central Pennsylvania.[11] On July 8, Sarah gave birth to Sarah
Maria Theresa McKean, who would be Thomas's favorite child.

McKean had stayed behind in York, where the Continental Congress—fewer than two dozen intrepid delegates—had relocated. Compared
to cosmopolitan Philadelphia, York was a small and bland city of less than
two thousand mostly German and Scotch-Irish inhabitants. It didn't matter
that there were few diversions because for the next ten months the delegates convened daily in a large room on the second floor of the town's brick
courthouse. They spent nearly every waking hour debating the Articles
of Confederation, military strategy, and the financing of an increasingly
costly war. Some members, though not McKean, questioned the leadership
of General Washington.

As the only member of Congress at the time who had served in the
Continental Army, McKean had credibility with his colleagues concerning military matters. He was appointed a member of a four-man committee that interviewed a Prussian named General Friedrich Wilhelm
August Heinrich Ferdinand, Baron von Steuben, who, inspired by the
Declaration of Independence, had traveled from Europe in 1777 to volun-
teer service to the Continental Army. In reality, von Steuben was neither
a general nor a baron, but he had been a Prussian soldier and understood
what it took to whip an army into fighting shape. It's not clear what about
von Steuben impressed McKean and his colleagues, but they sent him to
Valley Forge, and within weeks the self-styled baron was using the experience he had gained from fighting in the European Seven Years' War to
train American troops under the command of Washington. He quickly
rose to the rank of major general and inspector general, and the organization and discipline he promoted are credited with having helped to
change the course of the war.[12]

Back in Delaware the situation remained grim. In an address to the
General Assembly, McKean described what he found when he arrived in

New Castle on September 20: "all the public records and papers . . . and every shilling of the money in the treasury . . . and upwards of twenty-five thousand dollars . . . had been captured by the enemy." More concerning still, he found the state militia to be "dispirited and dispersed" and "many of them fled out of state for safety."[13]

In mid-October McKean wrote a long letter to General Washington describing the dire situation in Delaware and pleading for help from the general's army. Two days later Washington wrote back. Although he sympathized with McKean and the citizens of Delaware "who labour under very great difficulties," he regretted that the Continental Army could not do more to support them because "detaching part of our force might occasion the loss of a battle, which would endanger the safety of the whole continent." Washington did offer to send McKean a brigade of Pennsylvania militia at some point in the future but suggested that McKean should first drum up a Delaware brigade of "three or four hundred or more of militia."[14] McKean greatly admired General Washington, but he must have winced after reading such an obvious suggestion—especially since Delaware had already contributed hundreds of troops to the Continental Army, and he had been working tirelessly to recruit new soldiers. The British would occupy Wilmington for the next eight months.

# 10

## Alliance with France

**W**RITING TO HIS WIFE, ABIGAIL, FROM YORK WHERE CONGRESS HAD established temporary quarters, John Adams reported that "his spirits were not the worse for the loss of Philadelphia."[1] Yet, Adams had long recognized that without international support, the Continental Army was not likely to defeat a far superior British force. Only a few months after the vote in Congress for the Declaration of Independence, Adams had begun drafting a commercial treaty between France and the future independent colonies of the United States. Now, on the run from the British, Congress ordered on September 25, 1777, that its representatives in France, led by Benjamin Franklin, seek a treaty of alliance between the two countries as well as immediate military aid.

Although France was sympathetic to the American cause, its support for the colonies waxed and waned according to the fortunes of the rebels. After word reached France of the Declaration of Independence, the French foreign minister, Comte de Vergennes, expressed a greater openness to entering into a formal alliance with the United States. But upon receiving news of British victories over General Washington in New York, Vergennes's enthusiasm cooled, and the French deferred signing the treaty. Franklin's pleas nevertheless continued unabated. Primarily the result of both Franklin's persistence and popularity within the elite circles of French society and politics, France ultimately provided a secret loan and began offering clandestine military assistance to the Americans.

In February 1778, the British suffered a stunning defeat at the hands of the Revolutionary army. After what can only be described as a strategic failure of monumental proportions, British General John Burgoyne and 5,895 British and Hessian troops surrendered to Continental General Horatio Gates at the Battle of Saratoga. So unexpected and decisive was the defeat that, as the news spread, rumors circulated of a secret British peace offer to Franklin. Anxious to preempt the British, the French began negotiations with the Americans that would result in the signing of both the Treaty of Alliance and the Treaty of Amity and Commerce on March 14, 1778, guaranteeing French support for the American colonies if England "either by direct hostilities, or by [hindering] her commerce and navigation" interfered with French trade with America.[2]

Four days later the French ambassador informed the British government that France had officially recognized the United States as an independent nation. In response, Great Britain declared war on France, thereby engaging its principal European adversary in the American Revolutionary War.

McKean and the other members of Congress did not learn of the treaties until early May. When he heard the news, McKean was overjoyed and wrote to his wife, Sarah:

> The Treaty between the United States of America & the Most Christian king proves that the majesty of France is not only so, but also the most wise, most just, & magnanimous Prince not only in the world at present but to be found in history. The treaty was unanimously approved by Congress, and the King of France has the signal honor of the thanks of Congress.[3]

America's treaties with France had a profound effect on the British commitment to war. When Lord Howe learned of the treaty of alliance in the late spring of 1778, he had assumed correctly that France would declare war on Britain and told a Tory magistrate that the planned military campaign would be scrapped and his forces would now likely withdraw from Philadelphia. In fact, war planners in London had already made the decision that the British army in Philadelphia should fall back and relocate to New York. As rumors swirled of an impending evacuation, the most debated question in Congress was whether the Redcoats would leave by land or by sea.

General Henry Clinton replaced Howe and ordered the evacuation from Philadelphia of all twenty thousand troops, along with supplies and weapons. Tory sympathizers in the city were panicked to the point that one Loyalist described a "continual sense of terror, hurry, and confusion." When it became clear that most of Clinton's army would march out of the city, while cannons, livestock, and other supplies would be placed on ships to sail down the Delaware, many Loyalists begged to sail with the fleet. They emptied their homes of household items, knowing they were unlikely to ever return. One lady complained her "head grew dizzy with the bustle and confusion . . . carts, drays, and wagons, laden with dry goods and household furniture, dragged by men through the streets to the wharfs for want of horses: beds, boxes, trunks, chairs, tables, etc. turned out in the utmost confusion and haste."

On June 18, General Clinton led the British army out of Philadelphia.[4] Major Andre, who had occupied Benjamin Franklin's house, absconded with the renowned inventor's books, musical instruments, and even the equipment Franklin had used to conduct electrical experiments.[5]

⟶⟨⟨ ⟩⟩⟵

THE LAST BRITISH SOLDIER HAD BARELY DEPARTED BEFORE THOUSANDS OF displaced Philadelphians streamed into the city. After nine months in exile, they were eager to return to their homes, but their joy was tempered by what they found. Most of the shops had been either abandoned or shuttered. Trash and debris littered the streets and alleys. Benjamin Rush was not in the first wave of those to return, but he arrived two days later and observed, "The filth left by the British army in the streets created a good deal of sickness." Most disturbing, a miasma—the stench of death—hung in the air. Two thousand Americans had died during the occupation and had been buried in mass graves within the city.[6]

General Washington appointed Benedict Arnold military commander of Philadelphia, and Arnold marched into the city on June 19 with instructions from Washington to provide "security to individuals of every class and description." Washington had also been concerned about Tory smugglers transferring critical stockpiles needed by the Continental Army from Philadelphia to New York City and ordered Arnold to "prevent the removal, transfer or sale of any goods, wares, or merchandize, in possession of the inhabitants of the city." Arnold declared martial law but proved unable to do much about either the profiteering or the economic deprivation that continued to plague the city.[7]

Members of Congress slowly returned and convened at the state college because of the "offensiveness of the air in and around the State House," where, according to one member, "the enemy had made a hospital and left in a condition disgraceful to the condition of civility. Particularly offensive, before leaving, the British had opened a large square pit near the house, into which they had cast dead horses and the bodies of men."[8]

McKean was content to be back in Philadelphia, but his happiness was tempered by the realities of the economic crisis and the ongoing, grinding conflict. American rebels were dying at an alarming rate, as much from disease as from wounds on the battlefield. Congress continued to grapple with funding the war, and to McKean, it seemed to be increasingly consumed by petty infighting. Soon after Congress reconvened in Philadelphia, it authorized a wide-ranging investigation of American diplomacy. McKean was appointed to a special committee to consider issues such as whether America's foreign envoys, including both John Adams and Benjamin Franklin, had properly discharged their duties and whether the aid secured from France had been a loan or a gift. But the real question, unspoken, was which faction of the Congress—increasingly divided by ideology, region, and personal allegiances—would gain the upper hand.

Disgusted by congressional squabbling and backbiting in the midst of an existential threat, McKean invested little energy and time in the special committee, and his attendance at Congress tapered off. However, in April, the committee recommended that all of the American ambassadors should be recalled and that Congress should then vote on whether each ambassador should resume his post. The recommendation was accepted, and on April 22, the first vote was ordered on the recall of Benjamin Franklin from France. Silas Deane, a delegate from Connecticut, led the charge. Deane was a former ambassador to France who had been humiliated when he was recalled over questionable finances. Deane had nothing against Franklin personally; he was more interested in thwarting John Adams and Richard Lee and believed the recall of Franklin could shatter the Massachusetts and Virginia coalition that ruled Congress and had been responsible for embarrassing him. McKean's New York colleague Gouverneur Morris also supported Franklin's recall, but for a different reason: he wanted the job for himself.

After failing to appear in Congress for months, McKean suddenly showed up in Carpenters' Hall for the debate over the recall. He recognized that some in Congress seemed determined to turn "member against member, and the Congress against the states, particularly Pennsylvania and those of New England, and the states against Congress." His unexpected appearance alarmed Morris, who worried that McKean could tip the scales in favor of retaining Franklin. Morris tried unsuccessfully to postpone the vote in the hope that McKean might not be present at a later vote.[9]

Still, the vote on the recall of Franklin likely produced something of a dilemma for McKean. Although they respected each other, he and Franklin were not close friends. McKean could never forget or forgive Franklin's attempt to bring Pennsylvania and Delaware under the control of the Crown. On the other hand, McKean knew that Franklin was a patriot. He later explained, "I was reluctant to give up old servants for new men, whom I could not so well confide in." He also worried that the French would view Franklin's recall at such a critical moment in the conflict as an indication that America was reevaluating the alliance, and he believed a rupture in relations would be "disastrous." He voted against the recall, and in the end, just as Morris had feared, McKean's vote saved Franklin's post. The aging diplomat remained in Paris.[10]

That summer, John Adams, aware of the congressional debate and always anxious to guard his own reputation, wrote from his post in France a remarkable letter to McKean defending himself and disparaging Franklin. Adams called Franklin "a wit and a humorist." He conceded that the "old conjurer" might be "a philosopher," but Adams disdained, "he is not a sufficient statesman." The letter revealed Adams's insecurity as well as his competitiveness with his peers. Adams complained that Franklin was "too old, too infirm, too indolent and dissipated, to be sufficient to discharge of all the important duties."[11]

By the time McKean responded, Congress had reaffirmed its support for both Franklin and Adams. In his November 8 letter to Adams, McKean noted: "Since the date of your letter, I suppose you have been informed of what has passed in Congress respecting our foreign ministers, and particularly yourself." He then denounced the troublemakers in Congress, explained his support for Franklin, and offered Adams a rousing statement of encouragement that said as much about himself as it did Adams:

> Do not my friend be discouraged . . . difficulties, public and secret attacks, will eternally attend public Characters and high stations. The man who discharges his Trust with fidelity and according to the best of his abilities will always have the consolation of his own mind (a consolation the world cannot give) and he may be happy in the approbation of his country, but will never be miserable in the want of it—he will always also find a distinguishing, a worthy few, to support and applaud him.[12]

Debates such as those over Franklin's and Adams's recall led McKean to view the Congress as feckless and out of touch with the people. He feared that the more worrisome increasing dysfunction in Congress threatened to undermine a common vision of nationhood. He later described it as "a cabal, whose views I could not fathom." He wrote Richard Henry Lee, the Virginia statesman whose resolution had led to the Declaration of Independence, bemoaning the dearth of talent in the Congress: "There has been a virtuous band in Congress from the beginning of the present contest, but they were never so few, or so much opposed."[13] Although he didn't know it at the time, McKean was observing the increasing sectionalism, factionalism, and parochialism that would ultimately lead to the formation of political parties in America.

# 11

## The Treason Trials

O N HIS RETURN TO PHILADELPHIA, MCKEAN HAD BEEN HORRIFIED BY the condition of his adopted city and was well aware that General Washington had refused to agree to Article 10 passed by Congress "giving loyalists and deserters immunity from prosecution." Not that McKean was in the mood to forgive Loyalists. But many patriots took the law into their own hands and turned their wrath on Tories who had refused to sign "loyalty oaths," tarring and feathering them or hoisting them on liberty poles. In spite of his respect for Washington and his contempt for the conduct of British soldiers, the chief justice showed leniency to Loyalists after the British vacated Philadelphia, exemplified by the case of a British sympathizer named Samuel Chapman.

Chapman, a native of Massachusetts, had moved to Pennsylvania and joined the British army on December 26, 1776. He rose to the rank of lieutenant and fought near Philadelphia on April 30, 1778, at the Battle of Crooked Billet in which as many as a hundred Revolutionary soldiers were killed. Chapman was subsequently captured, sent to Massachusetts, and then extradited to Pennsylvania because of the role he had played at Crooked Billet. His Pennsylvania lawyer argued that he could not have committed treason because he left the state after the collapse of the proprietary government but before a new state constitution had been ratified.

He claimed Chapman had never "been a subject or inhabitant of the Commonwealth." However, the prosecution argued that a state constitution was nevertheless extant at the time, and in any event, treason was a common law crime. McKean believed the common law on treason lacked clarity and so gave narrow instructions to the members of the jury, who briefly deliberated and then acquitted Chapman. McKean's handling of the case lent credibility to the independence of the court and established his reputation as a moderate in the area of treason prosecutions.

Two other defendants who appeared before the McKean court in the fall of 1778 were not so fortunate. Abraham Carlisle and John Roberts, both elderly Quakers, were accused of "falsely and traitorously preparing, ordering, waging, and leveling a public and cruel war against the commonwealth." Carlisle, a successful carpenter, was charged specifically with having supplied information to the enemy as well as guarding the city gates during the British occupation. Roberts had none of the financial resources of Carlisle, and his alleged crimes were more ambiguous. He was accused of having ridiculed the American cause, predicting that the rebellion would fail, and encouraging others to support the Crown.

Carlisle's defense team included James Wilson, a friend of McKean's who also had signed the Declaration of Independence. Wilson stressed that Carlisle had never borne arms against the American cause, much less overtly harmed anyone. But the prosecution, headed by Joseph Reed, who served alongside McKean in Congress, produced a stream of witnesses who testified that Carlisle had guarded the northern gates of Philadelphia's city border and had encouraged a spy to provide information on rebel plans. McKean ruled that an accumulation of evidence over time could demonstrate allegiance to Britain and therefore treason. The jury deliberated for twenty-four hours and ultimately returned a guilty verdict. Wilson immediately filed an appeal, contending that the charges had not been drawn with "sufficient precision," but McKean, as chief justice, heard the appeal and, not surprisingly, upheld his original decision. He sentenced Carlisle to death by hanging.

Shortly after sentencing Carlisle, the court took up the case of Roberts, who confessed that he had tried to persuade individuals to support the

Crown. The case hinged on whether Roberts's intent was sufficient for an act of treason or whether he had to actually have successfully consummated a treasonable offense. McKean ruled the crime in this instance required that the jury find Roberts to have successfully enlisted others to the British cause. The defense conceded that Roberts recruited British sympathizers but also produced numerous witnesses who testified that Roberts had actually helped American prisoners gain access to their families. Joseph Reed, once again prosecutor for the state, introduced Roberts's confession into the record, and the jury convicted the elderly Quaker.

In late October, McKean sentenced Roberts. Sitting on the dais, McKean stared down at the old man and declared, "Treason is a crime of the most dangerous and fatal consequences to society. It is of a most malignant nature; it is of crimson color and scarlet eye." The chief justice then put the crime in a larger context, asking rhetorically how to punish someone "who joins the enemy of his country, and endeavors the total destruction of lives, liberties and property of all his fellow citizens, who willingly aids a cause which has been complicated with the horrid and crying sin of murdering thousands, who were not only innocent, but meritorious; and aggravated by burning some of them alive and starving others to death." McKean acknowledged Roberts had helped Americans, especially prisoners, and praised his "humanity, charity and benevolence," but, pronounced the Chief Justice, "the acts did not negate his greater crimes." He sentenced him to die by hanging, noting that he was showing leniency because in England traitors were drawn and quartered.

Over the next several days, dozens of petitions were filed with the Pennsylvania Assembly's Executive Council asking for clemency for both Carlisle and Roberts. Francis Alison, McKean's former instructor, was among those who pleaded for the council to pardon the two old men. And just days before the men were to be hanged, Chief Justice McKean and his associate justices wrote to the council asking for a pardon. It was vintage McKean—he believed the application of the law needed to be guided by compassion. In the end the pleas for mercy fell on deaf ears, and on November 4, Carlisle and Roberts were both executed. Joseph Reed, who had prosecuted the cases, expressed satisfaction that justice had been served. Reed focused less on the appropriateness of the sentence than on the fact that it had been applied equally to Carlisle, who was reasonably wealthy, as to Roberts, who was poor: "We could not have for shame have made an example of a poor rogue after forgiving the rich."[1]

Weeks later, in New York City, John Andre, the British officer and bon vivant who had lived in Benjamin Franklin's house during the British occupation of Philadelphia, read aloud at a Tory gathering a verse that he had written entitled "The Dream." Andre imagined a dreamlike metamorphosis in which General Washington became a gamecock, John Jay turned into a snake, and Thomas McKean was transformed into a bloodhound. In Andre's theatrical presentation, several judges were dispensing justice in Hell "and the first person called upon was Chief Justice McKean." Andre's voice rose as he described McKean's "more than savage cruelty, his horrid disregard to the many oaths of allegiance he had taken, and the vile sacrifices he had made to justice, in the interests of rebellion were openly rehearsed." The satirist bemoaned "the souls of Roberts and Carlisle . . . ordered to scourge him through the infernal regions." Andre's "Dream" was reprinted in the *Royal Gazette* and distributed among Loyalists throughout America. An anonymous reader commented on Andre's satire in the *Gazette*: "He who a band of ruffians keeps to kill, Is he not guilty of the blood they spill? Who guards McKean and Joseph Reed the vile, Help'd he not to murder Roberts and Carlisle?"[2]

One hundred eighteen individuals were ultimately indicted for treason in Pennsylvania. In McKean's court, only Carlisle and Roberts were put to death.[3] He believed in using the power of the court to send a strong message, but he was not, contrary to the view of his contemporaries and later by some historians, a "hanging judge" who sought vengeance or retribution. In the end, the treason trials enhanced McKean's reputation, but an aggrieved soldier would yet test his character.

—❦—

BRIGADIER GENERAL WILLIAM THOMPSON WAS A CONTINENTAL ARMY officer who had been captured by the British and imprisoned during the

Canadian expedition. The British subsequently released him on the condition that he could not be reinstated in the military until the Continental Army released a British solider of comparable rank.[4] This arrangement
represented a kind of honor code that existed between warring nations. He
had written General Washington, who responded that he would be "happy
to see you again with the army," but that it was "entirely out of my hands to
do anything," and "the matter therefore only lays with Congress."

Next, Thompson wrote to Chief Justice McKean, who referred the
matter to Thomas Bradford, the commissioner for prisoners and the man
responsible for prisoner exchanges and officer reinstatement. The months
passed, and Thompson, living in Philadelphia and unable to rejoin his military unit, spent his days frequenting the city's public houses. He increasingly and inexplicably blamed McKean for his purgatory, and one evening
in early November 1778, after several drinks, he boasted to a companion of
his intention to "whip [McKean] whenever he met him, unless Mr. McKean
would fight him as a gentleman which [he] believed him too great a coward
to do."

That same evening, McKean joined his fellow justices William Atlee
and John Evans, as well as Thomas Bradford, in Philadelphia's London
Coffee House. Sitting in one of the establishment's wooden booths, the old
friends were talking, laughing, and sipping draughts when General Thompson walked into the crowded tavern and stood at the bar. Bradford spied
Thompson through the candlelit haze of pipe smoke and told McKean that
Thompson could be reinstated in the Continental Army soon because they
were preparing to release a British prisoner. Anxious to relay the good news
personally to Thompson, McKean stood up and approached the general.
Thompson, however, was in no mood to receive the chief justice; he acidly
complained that McKean was unfairly keeping him out of the military and
that he had no means to support himself. When McKean tried to reason
with Thompson, the general shouted at him and then recalled that Mc-
Kean had sent him an insulting letter earlier in the year summoning him
to answer an accusation by another soldier that Thompson's servant was a
deserter. McKean asked to see the letter. Thompson's voice grew louder as
he continued to berate McKean, telling him that he didn't have the letter

because he had wiped "his arse with the paper." McKean then became irritated and, according to Bradford, declared Thompson was "no gentleman." When McKean turned his back to walk away, Thompson became enraged and looked as if he might physically assault the chief justice. McKean's friends and other patrons then stepped in to separate the two men. "Strike me if you dare," McKean bellowed. "I will make your heart ache if you do." Thompson yelled back, "Damn you I will make your bones ache first," and stormed out of the tavern.[5]

A week later, McKean reported the incident to Congress, alleging that Thompson's behavior had been a "gross insult to Congress." This set in motion a series of hearings that lasted for several weeks with the testimony of more than two dozen witnesses to determine whether Thompson was "guilty of an insult to the honor and dignity of this house, a breach of privilege." As the dispute dragged on, members complained that the entire incident was not worthy of their time. At last, on December 24 Congress voted that Thompson should apologize for "opprobrious language against, and scandalous reflections upon" a member of Congress.

Thompson offered a perfunctory apology to the Congress, but five days later wrote a letter published in the *Pennsylvania Packet* declaring that McKean had "behaved like a liar, a rascal, and a coward." He also challenged the chief justice to a duel. McKean replied that he could not "set the precedent obliging a member of Congress or a magistrate to subject himself to a duel with every person against whose opinion he gives his vote or judgment." McKean then used his most powerful weapon: the law. He sued Thompson for the "vile epithets" contained in his letter to the *Packet*.[6]

The controversy continued to simmer. McKean made public statements that he did not consider anyone who served in the military to be above the law, leading some of his antagonists to accuse him of having made an example of Thompson because he believed the military had grown too powerful. At the time, the military was held in high regard, certainly more so than officers of the court, and radicals alleged that the chief justice was antimilitary.

Months later, a Pennsylvania court vindicated McKean by awarding him nearly £6,000 in damages from Colonel Thompson. McKean "released the damages," asserting he "only wanted to see the law and facts settled."[7] In his view, allegations in the press that he was antimilitary were politically motivated and nothing more than thinly veiled attempts to discredit him as chief justice. He was, after all, the only signer of the Declaration of Independence present in Congress on July 4, 1776, who supported independence and then actually served in the military. None of the other delegates to Congress could claim that distinction. In his view, the Thompson affair was about libel and character assassination. It would not be the last time McKean would wrestle with issues of libel law.

# 12

## President McKean

T HOUGH THE BRITISH HAD VACATED PHILADELPHIA IN JUNE 1778, THE war was far from over. The last years of the decade were difficult ones for General Washington's Continental Army. By early 1779, in addition to the nearly twenty thousand highly trained, well-armed British soldiers, there were reportedly fifty thousand Loyalists in America who were either armed or ready to offer assistance to the Crown. This was more than double the number of troops that Washington had at his disposal.[1]

The Redcoats demonstrated their superiority during the summer of 1780. After enduring days of incessant bombardment, the Continental Army in Charleston, South Carolina, succumbed to the British Navy, and the entire American garrison of more than five thousand men was taken prisoner. Weeks later, on August 16, 1780, General Horatio Gates, a former British soldier who now commanded Revolutionary forces in the south, suffered a devastating defeat at Camden, South Carolina, when more than two thousand patriots were either killed or captured. Adding to the sense of despair, stories began to circulate that the British had undertaken a campaign of terror.[2]

McKean was incensed by reports of atrocities committed by British soldiers. He wrote to Sarah, deploring "the cruelty hitherto unthought even by themselves, such as murdering old men, ravishing women and little girls, burning houses with the inhabitants in them. . . . The militia have sent some hundreds of them to Hell in the midst of their iniquities and I have real reason to hope some hundreds more will be sent."[3] McKean had long believed in the legal justification for independence; British atrocities convinced him of the moral justification for the war. Yet his determination to drive the Redcoats from American shores was tempered by the realization that Revolutionaries lacked both organization and funds. In 1780, he wrote to Richard Henry Lee, noting the "deranged state of our finances," which "has given us infinite trouble and concern."[4]

By December, members of Congress had concluded that their only recourse was to seek another loan from the French. Having asked Benjamin Franklin to make similar appeals on many occasions, the members decided they should appoint a new special envoy better able to stress both the urgency and the importance of French assistance. They settled on John Laurens, a South Carolina aristocrat who was a key aide to General Washington. McKean was adamant that the appointment did not reflect a lack of confidence in Franklin, but Gouverneur Morris was not so charitable, declaring that the plan was "to remove Franklin indirectly, a thing which for obvious reasons could not be accomplished directly." Morris sniped that "we have sent a young beggar instead of an old one."[5]

General Washington, meanwhile, was growing increasingly discouraged. His troops, encamped in New Jersey, lacked food and clothing, and he had been forced to order confiscation of cattle and food stores from local farmers. Washington rued that his army had become "plunderers instead of protectors of the people."[6] The general understood America's deeply rooted suspicion of government power—it was, after all, against the abuse of such power that the Americans were fighting—but he had reluctantly come to the conclusion that the Revolution could succeed only by creating a central authority with the power to raise taxes and conscript soldiers. As he wrote to one Virginia delegate, "Unless Congress speaks in a more decisive tone; unless they are vested with powers by the several states competent to the great purposes of War, or assume them, as a matter of right . . . then our cause is lost. We can no longer drudge on in the old way. I see one head gradually changing into thirteen."[7]

There was one bit of good news in 1780. On the night of September 21, the Continental Army apprehended British Major John Andre near Tarrytown, New York, wearing an American uniform and carrying secret documents tucked into his boot. Major General Benedict Arnold of the Continental Army, who had served under General Washington, had provided documents to Andre detailing the fortifications and troop strengths at West Point. Arnold, angry that he had not been recognized for his courage and promoted, had changed sides in the war and had decided to secretly help the British capture the fort. After Andre was apprehended, Arnold escaped to New York City. One of the first officials to be informed of Arnold's treachery was McKean, who ordered a search for Arnold's personal papers and notified the Pennsylvania Executive Council of the developments. Arnold continued to evade capture and ultimately became a commander in the British army. Thirty-year-old Andre, on the other hand, who had once ridiculed McKean as a "bloodhound" and a hanging judge, was not so fortunate; he was convicted in a New York court of "being behind American lines under a feigned name and in a disguised habit"—and hanged. [8]

MCKEAN WAS GROWING INCREASINGLY WEARY OF CARRYING BOTH HIS federal legislative and state judicial responsibilities. On Christmas Day 1780, he wrote a long letter to his old friend John Dickinson, now the president of Delaware, complaining that, as both chief justice and congressman, he had been underpaid and overworked. He knew Dickinson, who also wore multiple political hats, would be sympathetic. McKean noted that he "had not been offered a farthing" for nearly two years and never even received compensation "as would defray" his personal expenses. He declared that his "health and fortune" were "impaired by unremitted attention to public affairs" and begged Dickinson to appoint "some other gentlemen as delegates." McKean opined on his need for "relaxation, which is absolutely as necessary . . . for the mind as for the body." It was a belated acknowledgment for McKean, who a decade earlier had been advised by Dickinson to "step back and enjoy life a little more."[9]

McKean ignored his own advice, and in March 1781 was back in Congress, which after a lengthy recess had reconvened for a ceremonial confirmation of the ratification of the Articles of Confederation. The Articles of Confederation had been conceptualized by Benjamin Franklin three decades earlier and then drafted in 1776 by a committee chaired by none other than John Dickinson. Although Congress had moved for ratification of the articles in 1777, now four years later there was an urgency, as delegates recognized that General Washington had been correct: the United States needed some form of a national government to bind the states together. Only then could America earn the international recognition and ultimately the support critical to the war effort.

After Maryland became the thirteenth state to ratify the articles on February 2, 1781, the United States became a confederation of sovereign states. Congress now had the authority to make treaties and alliances, raise an army and navy, and regulate the currency. But the articles also limited the power of the Congress, which was not empowered to levy taxes, regulate commerce, or even to write laws but only to recommend legislation to the states. And because the articles provided for neither an independent chief executive nor a federal court system, critical administrative and judicial functions remained the domain of the states as well.

One of the most significant features of the new framework was the office of president, a position with no inherent power but important because, as the presiding officer of Congress, he was charged with acting as an impartial moderator. The president sat in a large chair on a dais facing the other delegates and recognized those who wished to stand and be heard. When there was an important vote, the president summarized the issue at hand just as a judge might issue instructions to a jury.

After the Confederation entered into force and the United States formally emerged as a united, sovereign, and national state. Samuel Huntington, who had been elected president of the Continental Congress two years earlier, became the first president of "the United States in Congress Assembled." Although ultimate sovereignty continued to reside in individual states, members of Congress agreed to work together on important issues such as finance, foreign trade, and—the issue that dominated all others—the continuing conflict with England. The articles specifically stated that "all charges of war shall be defrayed out of common treasury which shall be defrayed by the several states." To support their work, Congress appointed a quasi-cabinet that included the wealthy Philadelphia merchant Robert Morris. He was given the title of Superintendent of Finance as well as Agent of Marine, two of the most powerful positions in the government, which meant that he controlled both the United States Treasury and its navy. Not surprisingly, Washington looked to Morris, and not President Huntington, to find the financial resources to fund the war effort. But since the state delegations refused to approve new taxes, Morris's hands were tied.[10]

In early July 1781, just a few days after the fifth anniversary of the Declaration of Independence, McKean wrote to his old friend Samuel Adams, who months earlier had retired from Congress for health reasons and had returned to Boston. McKean sounded a note of optimism about the direction of the war, reporting that the army under General Nathanael Greene, Washington's most capable and dependable officer, had been successful in defending both Georgia and South Carolina. He noted that a prisoner exchange had taken place in Augusta whereby "all the refugees and Tories taken in . . . have been given up for our militia taken by the enemy." McKean also cheerily wrote that "the Harvest in Pennsylvania and the adjoining states promises to be double in quantity than in any year during the last twenty" and that "the whole country teems with fruit." McKean was less sanguine about the political situation in Philadelphia. Once again, the colonies were leaderless: Samuel Huntington had resigned the presidency after serving less than six months in office under the Articles of Confederation.[11]

Huntington had never really wanted the position in the first place. His financial affairs were in disarray and his health was poor; he longed to be with his family in Connecticut and looked forward to resuming his career as a judge. Huntington had hoped to return to his home earlier but had been persuaded by his colleagues in the Congress to remain in Philadelphia until the articles had been ratified. In his letter to Adams, McKean warned that the experiment in national government might fail because "the honor [of serving as president] is gone a begging, as no one . . . seems willing to accept." He added that some of his colleagues in Congress "were so fond of having a great and powerful man to look up to, but that this they may liken him to a king."[12] Sam Adams knew that McKean was referring to Robert Morris, the wealthy Philadelphia businessman and political operator, whom they both distrusted and suspected of being a war profiteer. McKean remembered that Morris had initially opposed the Declaration of Independence, and he worried that now the arrogant businessman might become president.

Three days later, however, Congress nominated Samuel Johnston, a North Carolina lawyer who had been a member of Congress for only two years. But Johnston, like Huntington, turned down the offer because he, too, was in ill health, and he feared for the safety of his family back in North Carolina. With Huntington and Johnston both declining to serve, members of Congress faced a growing political crisis. The question on the minds of all the delegates was not only who was capable of leading the new nation but also who was willing to do so?

Caesar Rodney, McKean's Delaware colleague, recommended to the members that McKean be considered. Rodney noted that McKean had demonstrated a commitment to independence over many years and that he was known as a tireless public servant who had served on more committees in Congress than any of his peers. However, McKean had something of a reputation for arrogance, and his public spat with General Thompson also gave ammunition to the suggestion that he was antimilitary. In the formative years of the young republic, with political passions and wounds so raw, most public figures quickly found that they had some noisy detractors. McKean was no exception.

But he had many loyal friends, too, and on July 6 Caesar Rodney nominated him for president of the Continental Congress. Members of Congress voted by secret ballot and elected overwhelmingly the forty-seven-year-old chief justice as the first president of the United States chosen to serve after the Articles of Confederation had been ratified.[13]

Once again, McKean answered the call to service. Without the ability to raise revenue, he knew that under the Articles of Confederation his power would be limited, and he only agreed to serve as president for a short period of time—until a new president could be chosen or until there was a significant change in the conflict. It was a dark time in the struggle for independence; although he didn't know it at the time, his willingness to serve came at a critical juncture in the young republic.

McKean received letters of congratulation from across the country and around the world, including one from General Washington, who gushed that, on the basis of his "knowledge" of the new president's character, he was certain that the duties of the office would be executed with "greatest propriety." One of McKean's friends, Thomas Burke, who had served in Congress with him and who was now governor of North Carolina, wrote, "I am happy that the choice of Congress has fallen on a gentleman of your merit, and so long distinguished a firm and zealous patriot."[14] Writing from France, Benjamin Franklin didn't mention McKean's character, intelligence, or qualifications but simply congratulated him on "being called to the honorable and important Office of president."[15] Another friend, John Evans, a justice on the Delaware Supreme Court, writing from London, anticipated that McKean would be criticized for holding two prominent offices at one time, but Evans dismissed potential critics as "busy bodies" and assured McKean that he had "the approbation of the disinterested of the virtuous people."[16]

Since the American government contained neither a separate executive branch nor a judicial branch, as president of the Congress McKean undoubtedly occupied the highest-ranking official government position in America—even if it was a largely ceremonial one. Additionally, McKean continued to serve as Pennsylvania's chief justice. He was due a salary from the state of Delaware for his service in the Congress, but he had not been paid for years. Although he now had substantial real estate holdings, he probably could not have afforded to accept the uncompensated presidency had he not also maintained his salaried position on the bench.

Just as John Evans had predicted, some of the nearly dozen newspapers in Pennsylvania at the time criticized McKean for holding down the dual roles of chief justice of the Pennsylvania Supreme Court and president of the Continental Congress. Writing in Philadelphia's *Freeman's Journal,* also known as the *North-American Intelligencer,* an anonymous pundit using the nom de plume "Tenax" maintained that Pennsylvania's constitution was very clear that judges of the supreme court "shall not be allowed to sit as members of the Continental Congress, executive council, or general assembly, nor . . . hold any office, civil or military."[17]

McKean responded in a lawyerly fashion. He agreed that as chief justice of Pennsylvania he could not also be a member of Congress from Pennsylvania. In his view, however, Article 23 of the state constitution did not prevent him from serving as chief justice of Pennsylvania and simultaneously as president of the Continental Congress because in his capacity as a member of Congress he was representing Delaware. Moreover, he pointed out, there was ample precedent for plural office holding: he had, after all, been a member of Congress when he became chief justice, and no one had raised an objection at the time.[18] In the end, most members of Congress didn't much care about McKean's multiple offices. They were focused on one thing only: winning the war, which at the time was not going well.

The United States was essentially financially insolvent. Since independence, the Congress had issued paper as legal tender that totaled almost $250 million. But weeks before McKean's ascension to the presidency, the value of Continental paper had plummeted, as inflation, unchecked for years, spiraled out of control. Additionally, the states continued to issue their own currencies, the value of which varied widely. Counterfeiting, used by the British as a form of economic warfare; the spending of foreign loans before they were secured; and a British blockade of American merchant ships all contributed to the collapse of the Continental currency, which was nearly worthless by the time McKean took office.

Though he didn't particularly trust Robert Morris, McKean turned to him because he respected the financier's acumen. He also was aware that Morris had contributed a substantial amount of his own money to the Revolutionary cause. McKean asked Morris to find a way to fund the war, and Morris came up with a bold idea: he proposed that Congress establish a national bank, a financial institution that would be capitalized by the thirteen states and that would make loans to the war effort. Morris submitted his plan to Congress, where some members greeted it with skepticism because they assumed that Morris intended to run the bank himself and undoubtedly enrich himself in the process.

Though McKean worried about the concentration of so much economic power in one man, he supported the bank, which he believed would bring stability to the colonial economy and facilitate financing of the war effort. In truth, there were few other options. Some members of Congress proposed amendments to the Articles of Confederation giving Congress the power to require states to fulfill their obligations, but the legislation failed to pass. The states were already obligated to support one another—that was the purpose of binding them together under the articles—but everyone knew that individual state governments had no money either.[19] It was a predicament that McKean would long remember, one that would greatly influence his views on constitutional government in the years to come.

# 13

## The Siege of Yorktown

**D**URING THE WINTER OF **1780,** CAMPED AT **V**ALLEY **F**ORGE, **W**ASHING-ton's army suffered from a lack of food, warm clothing, and supplies and armaments. A year later, Washington divided the army into smaller units, but from his headquarters in New Windsor, New York, he complained to President McKean that his army still was not being adequately supported. In his new role, McKean tried to reassure General Washington that the healthy agricultural economy, especially in Pennsylvania, would ultimately provide adequate food to feed the troops.[1] The general had a very different view and dismissed McKean's cheerful optimism. The harvest in Pennsylvania might have been a good one, but Washington worried that the states had not adequately mobilized for war and complained to McKean "the fault must surely be our own" that "the bounties of providence necessary for our support and defense" were not reaching his army.[2]

The dearth of resources was undermining the morale of the troops, and Washington worried about his ability to hold the army together. In March, nearly a thousand members of the Pennsylvania brigade had mutinied and marched on the Congress because they had no winter clothes and had not been paid for months. Before they reached Philadelphia, where it was feared they might incite a riot, Washington's troops shot two soldiers. Three weeks later, when a handful of New Jersey militiamen rose up in mutiny, Washington ordered his troops to surround the mutineers, and they executed two of the ringleaders on the spot.[3]

Washington concluded that unless circumstances changed drastically, the Continental Army could not survive another year of war. Not only did the soldiers desperately need supplies but also the states needed a more unified political infrastructure. He implored McKean to keep him informed of Congress's work, telling the president that "he had often been left in the dark in matters which essentially concern the public welfare."[4] Privately, Washington had begun to contemplate a negotiated settlement with the enemy.

To make matters worse, by the late summer of 1781 McKean's sunny prediction of a bountiful harvest had turned dark. In a letter to his friend Arthur Lee, a diplomat, McKean warned that "famine will be added to the other calamities which already overwhelm us."[5] For the first time since becoming president, McKean expressed fear that the "government will find it impossible to support the war unless" it was "injected immediately with some hard money."[6] McKean was also receiving worrying reports from the field about the growing strength of the British forces, which were now commanded by a new, wily, and ruthless general.

Lord Charles Cornwallis had replaced Lord Howe as commander of the British troops in America. Cornwallis, who had been a Whig member of Parliament and had opposed continued British occupation of the American colonies, was well liked as a politician but had shown himself to be temperamental as a military leader. Notwithstanding his mercurial personality—or perhaps as a result of it—he was widely respected by his peers and greatly feared by his enemies. General Marquis de Lafayette, the French aristocrat who had joined the Continental Army and was one of Washington's most trusted generals, remarked that "Lord Cornwallis's abilities to me are more frightening than his superiority of forces. . . . I am devilishly afraid of him."[7]

To counter the British advantage in troops and armaments, President McKean encouraged a closer relationship with England's archenemy, France. On July 28, he again wrote Washington, and in an effort to bolster the general's spirits, informed him that Colonel Laurens, the American special minister to France, had assured McKean of "the sincere attachment of our good ally to our cause and country."[8] The fault lines between Anglophile and Francophile Americans had persisted for years, and McKean's overtures to the French were not uniformly appreciated. John Jay wrote McKean in September explaining that "an interest in the dignity of my country" led him to caution against permitting "the sovereign independent States of America submitting, in the persons of their ministers, to be absolutely governed by the advice and opinions of the servants of another sovereign." He added, "Nor is it clear that America, thus casting herself into the arms of the King of France, will advance either her interest or reputation with that of other nations."[9] But McKean was not particularly worried about America's reputation—he feared for its survival.

⊷⊷⊷

ONE OF THE MOST IMPORTANT OF WASHINGTON'S STRATEGIC WEAPONS WAS a retinue of spies that kept him abreast of British troop movements and war plans. The general asked McKean to share any military intelligence that crossed his desk, which he maintained, "If properly proved . . . may turn greatly to our advantage."[10] By virtue of his position as president and his past service on the Secret Committee, McKean had access to a wide range of informants, sources, and contacts. In July 1781, McKean forwarded to Washington a letter from Lafayette, who predicted "Lord Cornwallis intends to proceed with the rest of his army to New York, excepting perhaps his cavalry, which may be sent to Charleston."[11] A week later, McKean provided Washington with very specific information on British troop movements from an unidentified informant: "two battalions of light infantry of the Queen's rangers was certainly, and the guards with one or two British regiments and some cavalry, were [probably] embarked for New York."[12]

McKean's information substantiated the view of General Washington, who was also receiving intelligence from many sources that the decisive battle would be fought in New York. But in a letter written to Washington in early August, McKean provided startling news that suggested Cornwallis had drastically changed his strategy and ordered several ships from his fleet to set sail from the Potomac to the Chesapeake.[13] A few days later, after receiving additional reports, McKean estimated that three thousand troops were headed up the Potomac, although he maintained that Cornwallis himself had stayed behind in Portsmouth, Virginia. McKean's intelligence, although flawed in some important respects, provided valuable insight into the British strategic plan. Cornwallis had actually accompanied his entire army of more than eight thousand soldiers to Yorktown, Virginia, a tobacco port on the Tidewater peninsula. There, the British commander planned to resupply his war-weary army from His Majesty's ships. Washington was skeptical of McKean's information. He remained convinced that Cornwallis would make his stand in New York, and only after being pressed by his French ally Rochambeau, did the American commander agree to engage the British in the Chesapeake Bay.[14]

By the second week of August, Washington's troops and those of the French general Rochambeau were on the march from New York to Virginia to engage the enemy at Yorktown. Robert Morris, who continued to scour the states for funds, returned to Philadelphia on August 12, and the first person he met with was President McKean. Morris was having little luck extracting money for the war effort from beleaguered state governors, and his plan for a national bank had stalled. Neither man made any record of their discussion, but it was likely an uncomfortable meeting. McKean remained powerless to compel congressional action. He likely complained to Morris that at the time five states didn't even have representatives present in the Congress because either their legislatures had been slow to appoint delegates or the delegates who had been selected refused to serve, preferring instead to work at the state level on local issues.[15]

Though supplies lagged, the Continental Army continued its march from New York south to Virginia. On Thursday, August 30, General Washington and his top commanders, including Rochambeau, Knox, Sullivan, and Moultrie, riding ahead of the American and French armies, arrived at the outskirts of Philadelphia. They were greeted by a welcoming committee that included President McKean, who accompanied them as they rode on horseback through streets lined with cheering citizenry. At the City Tavern, McKean was among those who offered a toast to the generals and celebrated the impending arrival of the soldiers with a rum punch. Later that afternoon Washington went to the State House and delivered a brief speech to the Congress, which, though not written down, likely touched on the high-stakes significance of the impending military campaign. That evening, Philadelphia celebrated the arrival of Washington and his generals: bonfires blazed; men carried torches through the streets; and, on the waterfront, cannons fired salutes.[16]

Washington slept comfortably at the residence of Robert Morris, but not before the portly financier hosted a dinner in the general's honor, attended by the other military commanders and by the city's political elite. At dinner, President McKean raised a glass of Madeira in honor of General Rochambeau and offered a poetic metaphor, predicting that the alliance between France and America would end in victory over the British, or as he put it, "where lilies flourish, roses fade."[17]

The following day, the generals met outside Philadelphia and agreed on plans to coordinate their armies for a strategic assault on the British. The French planned to continue overland, while an American battalion sailed down the Chesapeake and would come ashore at Chester, Pennsylvania. The rest of the Continental Army planned to traverse the peninsula at the head of the Chesapeake and sail up the York River.

Two days later, on a hot Sunday afternoon, the Continental Army marched into Philadelphia. Although the troops were dirty and many were barefoot and clothed in rags, they paraded to fife and drum in a column that stretched two miles long. Once again, hundreds of citizens lined the streets to cheer. The soldiers were buoyed by the warm reception, but some reportedly resented seeing so many relatively prosperous and carefree civilians in the crowd. The soldiers from New England groused that they had not been paid in over a year. One officer later wrote in his diary, "Great symptoms of discontent appeared on the passage through the city."[18]

It wasn't just the soldiers who hadn't been paid. General Arthur St. Clair, a friend of McKean's, had written the president asking to "obtain some relief" because his lack of salary was "really robbing my children." Even General Washington worried that he had "neglected his private concerns." Washington, who was already a very wealthy man and who refused to accept a salary as general, nevertheless complained that his real estate holdings "might end in capital losses, if not absolute ruin."[19] McKean, whose own wealth was largely tied up in real estate and who constantly seemed to worry about money, likely shared similar misgivings, although he never publicly expressed them.

Fortunately, the American soldiers passed through Philadelphia before French soldiers arrived the next day; the Americans might have mutinied on the spot had they seen the French troops in their fresh uniforms: crisp, white broadcloth set off by colorful silk lapels bearing their regimental colors. The French officers wore pink and white plumes on their hats. McKean, standing with Washington and Rochambeau on the top steps of the state-house, reviewed the French as they paraded down Market Street. As the officers passed, McKean doffed his broad-brimmed black hat, bowing so low that other dignitaries feared he might topple forward. Not knowing exactly what the etiquette required, the other Americans copied McKean and bowed down as well.

That evening there were elaborate parties for the American and French military and diplomatic officers. Joseph Reed, president of the Pennsylvania Assembly, hosted the French officers, serving a banquet that featured soup made from a ninety-pound turtle.[20] In anticipation of engaging the British at Yorktown, the atmosphere at the dinner that night seemed almost festive. If McKean appeared outwardly ebullient and optimistic, he must have been privately fretful: he had just received word from Benjamin Franklin in France that troubles were looming at Versailles, where, as Franklin put it in his letter to the president, even "the best of friends may be overburdened . . . by too frequent, too large and too inopportune demands."[21]

Franklin's letter was two months old, but in more recent correspondence to Robert Morris he was even more direct and foreboding, writing that Prime Minister Vergennes's attitude toward the American Revolutionaries "terrifies me."[22] The American diplomat had promised Vergennes that America would draw no more loans on France after March 1781, but now, six months later, he told Morris that he had asked the French for yet another loan. America could not service its existing debt, but it needed more money to finance the war. That same day, Morris wrote to the governors of Delaware and New Jersey, declaring, "We are on the eve of the most active operations." He implored Rodney to find "hundreds of barrels of meat, two thousand barrels of rum, and five hundred bushels of salt" because "a body of soldiers" should not "starve in the midst of a plentiful country." General Washington also wrote to the governors "to enforce in the warmest terms the application of Mr. Morris."[23] And on the following day, President McKean joined the chorus, "We are all at the eve of a great event. . . . May God grant they be prosperous to us."[24]

Washington and his generals were greatly encouraged by the moral support they received in Philadelphia, but the commander worried privately that Cornwallis's well-equipped Redcoats would overwhelm his battered army. Although he had reconnoitered with Rochambeau, Washington had heard nothing from the other French military commanders, the Comte de Grasse and General Jean Nicholas Barras, both of whom had commanded fleets en route to the Chesapeake Bay. He implored General Lafayette, "If you get anything new from any quarter, send, I pray you, on the spur of speed, for I am almost all impatience and anxiety."[25]

On September 5, General Washington led his army out of Philadelphia. Late in the day, in Chester, a messenger delivered the latest intelligence from the Chesapeake: Count de Grasse had arrived in the bay with four large frigates, twenty-eight smaller ships, and over thirty-five hundred troops. Having routed the British naval force commanded by Admiral Thomas Graves, de Grasse was now firmly in control of Chesapeake Bay. With Lafayette's army to the west and de Grasse's fleet at sea, Cornwallis was penned between the French and American armies on one side and the French naval forces on the other. Washington was elated by the news.

Meanwhile, back in Philadelphia, in anticipation of perhaps the most decisive battle of the Revolution, President McKean continued to press the states to provide more troops and supplies. On September 11, he wrote to Governor William Livingston of New Jersey and Governor Joseph Reed of Pennsylvania informing them that "an act of Congress of yesterday contains a requisition of three thousand men of each of the states . . . to be properly officered and equipped . . . that the machinations of our enemies be entirely defeated."[26] Writing to General Washington that same week,

McKean passed along news of the requisition as well as intelligence that he had received that, "though not direct through any official or authentic channel, appears to be of sufficient consequence to be communicated to you without delay."[27] British reinforcements, perhaps ten ships, under the command of George Clinton, were on the way to rescue Cornwallis. McKean urged Washington to launch an attack as soon as possible. Washington responded immediately, "The intelligence is so important that I immediately transmitted it to Count de Grasse."[28] Still, Washington, confident for the first time in months, assured McKean that the "superiority" of de Grasse's forces, "even supposing [the British] should have arrived with ten ships . . . will be considerable."[29]

On September 28, General Washington made his final push toward Yorktown, leading his army through Pennsylvania countryside that he described in his diary as "beautiful fertile country." After a twelve-mile march, the Americans finally arrived at a clearing with a view of the enemy's redoubt. There, camped on a bluff overlooking the York River, directly across the water from the town of Gloucester, Virginia, were Cornwallis and his troops, numbering around nine thousand; they occupied the high ground, but the combined forces of the Americans and the French totaled almost nineteen thousand troops.[30]

On October 6, Washington wrote McKean an uncharacteristically optimistic letter: "I am not apt to be sanguine, but I think in all probability Lord Cornwallis must fall into our hands." The general, who had held together a ragged, underresourced army for over four years, predicted an outcome that would be "a most fatal stab to the power of Great Britain in America."[31]

Over the next ten days, as the Redcoats ran low on food and ammunition, French artillery bombarded British positions. Finally, at ten o'clock in the morning on October 17, a British officer climbed atop the ramparts at York waving a white flag. A missive from Cornwallis was soon delivered to General Washington, proposing "a cessation of hostilities for twenty-four hours and that two officers may be appointed by each side to meet . . . to settle terms for the surrender." Two days later, the articles of surrender were signed by General Washington and Lord Cornwallis near the banks of the York River.[32]

⟿⟿

IN PHILADELPHIA, PRESIDENT MCKEAN, UNAWARE OF CORNWALLIS'S SUR-
render, had written General Washington to tell him that a combination of
his responsibilities as chief justice of Pennsylvania and concerns about his
health had persuaded him to "resign the chair of Congress." He signaled his
intention to vacate the position in early November.[33]

Although there is nothing to suggest that McKean's health had seriously faltered, he had undoubtedly been frustrated by the five months he
spent as president of the Continental Congress. The Articles of Confederation had provided an important measure of cohesion to the thirteen
colonies by presenting a united front in appeals to foreign governments
for help, but it did not provide a framework for effective government at
home. As a delegate to the Congress, McKean had watched helplessly as
the Revolutionary army nearly fell apart on several occasions. As president, McKean could not conscript soldiers and was reduced to pleading
with governors to supply regular troops and militia for the war effort. Congress had the right to order the production and purchase of provisions for
the soldiers, but McKean could not force anyone to supply them or to pay
for them. Due to his great personal wealth and access to financing, Robert
Morris remained in many ways the most powerful member of the government. McKean wanted to return to his job as chief justice of Pennsylvania,
where he believed he could wield more influence and help to establish the
rule of law, not only for his state but for the entire nation.

Washington would not receive McKean's communication for several
days and in the meantime concerned himself with the preparation of a
report to the Continental Congress recounting the victory at Yorktown.
Jonathan Trumbull, the son of the governor of Connecticut and a close
friend of Washington's, had recently assumed the position of the general's
private secretary and was asked to write the report in the form of a letter to
President McKean.

Washington entrusted delivery of the letter to his trusted aide, thirty-
six-year-old Tench Tilghman. Tilghman hailed from a wealthy Maryland
family that had been divided by the war: two of his brothers were fighting

with the British. Before serving the general, Tilghman had been a successful merchant in Philadelphia, where he was acquainted with McKean. He accepted the honor of carrying the signed and sealed document even though he was seriously ill, suffering from a fever most likely brought on by malaria. He was also thoroughly exhausted, having assisted Washington in the round-the-clock negotiations that led to surrender and then joining in the celebratory drinking and feasting that followed.

Early in the morning on October 19, Tilghman climbed onto his horse to begin the three-hundred-mile journey to Philadelphia. A French cavalry officer accompanied him to the Yorktown waterfront where he boarded a small ship and sailed down the York River to Chesapeake Bay. Not until the next morning did he reach Annapolis, where he mounted a fresh horse and rode to his father's house in Chestertown, Maryland, arriving sometime in the evening. Tilghman, weakened by fever, collapsed into bed and slept until dawn the next morning. Back in the saddle once again, on his third horse in as many days, Tilghman rode all day and most of the night, finally reaching Philadelphia on October 22 at approximately two o'clock in the morning. The city's cobblestone streets were empty, and Tilghman was weak and drenched in sweat from his fever. He happened across an elderly German night watchman who guided him to McKean's mansion on Third Street. Tilghman rapped on the front door. President McKean, bleary-eyed and wearing a nightshirt, nevertheless warmly greeted him. Tilghman immediately handed over Washington's letter. McKean put on his reading glasses and read the letter by candlelight: "Sir, I have the honor to inform Congress, that a reduction of the British army under the command of Lord Cornwallis is most happily effected." Washington then matter-of-factly described the British army's capitulation and ended with an understated wish that the president and Congress "will be pleased to accept my congratulations on this happy event."[34]

As McKean read the general's news, his face lit up with excitement. He summoned an aide and ordered the bell in the State House to be rung. Word of the great victory spread as celebrants filled the streets in the early morning. One congressman, Elias Boudinot of New Jersey, recorded his feelings about the news in his diary: "God be praised."

At ten o'clock that morning, members of Congress, who had barely slept, gathered at the State House. Smiling and patting each other on the back, they took their seats in the assembly room. The room fell silent as the clerk stood and read aloud the dispatch from General Washington. When he finished, the members rose, threw their hats in the air, and shouted "huzzahs!" to fill the chamber. President McKean gaveled the assembly to order and announced the members should "go in procession to the Dutch Lutheran church and return thanks to God Almighty."[35]

Tench Tilghman needed several days to recover sufficiently to return to Yorktown and active duty. He had refused to accept any pay, a gesture of respect to General Washington, who was doing the same thing. Washington had praised Tilghman in his letter to Congress and urged the members to reward his aide's steadfast loyalty. Because there was no money in the Treasury, McKean entreated his fellow congressmen to contribute one dollar each to pay for the young colonel's room and board. They also voted to award him a horse and an "elegant" sword.

The following week, Congress sent a vote of thanks to the allied army in Yorktown, bequeathed a cannon to Count Rochambeau, and awarded General Washington "two strands of colours taken from the British army." The most serious issue before Congress was the fate of Lord Cornwallis. Several delegates wanted to see him hang in revenge for the atrocities his troops had committed in the Carolinas. In the end, a resolution calling for his execution was narrowly defeated, and he was ultimately exchanged for Henry Laurens, the American diplomat who had been taken prisoner by royal soldiers on his way to Paris.[36]

✦ ✦

IN EARLY NOVEMBER, MCKEAN RESIGNED THE PRESIDENCY OF THE Congress, having served less than four months. Before a new leader was chosen, he wrote a last letter as president, praising General Washington "for the conquest of Lord Cornwallis . . . and the wisdom and patience manifested in the Capitulation." He described the general as "the Deliverer of your country" and assured him that he was "held on the most grateful remembrance, and with a peculiar veneration, by all the wise and good in these United States."[37] In his last official act as president, McKean issued a national proclamation for a "Day of Thanksgiving and Prayer."[38]

A few weeks later, General Washington, writing from his home at Mount Vernon, congratulated McKean "on a release from the fatigue and Trouble of so arduous and important a task."[39] McKean had enjoyed only limited power as president but had employed a steady hand in keeping Congress engaged, providing intelligence reports to Washington, and maintaining close relations with France. The war was not over, but the victory at Yorktown was the turning point. Washington had once contemplated a negotiated settlement, but now it was the British who did so.

—⊱⊰—

McKEAN WAS HEARTENED BY WASHINGTON'S MAGNIFICENT VICTORY AND was encouraged by the progress that America had made toward an independent and democratic society in just five short years. But on a personal level, he was devastated. Just months after the battle at Yorktown, McKean's ten-year-old daughter, Mary, named after his first wife, succumbed to yellow fever and died. McKean rarely displayed emotion either in public or in prose and only referred to her somewhat wistfully in a letter to Samuel Adams as having been a "promising" girl.[40]

As he had previously in facing personal tragedy, McKean turned inward and focused on his work. Though the war dragged on, the terms of engagement were now different. Britain had all but given up its land war and had shifted to an economic embargo, using its vastly superior navy to disrupt trade and intercept American merchant ships on the high seas. In response, McKean joined others in the Congress in calling for the enlargement of the American navy, which had been established in 1775.[41] As always, the question was how to pay for it. He continued, somewhat reluctantly, to support the plans of Robert Morris to establish the First Bank of North America. But McKean had his own ideas about financing the war; he believed that the United States could assert "undisputed title to the Western lands, that belong to the Crown of Great Britain, and have been conquered by the blood and treasure of the United States."[42] Then, McKean proposed that the lands themselves could be used as collateral to obtain a loan—perhaps from the Netherlands. As it became evident years later, his vision of an expansionist America was very much in line with that of President Thomas Jefferson.

McKean was once again busy on the Pennsylvania Supreme Court. But his tenure was increasingly drawing detractors. One of his most vociferous critics was his former brother-in-law, Francis Hopkinson, who complained to Thomas Jefferson that in Pennsylvania "two or three leading members of the House drive the political Coach, the president is the footman of the chief justice [who] rides in the body of the carriage—and the people run whooping and hollering along side, choak'd with Dust and bespatt'd with Mire."

McKean's critics also increasingly included members of the press, especially the conservative editor of the *Independent Gazetteer* Eleazer Oswald. Oswald was tall, handsome, and supremely self-confident. He had served as a lieutenant colonel of artillery in the Continental Army. On October 1, 1782, he published an article criticizing the chief justice's decision in a court case involving two soldiers, rehashing the Thompson affair and accusing McKean of being antimilitary. Just as he had with Thompson, McKean considered the attacks libelous but was in no mood to relitigate his commitment to the military. The chief justice believed in free speech, but there were limits, especially when it involved criticism of him. He tried unsuccessfully, twice, to have Oswald indicted by a grand jury.[43] It was the first time on record that McKean attempted to use his power on the court to punish a detractor. It would not be the last.

# 14

## The Longchamps Affair

B Y THE FALL OF 1782, THE WAR WAS WINDING DOWN AS THE CONTI-
nental Army battled an increasingly dispirited and ineffective British
force. Nevertheless, General Washington, fearful that diplomatic efforts
might fail and that fighting might resume, was taking no chances. He
drilled his soldiers daily into an even more disciplined and cohesive force.
The effort did not go unnoticed by McKean. Though he was once again
devoting himself to his duties as chief justice, he wrote to John Adams, who
was representing the United States in the Netherlands, "Our army is better
clothed, better disciplined, in better spirits and more effective than any
period of the war; congress is still composed of virtuous men. . . . Money
seems to be our greatest want, and salutary steps are proceeding concerning
it; I flatter myself funds will soon be established sufficiently productive for
the public exigencies, but if this part should fail, we must rely somewhat on
our allies, our industry, economy and integrity."[1]

In fact, it was diplomacy that ultimately prevailed. Adams, Benjamin
Franklin, and Henry Laurens had been in Paris for several months patiently
negotiating a peace treaty, and on January 15, 1783, Britain declared an end
to hostilities with the United States. Three months later, on April 15, Congress ratified the preliminary Peace Treaty. Three days afterward, an elated
General George Washington announced publicly that the war was finally

over and peace at long last had been attained. He praised his soldiers for "erecting the stupendous fabric of freedom and empire on the broad back of independence." Over the next several weeks, Washington personally signed the discharge papers for thousands of soldiers who had served him—a sign of both the affection and the respect he felt for them. Horrified that the soldiers were being sent home with no reward for their service, Robert Morris wrote personal checks amounting to three months' salary, for each soldier. In cities around the country, Loyalists—more than a hundred thousand—packed their belongings and left for Canada or Europe.[2]

The end of the war prompted McKean to think that perhaps it was time to do something else with the rest of his life. After seven years on the bench, he was wearying of the job and briefly considered stepping down. He complained to his wife that he wished "the illiberal envious persons at Philadelphia were obliged to undergo the drudging of mind and body that I do, only for one circuit: They would not only be ashamed for their past parsimony and ingratitude, but serious of making me a proper compensation." McKean did not keep his musings to himself, and the idea of his retirement caused concern even among his adversaries. Joseph Reed, former president of the Pennsylvania Assembly, wrote to William Bradford, the Pennsylvania attorney general, that although "the Chief Justice not always pleases me in either law or politics . . . I should be sorry [if] he should leave the bench," and he predicted that McKean would "repent his decision."[3] McKean's former brother-in-law, Francis Hopkinson, had a less charitable view. He observed that power had a "tendency to debauch the best disposition," and then, referring to McKean, noted that when it "falls into the hands of a proud, capricious and ambitious man, its operation must be watched with a jealous eye."[4] But if McKean was seriously contemplating leaving public life, his plans were interrupted by a legal case with international significance.

❦

FRANCOIS BARBE-MARBOIS ARRIVED IN THE UNITED STATES DURING THE summer of 1783 to replace Charles Luzerne as French consul general when Luzerne was appointed ambassador. A year later, Marbois became entwined in controversy involving a French cavalry lieutenant named Charles Julian de Longchamps, who had settled in Philadelphia after fighting with the Continental Army during the Revolutionary War. Longchamps met a socially prominent young American woman, and after a brief courtship, the two eloped. The girl's family disapproved of the marriage and especially of Longchamps. The family planted stories in Philadelphia newspapers deriding Longchamps's "low and ridiculous origins" and branding him a fraud. To reclaim his good name, Longchamps appeared at the French consul's office with an armful of documents, which he claimed provided evidence of both his nobility and record of distinguished military service. He demanded the French government insist on an apology from the girl's family, but Marbois refused on the grounds that it was a private affair. Longchamps stormed out of the consul's office.

The next day, Longchamps alleged publicly that Marbois had slandered him by calling him a "rogue" and a "saucy devil."[5] He then renounced French citizenship and swore allegiance to the state of Pennsylvania. A few days later, Longchamps, now an American citizen, was walking on Market Street when, by chance, he encountered Marbois. The two men exchanged words, a heated argument erupted, and Longchamps struck Marbois with his walking stick. Strolling on the other side of the street, Ambassador Luzerne happened to witness the altercation. He reported the incident to the sheriff of Philadelphia and demanded that Longchamps be incarcerated and then extradited to France to stand trial. The sheriff agreed to arrest Longchamps for assault and battery but made clear to the ambassador that there was no existing legal authority to extradite Longchamps. Luzerne was incredulous and argued that Longchamps's hastily arranged embrace of American citizenship was nothing more than a cynical ploy, and he demanded that it should not interfere with the administration of French justice. The sheriff shrugged in response.

But the incident was far from finished. Marbois brought suit for personal injury in the courts of Pennsylvania. Because Marbois was of French origin and Longchamps claimed American citizenship, the lawsuit raised the issue of whether a foreign government had jurisdiction in the United States and what law would apply. The case fell to Chief Justice McKean.

Suddenly, the incident became a test of international law. Other countries with diplomatic representatives in America weighed in with Congress in support of the French position. The case put enormous pressure on the McKean court, which set bail many times higher than ordinary for an assault. Nevertheless, Longchamps paid the bail, walked out of jail, and promptly disappeared.[6]

The French ambassador was outraged that Longchamps had been released and appealed to John Dickinson, now the chief executive of Pennsylvania. Dickinson pleaded to the court that the honor of the commonwealth was at stake in the case. He demanded that Longchamps be tracked down and his bail revoked and that he be extradited to France. Notwithstanding his fondness for Dickinson and that he was himself a Francophile, Chief Justice McKean ignored the Pennsylvania chief executive and dismissed the assertion of French authority over the case. McKean argued that Longchamps had been legally released from jail on a properly issued writ of habeas corpus and once again refused to accept French jurisdiction. He was adamant that Longchamps would be tried in a Pennsylvania court under the laws of Pennsylvania.[7]

Longchamps was eventually located in a small town in central Pennsylvania living with his American bride. He was charged with assault under Pennsylvania law, and in October McKean presided over a crowded and sometimes acrimonious trial in the State House chamber. Longchamps was ultimately found guilty of "violent and opprobrious language" and of having assaulted Marbois. McKean sentenced him to two years' hard labor and fined him. By not returning him to French authorities, McKean asserted the primacy of the American legal system, and, in the process, laid the groundwork for making the United States a safe harbor for those fleeing persecution in their native lands. The Longchamps case set an important precedent regarding international claim to jurisdiction, and some legal historians believe that it contributed to the inclusion of the Law of Nations clause in the US Constitution, ratified later in the decade, which gives the American government the power to "define" the governing law (and punish violators) on the high seas.[8]

The front page of the *Boston Gazette*, November 26, 1787, contained a letter to the editor from "A Federalist" concerning the constitutional convention. *Library of Congress*.

After the surrender of General Cornwallis on October 18, 1781, General Washington notified President McKean of the great victory at Yorktown. Years later, President Washington declined to include McKean in his cabinet. *Picture Collection, The New York Public Library, Astor, Lenox and Tilden Foundations*.

Urbane and articulate, John Dickinson was McKean's closest friend, even though they differed on the issue of independence from Britain. *Print Collection, Miriam and Ira D. Wallach Division of Art, Prints and Photographs, The New York Public Library, Astor, Lenox and Tilden Foundations*.

In a letter written to Alexander Dallas two decades after the signing of the Declaration of Independence, McKean was the first signer to challenge the accepted view that the Declaration had been signed by all the delegates on July 4, 1776. *Manuscript and Archives Division, The New York Public Library.*

McKean's Delaware colleague Caesar Rodney played a critical role in the vote for independence, and later nominated McKean to be president of the continental congress. *The New York Public Library.*

When John Adams first met McKean at the beginning of the First Continental Congress, he found him to be one of the few "to see more clearly to the end of the business than any others of the whole body." They had a falling-out during the 1796 election, when McKean supported Thomas Jefferson. *Fiske*, How the US Became a Nation *(Boston: Gin & Company, 1904). http://etc.usf.edu/clipart/0/81/adams_4.htm#*

Young Thomas McKean made a name for himself in the courtroom as a skilled and artic- ulate advocate for his clients. *Print Collection, Miriam and Ira D. Wallach Division of Art, Prints and Photographs, The New York Public Library, Astor, Lenox and Tilden Foundations.*

McKean with his son Thomas
McKean Jr. McKean had six
children with his first wife and
five with his second. *Charles
Wilson Peale, 1787. Philadelphia
Museum of Art.*

Sarah Armitage, McKean's
second wife, with their daughter
Sally. Sarah was the half-sister
of Francis Alison's wife.
*Charles Wilson Peale, 1787.
Philadelphia Museum of Art.*

Thomas McKean around the time of the Declaration of Independence. He wore multiple political hats and played a significant role in delivering the delegations of both Delaware and Pennsylvania in support of independence. *Courtesy of Delaware Department of State, Division of Historical and Cultural Affairs. Delaware State Museums.*

Irish-born Francis Alison, a minister and teacher, had a profound effect on young Thomas McKean, who spent nearly a decade at Alison's school in New London. His classmates included two other eventual signers of the Declaration of Independence. *From the University Archives and Records Center, University of Pennsylvania.*

The British passed the Stamp Act in spring 1865. McKean not only kept his court open but refused to use stamped documents. *Arthur C. Perry,* American History *(New York: American Book Company, 1913). http://etc.usf.edu/clipart/45100 /45198/45198_stamp.htm#*

Philadelphia was one America's most important cities in the mid-eighteenth century. This image of the Jersey Shore/East Prospect extends from present-day South Street to Vine Street, with the existing city shown in great detail. Several steeples break the skyline, including those of the State House at left and Christ Church in the center. *Print Collection, Miriam and Ira D. Wallach Division of Art, Prints and Photographs, The New York Public Library, Astor, Lenox and Tilden Foundations.*

Independence Hall was where delegates to the Second Continental Congress passed the Declaration of Independence. It was also home to the Pennsylvania Supreme Court on which McKean served as Chief Justice. *John Gilmary Shea, The Story of a Great Nation (New York: Gay Borthers & Company 1886). http://etc.usf.edu/clipart /5600/5625/independence _hall_1.htm#*

The *First Continental Congress* met in Carpenters' Hall from September 5 to October 26, 1774. The Pennsylvania State House (*Independence Hall*) was being used by the more conservative *Provincial Assembly of Pennsylvania*. *Benson J. Lossing*. The Pictorial Field-Book of the Revolution (*New York: Harper & Brothers, 1851*). *http://etc.usf.edu/clipart/13800/13847/carpenters_13847.htm#*

RIGHT: As Chief Justice of the Pennsylvania Supreme Court for over two decades, McKean cut an imposing figure. He modeled himself after English jurists but helped develop American jurisprudence. *Wikimedia.*

BELOW: McKean likely signed the Declaration of Independence in early 1777. *University Archives and Records Center, University of Pennsylvania.*

McKean and his family lived in one of the grandest houses in Philadelphia. Duche House, modeled on the design of an English palace, was previously owned by a Tory sympathizer. *The New York Public Library.*

# 15

## The End of War

THE END TO THE WAR RAISED IMPORTANT QUESTIONS ABOUT THE RULE of law in Pennsylvania and throughout America. Although Chief Justice McKean and his court had adopted English common law for Pennsylvania, one of the most vexing questions was how to deal with those who had remained loyal to the Crown during the Rebellion. Should these individuals be excused—or should they be punished? The Pennsylvania radicals with whom McKean had sided in the past were in no mood to forgive British collaborators, and under state law Tory property could be seized by the state and sold.

Pennsylvania radicals also saw the end of the war as an opportunity to confiscate the proprietary lands of the Penn family. The Supreme Executive Council, populated by radicals, contended that as proprietors the Penn family had acted as trustees for the Crown. They also argued the Penn family simply had too much money and owned too much land, both of which were deemed detrimental to the interests of a budding democracy. The council asked that lawyers draw up a report to be presented to Chief Justice McKean for his consideration.

McKean saw no conflict between wealth and democracy. He felt strongly that individuals with property, as long as it has been legally purchased or inherited, should make the larger decisions for the rest of society.

When the case of the Penn family came before him, McKean ruled that not only had the original grant to them been legal but also the property had passed through the family by means of legal inheritance. Because the Crown had also persecuted the Penns, McKean did not regard the family as the Crown's "trustees" and saw no reason to confiscate their property.[1] Years later, McKean would serve as a pallbearer at the funeral of former governor John Penn.[2]

McKean did enforce the law of confiscation as it pertained to British sympathizers. In fact, he personally benefited from the law when he acquired one of the finest houses in Philadelphia from Jacob Duche, a Tory sympathizer, who years earlier had been a classmate of his at Dr. Alison's academy. Making the acquisition even more controversial, and adding to the family enmity stoked between him and Francis Hopkinson, Duche had grown up to be a prominent Anglican minister and had married Hopkinson's sister Elizabeth. Duche gave the invocation at the first Continental Congress, but he never fully embraced the independence movement. After writing General Washington a letter pleading with him to surrender to the British, Duche was branded a Tory and ostracized by the post-Revolutionary political establishment of Philadelphia.[3]

Francis Hopkinson resented that Thomas McKean would turn Elizabeth out of her home, but the chief justice was undeterred. McKean purchased the house at public auction for 7,750 pounds and 232 bushels of wheat, a bargain even by the standard of the times. Hopkinson may have considered McKean callous and unethical, using the law to his advantage, but he was hardly alone. Among his neighbors was John Dickinson, who had purchased at a discount the confiscated mansion of British collaborator Joseph Galloway.

McKean's new home provided ample space to accommodate his growing family, which now included Sophia Dorothea McKean, his tenth child, born on April 14, 1783. Built on the blueprint of a wing of the Lambeth Palace, the elaborate Tudor home of the Archbishop of Canterbury in London, the house was situated on the east side of Third Street and stretched a full city block from Pine Street on the south to Union Street on the north. Besides the main house, the property included a coach house and stables.

The residence was three stories high, with a large, ornate living room well suited to entertaining and multiple bedrooms on the top floor.[4]

McKean had grown wealthy buying and selling property, and after moving into the Duche House, he and his family adopted a more opulent lifestyle. They dressed in fashionable clothing imported from England. He furnished his house with hand-carved furniture manufactured by local craftsmen, and he purchased fine china decorated with his family crest: a blue eagle, wings splayed, clutching a serpent in its talons. He bought a gold-tipped walking stick and eyeglasses from T. B. Freeman, the finest store in Philadelphia. And he commissioned his portrait, and those of his family members, to be painted by such notable artists as Gilbert Stuart, the leading society painter of the day, and Charles Wilson Peale, a good friend as well as a political activist.

McKean's newfound and newly visible wealth clearly rankled Francis Hopkinson, who anonymously wrote in one Philadelphia newspaper about seeing the chief justice "in the morning, strutting his pavement in red slippers, plaid gown and starched cap."[5] McKean may have enjoyed the comforts of the Duche House, but material success was not what ultimately motivated him. He remained determined to establish a truly American system of government with the rule of law as its cornerstone. With that goal in mind, he decided to expand Pennsylvania's judicial system to the far reaches of the state.

✦

IN 1786, CHIEF JUSTICE MCKEAN TRAVELED BY HORSE-DRAWN CARRIAGE with a small entourage across the Allegheny Mountains to Pittsburgh, some three hundred miles west of Philadelphia. At the time, Pittsburgh had fewer than five hundred residents and was the westernmost town of any prominence in a country that still clung to the East Coast and was years away from fulfilling its westward destiny. There, McKean convened the region's first oyer and terminer court, or criminal court, bringing the rule of law to the nation's frontier. As chief justice, he subsequently made several trips a year and was often gone from home for weeks at a time.

The trips were challenging in part because of the unpredictability of the weather. A rainstorm, with severe thunder and lightning, could come up over the mountains in what seemed an instant. In summer, the sun and heat could be oppressive, and in winter the wagon roads could be icy and impassable. Travelers during the late eighteenth century typically stayed in inns and rooms above taverns, and the accommodations were uniformly primitive. John Adams, who traveled from his home in Braintree, Massachusetts, to Pennsylvania on many occasions, described the taverns "as full of people drinking drams, toddies, carousing. . . . Here the time, the money, the health, of many that are old, are wasted: here disease, vicious habits, bastards and legislators are frequently begotten." One of the original justices of the supreme court, required to ride circuit, complained that he had been forced to "share a bed with a man of the wrong sort."[6]

When away from home, McKean wrote frequently to his wife, Sarah, describing his travels, which typically entailed riding over a hundred fifty miles on rough and mountainous roads. His stamina far outpaced that of his colleagues on the court. Justice William Bradford recounted one memorable occasion when McKean's carriage broke down along the way. Undeterred, the chief justice abandoned the conveyance, detached its frame from the two horses pulling it, and rode bareback to complete the journey. On another occasion, after a particularly tough trip over rocky terrain, the chief justice noticed that his colleague on the court, Benjamin Rush, "was a little fatigued." Because they had still had "upwards of a hundred miles to ride yet over some of highest mountains and worst roads in the world," he advised Rush to stay behind and rest.[7] McKean, however, continued the journey. The truth was that he rather enjoyed riding circuit. Before one sojourn he wrote to George Washington, "My health requires a ride in the country and my mind some relaxation."[8]

Initially, McKean was not particularly fond of western Pennsylvania, which he referred to as being in a "middle state of civilization."[9] His disdain was based on not only the accommodations but also the coarseness and brutality that he observed as a part of frontier life, reflected in the cases over which he presided. He adjudicated the trials of Patrick McSherry Jr., who was convicted of butchering John Weigert with a sickle; of John

McDonald, who burned Laurence Kreamer's wife and son alive in their house; and Margaret Angle, a spinster charged with killing her "new born male bastard." There was still the threat of an Indian attack in western Pennsylvania, and one of his most celebrated cases involved a Native American named Mamachtaga, who was convicted of murdering a white man and who was sentenced to hang.[10]

McKean may have considered western Pennsylvania primitive and rough, but his contempt was tempered by a sense of civic duty. Whenever there, he took the opportunity to educate the public on the value of democratic institutions. The holding of court was an important event for the small towns he visited, and his courtroom was often packed with curious onlookers. Resplendent in his velvet robes and powdered wig, McKean cut an imposing figure. After bringing down the gavel to quiet the room, he frequently waxed philosophically on the importance of the rule of law in a democracy and often digressed into long monologues about subjects such as the value of education in a civilized society and the responsibility of citizenship. These were important topics for a poor and sparsely settled part of the country. Some considered the judge to be pompous and didactic, but his efforts to spread democracy and fortify the law gained the respect of many. His reputation and stature continued to grow throughout Pennsylvania.

Years later, McKean revised his opinion of western Pennsylvania. He referred to its inhabitants as "decent & orderly as any persons in the oldest settled counties in Pennsylvania," and he expressed his gratitude that they "paid as much attention and respect to the Judges in every way practical as in any part of the state."[11] His view may have been influenced by the fact that they turned out to be among his most reliable and loyal political supporters.

McKean had been regarded as a progressive in Congress, especially with respect to the question of independence from Britain. On the bench, however, he was a strict constructionist, a judge who interpreted the law, where it existed, in its most literal form. Nowhere was this more evident than on the issue of slavery, where his thinking was paradoxical. While serving in the Delaware Assembly in 1774, McKean had delivered one of the most celebrated speeches of his career to an overflow audience in the courthouse at Lewes. In remarks that were very progressive for the times, he expressed hope for "some honourable and safe expediant to put an end to our African slavery, so dishonourable to us, and so provoking to the most benevolent parent of the universe."[12] Yet a decade later, while serving as chief justice of Pennsylvania, McKean presided over a case involving a slave named Francis Belt, who had accompanied his "master" Philip Dalby, a Virginia plantation owner, on a visit to Philadelphia. The Philadelphia Abolition Society encouraged Belt to look to the Pennsylvania courts for his freedom, and Belt petitioned the Pennsylvania Supreme Court. General Washington, acquainted with Dalby, took a keen interest in the facts of the case and called it "a vexatious lawsuit." The future president, an owner of slaves himself, criticized the Abolition Society for "acting repugnant to justice so far as its conduct concerns strangers."[13] Even though Pennsylvania had passed the Gradual Abolition Act in 1780, McKean sided with Dalby because the law in Virginia was clear: slaves were private property, and the chief justice viewed the case as a matter of states' rights.

On another occasion, in a case over which he presided involving the status of a runaway slave, McKean adopted a decidedly racist tone. In issuing instructions to the jury, he argued that blacks were neither the moral nor intellectual equivalent of whites.[14] This placed him in sync with many of the Founding Fathers, including Franklin, Washington, and Jefferson, who had all owned slaves but ultimately revised their views and condemned slavery as an institution. Among the founders, only John Dickinson actually freed his slaves in the period between 1776 and 1786. Near the end of his career, however, McKean once again condemned slavery and embraced the concept of its "abolition" as "being within reach of the federal government."[15]

McKean seemed conflicted over the role of women in society as well. As chief justice, one of his responsibilities was to rule in cases of divorce. In every case before him, no matter the facts, he ruled in favor of the male whether or not he was the defendant or the plaintiff, an outcome entirely consistent with British precedent as well as American mores at the time. On the other hand, McKean supported women's education, a highly progressive view during the era. In a letter to President Jefferson, Madame

Marie Rivardi, headmistress of a girls' academy, asked that he provide federal support for her school and gushed, "Governor McKean is a patron."[16]

Perhaps McKean's view of women was most clearly revealed in his relationship with his wife Sarah. One episode stands out: a few years after he became chief justice, McKean decided that he wanted to buy a country estate so that, as he explained to Sarah, he might "live cheap and spend the remainder of my days in comfort."[17] Over the years he had acquired several parcels of land in and around Philadelphia and told his wife that he would sell a few of them to raise the necessary funds to purchase a country house. The discussion of financial and property issues between husbands and wives was somewhat unusual during this era, but Thomas respected Sarah's good judgment.

Sarah was also a landowner; she had inherited several parcels of land from her family and was wealthy in her own right. While she was out of town visiting friends, McKean sold a parcel of property as he had told her he planned to do. But unbeknownst to her, he sold a parcel of her property. When Sarah later learned of the transaction, she was furious and apparently let her husband know it, for he rather sheepishly wrote her, "I thought you loved the country life, but now you seem to prefer the town. Fine, we will continue in town." And then, in a feeble attempt to justify the sale of her property, he declared, "The general character of the ladies is, that they are fickle, ever changing, & never satisfied, but I flattered myself you were an exception." A few months later, when the family finally purchased a house in the country, it was Sarah who made the decision, not the chief justice.[18]

McKean's relationship with Sarah was different from the way other prominent men of the day treated their wives. They discussed everything from finances to the arts to current events, and he encouraged her political activism. Sarah served as a prominent member of the Ladies Association, an organization founded by Esther de Berdt Reed, who recommended that American women renounce "vain ornaments" such as fashionable clothing and elaborate hairstyles and donate the money to the troops as an "offering of the ladies." In the summer of 1780, Sarah joined three dozen Philadelphia women and raised over 300,000 Continental dollars for the soldiers

from nearly sixteen hundred people. Even counting for the massive inflation of American money, it was a substantial sum.[19]

Judge McKean was proud of his wife's important work and dedication
to the cause of American independence, but his relationship with her was
another example of the contradictions in his life, both public and private.
In the same way that he seemed to embrace abolition, yet backed slave
owners from the bench, McKean respected his wife's independence and
intelligence, but ruled in favor of men in every domestic lawsuit. In some
respects, these contradictions were part of the evolution of the United
States itself, where individual rights collided with the more rigid mores of
an earlier era. In the end, at least, on the public side of his life, McKean
usually fell back on the strict interpretation of English law that had been
passed down through the decades in Pennsylvania.

# 16

## "An Assembly of Demigods"

"**W**E SEEM AFRAID," CHIEF JUSTICE McKEAN WROTE TO JOHN Adams in the spring of 1787, "to enable anyone to do good lest he should do evil." McKean was writing John Adams after reading his three-volume work, *Defence of the Constitutions of Government of the United States of America*.[1] At the time, Adams represented the United States in London as its chief diplomat. Aware that the Articles of Confederation continued to provide an insufficient governing framework and that support for a stronger central government was gaining ground in America, Adams had felt compelled to provide the conceptual structure for constitutional governance. He spent evenings writing feverishly in his London library, books stacked about him, marking quotations and passages from the works of philosophers, historians, and political theorists, including Machiavelli, Locke, Hobbes, Milton, Aristotle, Montesquieu, and Plato. Adams had drawn from over fifty books in his research, and although the tome's narrative was choppy, interrupted with historical references—though with few citations—McKean found the book to be a thoughtful, high-minded analysis of what a future American government should look like.[2]

In his book, Adams was especially critical of vesting excessive power in a unicameral legislature. "What was to restrain it from making tyrannical law?"[3] Besides Georgia, Pennsylvania was the only state in the country with a unicameral legislature—it would not be altered until 1790. Adams argued that effective governance required checks and balances, and that meant a bicameral legislature as well as equally strong executive and judicial branches.

Adams's views resonated with McKean. "The balance of the one, the few, and the many," McKean acknowledged to his friend from Massachusetts, "is not well poised in this state." The chief justice complained, "The legislature is too powerful for the executive and judicial branches of the government . . . it can too easily make laws, and too easily alter or repeal them." He agreed with Adams that "we must have another branch, and a negative in the executive, stability in our laws, before we shall be reputable, safe and happy."[4]

As a result of his time as president of the Congress, McKean understood better than most the shortcomings of the Articles of Confederation. He recognized that the thirteen states needed something more than shared values and vague concepts of comity in order to function effectively. But McKean did not completely accept Adams's recommendations for a new national government. "In general," McKean confessed, "I dislike innovations, especially in the administration of justice; and I would avoid tampering with constitutions of government, as with edge-tools." Perhaps as chief justice of one of the—if not the—most powerful states in the country, he didn't relish the prospect of competing with a potential federal court.[5]

Still, McKean found himself "in concurrence in all the sentiments" of Adams's work. Sharing McKean's approbation, Thomas Jefferson praised the book's "learning and good sense," and even James Madison, who didn't much like Adams, admitted that the book had "merit."[6]

―⧓―

FEW POLITICAL LEADERS WERE ANXIOUS TO INCREASE THE POWER OF THE federal government, but most also considered, as Joseph Ellis has written, "the status quo as wholly unacceptable."[7] Alexander Hamilton had been the first to propose a convention to reform the articles, but for two months Congress could not even muster a quorum to evaluate on the proposal.

However, on February 28, Congress at last voted to hold a convention in May to consider a new constitution.

Three weeks after McKean sent his letter to Adams, delegates to the Constitutional Convention began gathering in Philadelphia for the "sole and express purpose of revising the Articles of Confederation."[8] The fifty-five delegates who arrived in Philadelphia over the course of several weeks were already in general agreement that an effective central government with a wide range of enforceable powers should replace the weaker Congress that had been established by the Articles of Confederation. There was not significant diversity among the group: all were white males and most were extremely wealthy. Nonetheless, when Thomas Jefferson, who was representing the United States in Paris, learned of the roster of delegates to the Constitutional Convention, he was impressed, writing to John Adams in London, "It really is an assembly of demigods."[9] McKean was not a delegate to the convention that included many of his former colleagues: three had attended the Stamp Act Congress; seven were present in the First Continental Congress; eight signed the Declaration of Independence; and forty-two served under the Articles of Confederation.

Once again, as they had done in 1776, delegates met in the large room on the first floor in the Pennsylvania State House. This time they were not there to debate separation from an empire but rather the principles on which a new government would be founded. The Pennsylvania delegation included James Wilson and Robert Morris as well as Benjamin Franklin. The most celebrated delegate was General Washington, representing Virginia, who after prodding from both Hamilton and Madison had agreed to serve. The general arrived in Philadelphia in late May and was again comfortably ensconced at the palatial home of Robert Morris. On the first day of the convention, May 25, Morris nominated him to preside over the proceedings. In his typically understated manner, Washington noted in his diary, "Working by unanimous vote I was called up to the Chair of president of the body."[10]

On July 4, 1787, Washington invited McKean and other "signers" to join him at Epplee's Tavern to honor the eleventh anniversary of the Declaration of Independence. As they toasted past accomplishments, the city celebrated with parades, fireworks, and artillery salutes. The *Pennsylvania Herald* published an editorial challenging the delegates to provide "a system of government adequate to the security and preservation of those rights . . . promulgated by the ever memorable Declaration of Independence."[11] A few weeks later Washington dined at the chief justice's house and complained that as the presiding officer of the convention he was forced to listen to endless debates over technicalities in the proposed constitution. The general's impatience belied the fact that the delegates were making slow and steady progress.

By late July, the debate had intensified and had become focused on two streams of intellectual thought: the Virginia Plan drafted by James Madison, and the New Jersey Plan drafted by William Paterson. Madison's plan recommended a consolidated national government, generally favoring the most populated states, while Paterson's decentralized approach generally favored smaller states. The delegates spent hours upon hours debating the virtues and pitfalls of these two plans. In the end, the Connecticut Compromise, or the "Great Compromise," as it came to be known, settled the question by creating both a House of Representatives and a Senate. In the House each state would be apportioned seats in Congress based on population and the people would elect their representatives, while in the Senate, each state would have two senators generally to be elected by their respective legislatures.

The Great Compromise had ended the stalemate between "patriots," who had sided with Paterson, and "nationalists," who had sided with Madison, and allowed the drafters to produce a final document for consideration by the convention. A number of delegates were disappointed that the final document represented a patchwork of what they viewed as unfortunate compromises; some left before the final ceremony, and three refused to sign.[12] On September 17, thirty-nine delegates approved and signed the constitution. Benjamin Franklin summed up the feelings of many of his colleagues when he addressed the convention, "There are several parts of this Constitution which I do not at present approve, but I am not sure I shall never approve them." He would accept the constitution because, as he put it, "I expect no better and because I am not sure that it is not the best."[13] Now it was up to the individual states to ratify it.

⚊⚊⚊

THE PENNSYLVANIA GENERAL ASSEMBLY, WHICH HAD RELOCATED TO THE grand hallway on the second floor of the State House during the last twelve days of the convention, received a copy of the constitution soon after the document had been signed. This would be the first test of the new constitution, and almost immediately, the assembly began to debate its merits, quickly dividing into two groups: Federalists, who supported the constitution, and Antifederalists, who opposed a national government.[14]

The Antifederalists organized against ratification by writing newspaper articles and letters and by distributing pamphlets. They described what they viewed as the proposed document's myriad flaws, which they attributed to a "detestable conspiracy." The Antifederalist campaign focused especially on western Pennsylvania, where one pro-constitution newspaper editorialized "the people is most easily deceived."[15] Antifederalists tried to frighten citizens by predicting that a federal constitution would lead to "aristocracy, monarchy, and oligarchy." But they didn't really have an alternative.[16]

Those who favored the constitution had the momentum. Most importantly, the support of heralded leaders such as George Washington and Benjamin Franklin gave confidence to average citizens. Franklin, who had served as a delegate to the Federal Convention, was also "president" of the Pennsylvania Assembly, which at the time comprised a majority of nationalistic legislators. On September 29, 1787, with Franklin presiding, the assembly settled on November 6 to hold a statewide election for delegates to the convention and on November 21 as the date to open the ratifying convention.[17]

In a surprise move, Pennsylvania's Federalists persuaded McKean to stand as a candidate for delegate to the ratifying convention. Federalists were aware, as one supporter of the constitution put it, that McKean had "long associated with radicals."[18] They nevertheless also recognized from observing his work on the bench that he was in many respects a conservative and therefore might have an independent perspective on the constitution if not outright sympathy for the Federalist view.

McKean agreed to join forces with his former adversaries because, as he explained in a letter to a fellow justice of the Pennsylvania Supreme Court, "Those, who have the least at stake and who know the least about government, are the most busy." With McKean now on their side, Pennsylvania Federalists believed they had scored a propaganda coup, or as a Constitutionalist characterized it: McKean "will be proof that the Federalists do not go upon party distinctions." On November 6, he was elected as a Federalist delegate, one of forty-six statewide. The Antifederalists had only managed to elect twenty-three delegates.[19]

While Frederick Muhlenberg presided over the convention, McKean and James Wilson—who had represented Roberts and Carlyle in the 1778 treason cases—led the pro-constitution forces. Wilson had worked in the law offices of John Dickinson and had been elected in 1775 to the Continental Congress, where he had gained a reputation as hard working, disciplined, and earnest. Tall and well dressed, he wore thick spectacles, and one delegate described him as "rather imposing . . . and not persuasive."[20] But this view was not universally shared; no one doubted Wilson's intelligence, and another delegate remarked that Wilson impressed "not by the force of his eloquence, but by the force of his reasoning."[21] He and McKean shared a Scottish heritage (though McKean claimed Irish ancestry as well) and were fond of each other, perhaps because they shared the distinction of not being particularly well liked among their peers.

⊷╬╀⊷

"WE DO NOT COME HERE TO LEGISLATE," MCKEAN TOLD THE DELEGATES who had gathered in the Assembly Hall at the State House on November 24, the first full day of debate. "We have no right to inquire into the power of the late Convention or to alter and amend their work," McKean declared. "The sole question before us is, whether we will ratify and confirm, or, upon due consideration, reject in the whole, the system of federal government that is submitted to us."[22]

Ratification, in other words, meant an up or down vote. The Federalists could have called for a vote immediately, but McKean felt that it was important "not to preclude, but to promote a free and ample discussion of the Federal plan."[23] The Pennsylvania Convention met for five consecutive weeks. With each passing day the debate became increasingly tedious as delegates often covered the same ground. The Antifederalists never seemed satisfied; they continually worried that a federal constitution would diminish the power of the states. Wilson paced the floor, answering questions and endeavored to persuade his colleagues with logic and legal reasoning. Dr. Benjamin Rush often joined in the debate. So did McKean, who on November 28 addressed the delegates on the importance of establishing a national identity: "I earnestly hope . . . that the statutes of the federal government will last until they become the common law of the land, as excellent and as much valued as that which we have hitherto found dominated the birthright of an American."[24]

McKean favored a national constitution because he believed it provided structure to the national government through a system of checks and balances. Using language that presaged Chief Justice John Marshall's seminal 1803 decision in the case of *Marbury v. Madison*, McKean praised judges who would "decide against the legislature in favor of the Constitution" and thereby restrain the legislative branch. By this point, McKean recognized that a United States Supreme Court would eventually eclipse the states' highest courts, but he believed it was critical to the smooth functioning of the government. In his arguments for the constitution, McKean's leitmotif was that it would firmly establish the rule of law in America.[25]

———

BY EARLY DECEMBER NERVES BEGAN TO FRAY AND THE PATIENCE OF THE delegates, including McKean, had begun to wane. For many years, McKean had claimed both Delaware and Pennsylvania as his home, but the two

states came down on very different sides in the debate over a federal constitution. Delaware, not Pennsylvania, became the first state to endorse the
document on December 7, 1787, when after only four days of debate its
assembly unanimously ratified the new constitution.[26]

The following day in Philadelphia, the debate in the Assembly Hall
focused on trial by jury as a fundamental right in a democratic society.
Antifederalist delegate John Smilie pontificated on the virtues of jury trial,
making numerous references to English precedents. After listening quietly
for several hours, Chief Justice McKean arose and groused that everything
he had heard over the many weeks of debate, all the objections to the constitution, could have been delivered in two hours. He noted that Smilie's
tedious discourse on trial by jury was completely irrelevant. As he concluded his remarks, a burst of loud, spontaneous applause erupted from the
audience that packed the second-floor gallery.

Smilie bolted upright from his chair, gazed up to the gallery, and then
pounded his fist on the table. "No, Sir, this is not the voice of the people
of Pennsylvania." He continued, "And were this convention assembled at
another place, the sound would be of a different nature, for the sentiments
of the citizens are different indeed." Smilie then accused the chief justice
of treating the opposition with contempt and speaking with "a magiste-
rial air." He added defiantly, "Were the gallery filled with bayonets, such
appearance would not intimidate me . . . in the conscientious discharge of
a public duty."[27]

As Smilie sat down, McKean rose slowly to his feet again. With what
one can only imagine was a wry smile, the chief justice looked at Smilie
and said, "The gentleman is angry, sir, because other folks are pleased." He
accused Smilie and the other Antifederalists of refusing to listen to reason.
He mocked what he viewed as their relentless negativism and cynicism,
their tendency to pose unanswerable hypothetical questions. "If the sky
falls," McKean declared, "we shall catch larks, if the river runs dry, we shall
catch eels." McKean concluded their behavior amounted "to a sound . . .
the working of small beer."[28]

On December 10, McKean attempted to recapitulate the arguments
of the Antifederalists and then offered his peroration. He elaborated on

an argument that Benjamin Franklin had made to the delegates in the late summer of 1787, when the aging statesman said, "There is no form of government but what may be a blessing to the people if well administered." However, McKean carried Franklin's argument a step further:

> Though a good system of government is certainly a blessing, yet it is on the administration of the best system, that the freedom, wealth, and happiness of the people depend. Despotism, if wisely administered, is the best form of government invented by the ingenuity of man.[29]

McKean, of course, believed democracy to be the best form of government, but he was trying to make the case that even a wise autocrat could theoretically govern effectively: "The best government may be so conducted, as to produce misery and disgrace, and the worst so administered, as to ensure dignity and happiness to a nation."[30] In McKean's view, the constitution's success would ultimately depend on leadership.

However, McKean's words were poorly chosen, and Antifederalists pounced. Quoting his remarks out of context, they alleged the chief justice had embraced a return to a monarchy and even endorsed despotism as a legitimate form of government. McKean was pilloried in a number of newspapers around the country, including the *Boston Gazette*, where "Publicola" a pen name for his old friend Sam Adams, ridiculed him as an antidemocratic tyrant.[31]

———

ON DECEMBER 12, DELEGATES TO THE PENNSYLVANIA STATE CONVENTION voted 46 to 23 in favor of ratification: not a single delegate had changed his mind in over five weeks of debate. In the immediate aftermath of the vote, the bells of Christ Church rang out and members of a militia artillery guard standing shoulder to shoulder on the Market Street docks fired a salute thirteen times. At the Sign of the Rainbow Tavern, and in other taverns across the city, patrons raised their glasses thirteen times in honor of the new constitution. That evening, a boat mounted on a wagon and pulled by five horses paraded through the city streets with a placard proclaiming the "fixed expectation of commerce and navigation under this happy government."[32]

But the news was met by rioting in some quarters of Pennsylvania. In Carlisle, a crowd of Antifederalists disrupted a pro-Federalist celebration. The next day, the Antifederalists gathered in the town square, and after parading the effigies of Wilson and McKean in a cart through the streets, burned them. One of the Antifederalist mob later recalled that the chief justice's effigy was dressed in "a good coat . . . a pretty good hat and wig and Ruffl[e]d Shirt." McKean had become a symbol of class authority, and by fashionably outfitting him and then burning his effigy, the mob challenged not only one of the state's most powerful political figures but also the entire political establishment. No one seemed to remember that McKean had once been aligned with Pennsylvania's radicals and that he had played a pivotal role in the state's support for independence in 1776.[33]

Even Philadelphia's political firmament became polarized by ratification. Only days after the vote, David Rittenhouse, a renowned scientist and patriot who had died six months earlier, was celebrated at a memorial service at Christ Church in Philadelphia. Dr. Benjamin Rush, who had opposed the Constitution, led the accolades for his departed friend. At the conclusion of the service, members of the Philosophical Society, where Rittenhouse had been a member, retired from the church to their own hall. McKean offered a pro forma resolution complimenting the doctor's eulogy, but surprisingly his benign tribute engendered significant opposition. Indeed, the intensity of feeling in the room rose to a fever pitch, with men jeering at each other. Pennsylvania's clerk of courts Alexander Dallas and other Jeffersonians heartily approved of Rush's performance and enthusiastically supported McKean's resolution. But the doctor had inadvertently ignited a tinderbox when he innocently referred to Rittenhouse's "republicanism" and faith in "democratic institutions." Federalists expressed outrage that Rittenhouse's memory should be used to advance the political fortunes of their opponents. They refused to condone Rush's eulogy of Rittenhouse because he had not supported ratification.[34] McKean was stunned and irritated—he had, after all, led the charge for the Federalists during the debate over ratification of the Constitution and believed he was owed their respect if not their gratitude.

The Federalists and the Antifederalists identified themselves solely on the basis of their view on the desirability of a federal constitution. They did not embrace a broader ideology, had no party leadership, and were not organized in any fashion. Nevertheless, the dispute at the Philosophical Society foreshadowed the emergence of political parties in America. And notwithstanding his irritation with Federalists at the Philosophical Society, McKean's tilt toward federalism became even more pronounced over the issue of freedom of speech.

⊸⊷⊷⊷

PENNSYLVANIA'S CONSTITUTION HAD GUARANTEED BOTH FREEDOM OF speech and freedom of press. However, none of the first nine states to ratify the federal constitution, including Pennsylvania, recommended an amendment guaranteeing freedom of speech or press. Indeed, Wilson and McKean, the leaders of the ratification convention, had rejected a proposal for such an amendment.

Newspapers during this era were not held to modern-day standards of objectivity and often printed scurrilous, unverified information about individuals. In Pennsylvania, the Antifederalists justified their view of free speech by quoting directly from the state constitution, which stated, "Freedom of the press ought never to be restrained." This proposition was tested when McKean's old nemesis, Eleazer Oswald, the publisher of the *Independent Gazetteer* and by this point an ardent Antifederalist, published a series of articles both mocking and critical of Andrew Brown, a prominent Federalist and the former publisher of the *Federal Gazette*. Brown demanded that Oswald reveal the identities of the authors of the articles, and he threatened to sue Oswald if the publisher resisted. Oswald acknowledged that articles in his paper contained a "proportion of invective and abuse" toward Brown, but he nevertheless referred to him as a "hand-maid" of the Federalists and refused to divulge the names of Brown's critics.[35] True to his word, Brown brought suit for libel against Oswald.

Oswald moved to have the case dismissed, and he argued gratuitously that it should never come to trial because Chief Justice McKean was biased and he would not get a fair trial in Pennsylvania. This infuriated McKean, who invoked the doctrine of constructive contempt and had Oswald arrested and imprisoned. But Oswald would not back down, and he used the *Gazetteer* to attack McKean and his allies on the court for blatantly trampling his rights and, by extension, the rights of every citizen in Pennsylvania. He argued that libel was "incompatible with law and liberty" and that it was "destructive of the privileges of a free country." He demanded a jury trial and accused McKean of "oppression." But he took his public attack on the chief justice a step further by referring obliquely to McKean's appearance a year earlier during the July 4 ratification celebration; he described him as "the whore of Babylon" who "wore scarlet robes while riding in a chariot-like float."[36]

McKean was especially sensitive about ad hominem attacks on his character. As far as he was concerned, Oswald's diatribes went beyond the bounds of personal decency and insulted not only him but American patriotism as well. The chief justice ordered the thirty-three-year-old editor to appear before him in court and lectured him: "Libeling is a great crime, whatever sentiment may be entertained by those who live by it." The chief justice declared Oswald had willfully attempted to "dishonor the administration of justice." Most importantly, McKean laid down an interpretation of libel that became the standard not only for Pennsylvania but many other states as well: "There is nothing in the constitution of this state respecting the liberty of the press, that has not been civilized by that kingdom [England] for nearly a century past." As Oswald stood before the bench, McKean told the editor, "Your circumstances are small but your offense is great." The chief justice denied that Oswald was entitled to a trial by jury. "Whether the publication amounts to a contempt, or not, is a point of law, which after all, is the province of the judges, and not of the jury, to determine." McKean fined Oswald and threw him in jail for one month.[37]

But Oswald was still not finished. He asked the assembly to impeach McKean for gross violations of judicial procedure. He claimed that McKean's punishment was personal retribution. He complained that there had been no grand jury indictment, no trial by jury, and that McKean had had a personal vendetta and therefore an interest in the outcome of the case. Although many members of the assembly agreed with the editor, none was willing to confront the chief justice directly, and the impeachment charges were never filed.[38] The incident revealed how far courts had progressed in Pennsylvania and how much authority McKean now wielded.

# 17

## Rule of Law

PENNSYLVANIA HAD VOTED TO RATIFY THE CONSTITUTION, BUT IT would take several months before a majority of the states followed suit. Finally, on June 21, 1788, Virginia and New Hampshire delegates voted in favor of ratification. Twelve years after the Declaration of Independence, six years after the Treaty of Paris, and one year after the Constitution had been adopted by the convention, America became a nation. Written primarily by James Madison, the Constitution brilliantly conceptualized a system of checks and balances among judicial, legislative, and executive branches. Now Madison and other members of Congress prepared to convene in New York and elect the nation's first president.

On his way north to New York from Virginia, Madison stopped in Philadelphia for a few days. There, he made the acquaintance of one of Sally McKean's closest friends, a pretty young socialite named Dolley Payne, who two years later married John Todd Jr., a Quaker lawyer. Madison also attended a dinner party at the home of Dr. William Shippen, where he, Shippen, and Thomas McKean reminisced about the road to nationhood and discussed the challenges ahead. They agreed that George Washington, the undisputed hero of the American Revolution, would be the natural choice to lead the country.[1] What McKean didn't reveal to either Shippen or Madison was that he hoped to serve the new president. As one of the most respected jurists in the country, McKean now wanted to play another role on the national stage—perhaps as the chief justice of the new Supreme Court or as America's first attorney general.

→‹‖›→

AMID GREAT ANTICIPATION, PRESIDENT-ELECT GEORGE WASHINGTON arrived in New York in early April 1789. He entered the city riding on a white steed, tipping his hat as he passed by the nearly twenty thousand cheering citizens who lined both sides of Manhattan's narrow streets. The British had occupied Manhattan during the war, and now in the aftermath, the city's designation as the capital of the United States was an especially sweet irony for its residents. Washington moved into the Samuel Osgood house, an impressive mansion at the northeast corner of Pearl and Cherry Streets. Once settled, he immediately set about organizing a government.

In late April, McKean wrote a lengthy letter to the new president expressing "an ambition to take a share in Your Excellency's administration." He offered his services "in the judicial department" and, although he had known Washington for nearly two decades, felt obligated to describe his professional background in great detail. He "had begun the study of the law at age sixteen," and his career culminated with his appointment as chief justice of Pennsylvania, a position he had "held near twelve years, having been twice chosen by unanimous ballot." Perhaps sensing that he had gained more than a few detractors along the way, McKean wrote, "My character must be left to the world." But he quickly added that his integrity had never been questioned and "no judgment of the supreme court of Pennsylvania since the Revolution has been reversed or altered one iota." McKean closed his appeal to the new president with a very personal commitment: "If you shall approve of this overture, I promise you to execute the Trust with assiduity and fidelity and according to the best of my abilities."[2]

Washington likely received the letter around the time of his inaugural address, a brief and somewhat bland speech delivered in the great room in Federal Hall. In the days that followed, McKean was undoubtedly hopeful.

He had enjoyed one of the most distinguished careers of anyone of his generation. Although his influence had been limited as president of the Continental Congress, he had done everything he could to support Washington as commander of the Revolutionary Army. And only a few years earlier, he had supported Washington in a politically charged legal dispute over land the president-elect owned in western Pennsylvania. McKean may have thought Washington owed him a favor.

Before the Revolutionary War, the British had awarded General Washington nearly three thousand acres of land in western Pennsylvania for his service during the French and Indian War. But during the time that he commanded the Revolutionary Army, squatters had settled on his land, built farms, and laid claim to the properties. The squatters called themselves "Covenanters" after the seventeenth-century Scotsmen who opposed King Charles II. Washington was outraged by what he considered their bold effrontery, writing that "to deprive me of the little I have, is, considering the circumstances under which I have been and the inability of attending my own affairs, not only unjust, but pitifully mean."[3] It was a dubious claim from one of the richest men in the country.

The Covenanters would not relent. They hired Hugh Henry Breckinridge, a colorful and accomplished attorney from Pittsburgh, to represent them. Breckinridge had won renown for having hauled a printing press over the Alleghenies and launching the first newspaper in the West. He relished the notion of a legal battle with someone as celebrated as General Washington.

The trial began on the afternoon of October 24, 1785, with Chief Justice McKean presiding. General Washington had spent months pulling together a body of evidence; he wanted to attend the proceedings but was unable because of illness. He retained a local attorney, Thomas Smith, to represent him. Smith was well liked and had a sterling reputation but had never before represented such an august client. Smith was visibly nervous and stuttered as he presented the defense before Chief Justice McKean. He rambled on about Washington's service to the nation and contended that the general's military obligations had limited his ability to attend to his personal and business affairs. Under the circumstances, Smith declared, it would not be fair to give away land that rightly belonged to the hero of the Revolution.

After delivering his opening remarks, Smith sat down and Breckinridge stood before the jury. He declared that his case was simple: since the settlers had improved the land, and Washington had not set foot on it for several years, the general no longer had any legal claim. McKean sat stone-faced. His grandfather had been a Covenanter in Scotland, but the chief justice did not allow his ancestry to influence his adjudication of the case. He barred the introduction of any evidence related to improvements to the land because it could not be authenticated. This was a serious setback for the settlers, but Breckinridge pressed ahead, arguing that the settlers had actually occupied the land before Washington gained title to it. He proved it by submitting receipts predating the transfer of title for materials that had been purchased to improve the land.

By the closing arguments, Smith anticipated a verdict against his client. As he put it, "We had very strong prejudices, artfully fomented, to encounter."[4] Yet, to his great surprise, he prevailed with the jury. It's not clear whether the outcome resulted from Smith's persuasiveness, Washington's celebrity, or perhaps McKean's strict instructions to the jury. Whatever the reason, General Washington must have been pleased by the result.

Four years after the "Covenanters" case, President Washington overlooked McKean for membership in his cabinet. There is no record that he even responded to McKean's letter. In the end, Washington turned to Edmund Randolph, a fellow Virginian, descended from one of the oldest and most prestigious families in the country, to be his attorney general. He chose John Jay as chief justice of the United States. Jay was a prominent lawyer in New York and had extensive foreign policy experience as well. Among the other three justices chosen by the president were John Rutledge, who resigned two years later without ever having heard a case on the court, and Robert H. Harrison, who declined his commission on the grounds that circuit riding was too arduous. James Iredell, who replaced Harrison, was not confirmed by the Senate for several months and then did not show up for the first meeting of the court. Washington's final pick for the court, undoubtedly hurtful to McKean's pride, was James Wilson,

McKean's Pennsylvania colleague, who had neither the experience nor the stature of Pennsylvania's chief justice but who had played a pivotal role in both the constitution and ratification conventions.[5]

⊷ ⊷

IF MCKEAN WAS DISHEARTENED BY THE PRESIDENT'S DECISION NOT TO appoint him either to his cabinet or to the Supreme Court, he didn't reveal it—at least initially. He continued to be a great admirer of President Washington. But watching from the sidelines, he grew increasingly concerned as Secretary of State Thomas Jefferson and Secretary of Treasury Alexander Hamilton competed for influence within Washington's inner circle. Hamilton pushed for more centralized government control, and his plans for a national bank and retirement of the public debt stirred controversy among the public and roiled the administration.

McKean had supported a federal constitution, and he favored what historian Gordon Wood has described as the "preoccupation of the Federalists. . . . Tying people together, creating social cohesiveness, making a single nation out of disparate sections and communities."[6] Like them, he wanted strong state and federal courts because he viewed the judiciary as the bulwark against an unruly democracy and the rule of law as the most effective check on ever-changing popular attitudes. Moreover, McKean agreed with the Federalists, who had pushed for the Judiciary Act of 1789 to give concurrent original jurisdiction to the state courts. Yet McKean was not entirely comfortable with the emergence of political parties and still refused to commit himself to one.

⊷ ⊷

MCKEAN REMAINED ON THE PENNSYLVANIA SUPREME COURT DURING THE 1790s, accruing even greater power during the last decade of the eighteenth century than he had the decade before. During this period, McKean's court was arguably more powerful than the US Supreme Court, which moved from New York to Philadelphia in early 1791 and convened across the hallway from Pennsylvania's highest court. Even after members of the Supreme Court settled into what they thought would be their permanent home, they spent the following eighteen months debating and bickering over policy and procedure. The justices worked out some of the thorniest procedural issues, but the court decided only a handful of cases in its first years. Chief Justice John Jay was bored, and he disdained circuit riding. He so disliked his job that in 1793 he ran for governor of New York. He lost, but two years later, he ran again and this time won. Jay happily resigned from the court.[7]

Pennsylvania's highest court became even more influential when McKean's colleague and friend Alexander J. Dallas assumed the unofficial role of supreme court reporter. Dallas had been born in Jamaica, in British West Indies, and was educated in London. He immigrated to Philadelphia in 1783 and was admitted to the bar two years later. Under Governor Thomas Mifflin, he was appointed clerk of courts in Pennsylvania and worked closely with McKean, developing a deep respect for him. Dallas recognized that the US Supreme Court had no written precedent on which to base its decisions, but under McKean, the Pennsylvania Supreme Court had been developing a body of "American" law, based largely on the English antecedent and foundation, for over two decades. Dallas set about researching and writing a multivolume work entitled *Reports of Cases Ruled and Adjudged in the Courts of Pennsylvania Before and Since the Revolution*. McKean, who by this time had been chief justice for fourteen years, made available to Dallas his extensive collection of personal notes about the cases he had adjudicated. This gave Dallas important context for his work, and when he finished the tome, he dedicated it to McKean.[8]

The chief justice sent a copy of Dallas's *Reports* to Lord Mansfield, the celebrated English jurist, with an accompanying letter that identified himself as "the first Chief Justice of a new Republic in America," who endeavored "humbly to imitate your right example."[9] Mansfield had served as the lord chief justice of England and was now an elderly, senior statesman, but he replied to McKean that the reports "showed readiness in practice, liberality in Principle, strong reason and legal learning; their method too is clear and the language plain."[10] Mansfield's approval undoubtedly pleased McKean, but more significantly, Dallas' Reports became a touchstone for courts throughout the country, including, as Dallas had envisioned, the US Supreme Court.

As America entered a new era of constitutional government, McKean's political leanings remained somewhat difficult to ascertain. He continued to be leery of what he viewed as a Federalist tilt toward Britain over France in foreign relations. He was more moderate on economic issues than most Federalists, but he appreciated that Hamilton's policies had brought the nation greater prosperity. This was especially evident in Philadelphia, where exports had grown to $7 million a year, representing nearly a fourth of all American trade. And he continued to find himself in agreement with Federalists on most legal issues, including freedom of speech.

⊷⊱ ⊰⊶

MCKEAN'S LONGEVITY AND STATURE ON THE STATE SUPREME COURT MEANT that he was one of the most celebrated individuals in Philadelphia. He was a member of the prestigious Philosophical Society of Philadelphia, which had been founded by Benjamin Franklin and which included many of the most learned and prominent persons in the city. Though McKean's heritage was Scottish, his father, William, had emigrated from Ireland and married Letitia, an Irish American, and so McKean identified himself as an Irish American. In early 1790, he helped found and was subsequently elected president of the Hibernian Society for the Relief of Emigrants from Ireland. The society raised funds for Irish immigrants, and its members greeted every ship from Ireland that arrived at Philadelphia's port. They helped Irish families with housing, work, education, medical care, and even legal advice. As historian Douglas Bradburn has observed, during his time as president of the society, McKean "connected the poor immigrant Irish and Irish emigres, to the local and national Republican elite, helping to consolidate the power of the Irish to mobilize an ethnic solidarity across class and religious lines."[11]

At the same time, he and the members of his family enjoyed a rising social status, although they would never penetrate the elite echelon because the McKeans were not one of the "original" families of Philadelphia. After the federal government moved from New York to Philadelphia in early December 1790, McKean and his teenage daughter Sally attended the new president's "levee," a weekly open house held at the president's rented home, the Masters-Penn House. One contemporary observer described the levee as "part imperial court ceremony replete with choreographed bows and curtsies, part drop-in parlor social," striking "the proper middle note between courtly formality and republican simplicity."

After she and her father attended the levee, Sally wrote a letter to a friend in New York and recalled the splendor of the house and the elegance of the party: "You never could have had such a drawing room. It was brilliant beyond anything you can imagine, and though there was a great deal of extravagance, there was so much of Philadelphia taste in everything that it must have been confessed the most delightful occasion of the kind ever known in this country."

Indeed, the Masters-Penn, located on 6th and Market Streets, epitomized "Philadelphia taste." The mansion was built during the 1760s by Mary Lawrence Masters, widow of William Masters, who was one of the richest men in the colony. Mrs. Masters gave the house, reputed to be the largest in Philadelphia, as a wedding present to her daughter, Polly, who married Richard Penn, the governor of the colony and grandson of William Penn, founder of the colony. Before the British marched on Philadelphia, Mrs. Masters and the Penns fled to England. General Howe lived in the house during the British occupation, and after the city was liberated, Benedict Arnold moved in. The house was seriously damaged by fire in 1780 but was subsequently bought and renovated to its former grandeur by Robert Morris, who donated the house to the nation for use by the new president.

The excitement created in Philadelphia by the Washington presidency was dampened when Benjamin Franklin died in January. Franklin, one of the most venerated American patriots of the Revolutionary era, was eighty years old and had been ill for some time. Although Franklin and McKean had never been particularly close friends—they were of different generations and McKean had none of the wit, charm, or intellectual breadth of Franklin—they shared a passion for independence and enjoyed a mutual admiration. McKean was one of six pallbearers at Franklin's funeral, which included a procession from the statehouse to the cemetery at Christ Church past thousands of onlookers who mourned the loss of one of America's towering Founding Fathers.[12]

McKean's role as a pallbearer underscored that he was one of the most important political figures not only in Pennsylvania but in the country. Although the chief justice was respected, he also had gained a reputation for arrogance. One story about McKean that circulated told of his receiving a legal brief addressed to "the right Honorable Thomas McKean, Esq., Lord Chief Justice of Pennsylvania." Without a trace of irony or humor—or humility—McKean reportedly declared from the bench, "These are perhaps more titles than I can fairly lay claim to, but at all events the petitioner has erred on the right side."[13] It was the kind of pomposity that prompted the editor William Cobbett, who wrote under the nom de plume "Peter Porcupine," to direct frequent and vicious personal attacks at McKean. Cobbett castigated the chief justice as "tyrannical," a "[political] trimmer," a "base coward," a "drunkard," a "sneaking sycophant," a "companion of a herd of Scottish malcontents," and a man often seen "brawling and boozing in public houses with the rabble."[14] Cobbett's aspersions may have been excessive and mean-spirited, but none of it helped McKean's reputation and only underscored that along with political influence and social status came antagonism and controversy. Just as he had done with Oswald, McKean would see to it that Cobbett paid a high price for his disrespect.

# PART III

# THE POLITICIAN

# 18

## The Tides of Change

HISTORIAN GORDON WOOD HAS DESCRIBED THE 1790S AS "THE MOST awkward in American history." Wood writes that "everything was changing and moving much too fast."[1] As a result of the Paris Peace Treaty, the size of the nation had doubled and was now greater in area than England, France, Spain, Italy, and Germany combined. Though the population was still small by European standards, it had soared in the previous fifteen years and now stood at four million, including seven hundred thousand slaves, the vast majority of whom were owned by planters in Virginia, Maryland, and the Carolinas. Most Americans lived along the eastern seaboard; everything else was wilderness, sparsely occupied by Native Americans, estimated at around a hundred thousand in number. The promise of cheap land meant that every day wagons headed west to the new states of Kentucky and Tennessee. The majority of Americans lived on farms, and the decade would see a rise in demand for agricultural products, but wages were still low. There was no standard American currency, which meant that foreign currencies as well as those of individual states were in use, making interstate trade extremely difficult. Canals were being built, but the roads were generally very poor, especially in the South. The Continental Army had atrophied to seven hundred officers and men, and the navy, once a growing force, had disappeared. General Nathanael

Greene, the Revolutionary War's most celebrated American general after Washington, had written to his former commander: "Many people secretly wish that every state be completely independent and that as soon as our public debts are liquidated that congress should be no more."[2] America may have been a nation, but it still lacked a national identity.

—— ——

JUST AS IT HAD UNDER THE ARTICLES OF CONFEDERATION, THE UNITED States government teetered on the edge of bankruptcy. To meet the challenge, President Washington had appointed Alexander Hamilton to be secretary of the treasury. Born out of wedlock in the West Indies and orphaned at age thirteen, Hamilton had attended King's College (now Columbia University) in New York City before becoming Washington's most trusted wartime adviser, and later one of the chief defenders of the US Constitution in the *Federalist Papers*.

As treasury secretary, Hamilton placed the federal budget on a more solid footing by renegotiating foreign debt, estimated in excess of $40 million. Though he succeeded in levying excise duties and customs taxes, debt payments outpaced revenue. Hamilton believed that for the United States to have international credibility, it would have to pay off its debt. To raise additional funds for the US Treasury and balance the budget, he counseled President Washington to impose a federal excise tax on spirits. Opposition to the tax was widespread, but nowhere more than in western Pennsylvania, where spirits were cheaper than in the eastern part of the state, and where in every village and hamlet some family's livelihood depended on the operation of a still.

Dissent turned violent in one Pennsylvania county after a federal revenue inspector, John Neville, attempted to serve process on distillers who had not registered with the authorities the previous year. In Cumberland County, a mob of a few dozen angry citizens surrounded Neville's home and fired gunshots into the house, where he and his wife had barricaded themselves. Neville was well armed and managed to ward off the attackers. But the next day a mob of five hundred angry protesters returned. Neville and his family had wisely fled hours earlier, but the mob burnt his house to the ground. Fearing that local constables could not contain the situation, the US attorney for the region appealed to the federal government for support.

During the summer of 1794, most members of the national government vacated Philadelphia in the midst of another outbreak of yellow fever. The year before nearly four thousand residents had died from the disease that had no cure and that killed most of whom it infected. Nevertheless, this summer President Washington remained in the city. He summoned his most trusted advisers to his residence, including Alexander Hamilton, to advise him on the crisis in western Pennsylvania. The president was sensitive to the fact that the rebellion was as much a state issue as a federal issue, so he also asked a handful of Pennsylvania officials, including Chief Justice McKean and Governor Thomas Mifflin, a Federalist and signer of the Constitution, to join the meeting. Sitting in the parlor of the Masters-Penn House, Hamilton advocated for "a competent force of Militia" to "be called forth to suppress the insurrection and support civil authority." After much discussion, it was clear that he and the president tended to view the insurrection as a national security issue requiring a firm response that would send a message about the young republic's viability.[3]

McKean would have been conflicted over how to handle the rebellion. On the one hand, the controversy would have recalled for him the resistance to the Stamp Act—in which he had played an important role—and opposition to a perceived unfair tax. On the other hand, McKean had briefly served as president and knew how difficult it was for the country to function and maintain unity without revenue. In the end, he viewed the incident fundamentally as a law enforcement issue and warned the president that "the employment of military force . . . would be as bad as anything the Rioters had done—equally unconstitutional and illegal." He argued that the insurgents could be prosecuted and punished without resorting to force. Governor Mifflin doubted Pennsylvania's militia would be up to the task of suppressing a full-fledged insurrection but did not want the federal government to usurp his authority. He opted to appoint a state commission, which included McKean, to meet with the rioters in a last-ditch effort to avoid bloodshed. President Washington was deeply skeptical that Mifflin's commission would accomplish anything, but he respected both the chief justice and the governor and agreed to let them try to settle the issue.

In early September, McKean and the members of the state commission traveled to Cumberland County and convened a public meeting in the county courthouse. One after another, residents stepped forward to complain about the tax and describe their dire economic conditions. Many recounted how they had been encouraged by locally elected officials to resist the tax. The testimony had little effect on McKean, who sharply criticized the rioters. Pointing out that members of the assembly who offered support to the insurgents should have instead worked to uphold the law, McKean insisted that they be recalled from office. As word of the chief justice's reprimand spread, a crowd gathered outside the courthouse, cursing the chief justice and pelting the building with stones. After several hours the crowd dispersed, but a few days later, the local sheriff identified several of the protesters, and McKean ordered their arrest. That action prompted a mob of nearly two hundred men to gather in the town square of Carlisle; angry protesters denounced the government and fired their guns in the air. McKean, who had left Carlisle only hours before, was burned in effigy.

McKean's failure to restore peace to the region persuaded President Washington that the insurrection needed to be quelled by military force. Not willing to take any chances, Washington dispatched an overwhelming force of thirteen thousand armed militia under the joint command of Alexander Hamilton and Henry "Light-Horse Harry" Lee to suppress the insurgency. Before the army arrived in Carlisle, the rebels returned to their homes, and there was no confrontation. However, Lee subsequently arrested twenty men, who were prosecuted; most were acquitted, and those who were convicted were later pardoned. The excise tax remained in effect, although it proved difficult to collect and was largely ignored.

Washington's forceful response to the crisis, known as The Whiskey Rebellion, demonstrated that the new national government had both the will and the power to suppress violent resistance to its laws. Though his own mission to restore order in central Pennsylvania had failed, McKean continued to believe that the federal government had precipitated the crisis in the first place and that sending in the army was an overreaction. In his view, it was symptomatic of the fact that the federal government had grown too powerful. Although he greatly admired President Washington, McKean was increasingly concerned that Secretary Hamilton was pushing the president, and with him the American government, in the wrong direction. The Whiskey Rebellion was one example of overreach, but for McKean, American foreign policy became an even greater cause for concern.

⟶⟵

IN 1794, PRESIDENT WASHINGTON DISPATCHED JOHN JAY, CHIEF JUSTICE of the United States, to London to negotiate with the British an end to their interference with United States trade. For some time, the Royal Navy had been intercepting American vessels conducting commerce in the French West Indies. Jay, of course, had cautioned McKean years earlier, during the War for Independence, about becoming too beholden to the French. Although McKean was skeptical, Jay's mission was widely supported. Even Secretary of State Jefferson, who was daily growing more estranged from the administration, shared the president's hope that "Jay's Mission may extricate us from the event of war."[4]

Over the course of several months, Jay successfully negotiated an arrangement with the British that went far beyond the American and British confrontations at sea. The chief justice persuaded the British to withdraw their troops from pre-Revolutionary forts west of Pennsylvania and north of the Ohio River that had been mutually recognized as American territory in the Treaty of Paris of 1783. Jay also reached agreement on the legacy of wartime debts and on the arbitration of the American-Canadian boundary. Finally, the treaty established a global trading regime between the British Empire and the United States, but by leaving open the question of neutral rights, failed to include adequate protections for America. Moreover, Jay angered many Americans by failing to negotiate compensation for stolen slaves and by conceding American responsibility to pay British merchants for pre–Revolutionary War debts. Because it seemed to favor British concerns in too many areas, Jay's Treaty created a political firestorm throughout the United States. Notwithstanding the treaty's commercial benefits, the War for Independence simply remained too raw for many Americans skeptical of any deal with Britain and wanting nothing to do with their former adversary.[5] McKean counted himself a member of this group.

In late June 1795, weeks before the Senate was to consider ratification of Jay's Treaty, an antitreaty meeting was held in the State House yard in Philadelphia. On the stage Clerk of Courts Alexander Dallas, Speaker of the Pennsylvania Assembly Frederick Muhlenberg, and Associate Justice William Shippen joined Chief Justice McKean. At one point, Congressman Blair McClenachan raised the treaty above his head and shouted, "What a damn treaty!" The crowd roared. The parchment was then attached to a pole and paraded first to the house of the French ambassador, where the crowd shouted their approval, and then to the house of the British ambassador, where it was burned.[6] Secretary Hamilton's successor at the treasury, Oliver Wolcott Jr., whose father, like McKean, had been a signer of the Declaration of Independence, characterized McKean and other protesters' behavior as representing "the ignorant and violent class of the community."[7] Alexander Hamilton pronounced, "The cry against the treaty is like that against a mad dog."[8]

The Senate finally ratified the Jay Treaty in February 1796. Ratification had a profound effect on American politics, galvanizing opponents, further dividing the country, and leading ultimately to the formation of political parties in the United States. The fledging Republican Party grew in both numbers and stature, while the Federalists consolidated their dominant position in the government. Thomas Jefferson, who had grown increasingly disillusioned with President Washington and Secretary Hamilton, resigned as secretary of state and returned to his mountaintop home in Virginia. He and Vice President Adams, both friends of Thomas McKean and once close friends themselves, became the leading competitors to succeed President Washington in the election of 1796 held that fall.

# 19

## The Election of 1796

VICE PRESIDENT JOHN ADAMS HAD ASSUMED FOR SOME TIME HE WOULD inherit the office of president. He had shown great loyalty to President Washington and never complained publicly about spending endless hours presiding over tedious senate debates. Thomas Jefferson, on the other hand, had left Philadelphia and government service two years earlier and had returned to Monticello, where he hoped to be the "most ardent and active farmer" in Virginia.[1] But James Madison touted a Jefferson candidacy and ultimately persuaded the primary author of the Declaration of Independence to pursue the presidency.

For the first time in the young country's history, candidates would openly identify themselves as members of a political party. Other trappings of the American political scene emerged, such as campaign rallies and slogans. Although the two candidates made very few public appearances, they left the campaigning to surrogates, who wrote favorable stories about their preferred candidate in the press while attacking the opponent in newspapers and pamphlets. The Republicans lambasted Jay's Treaty as a mistake of monumental proportions, while the Federalists tied the Republicans to the excesses of the French Revolution. Adams was caricatured as a monarchist; Jefferson was portrayed as a wild-eyed atheist, radical dreamer, and, worst of all in their view, a Francophile.

THERE WAS NO NATIONAL ELECTION DAY AS THERE IS TODAY; RATHER, OVER the course of several months, each state held its own. As the campaign progressed over the summer, the president and Mrs. Washington invited Chief Justice McKean and his youngest daughter, Sally, to a small dinner at the Masters-Penn House. It was typical of the gatherings Mrs. Washington liked best, with a mix of close friends, socialites, and government officials.

Sally McKean, age nineteen, was extremely pretty with dark hair and blue eyes. One of her best friends growing up in Philadelphia was Dolley Payne, who would later marry James Madison. The young women were two of the most beautiful and most eligible in Philadelphia society. Wearing the latest fashionable attire, they often attended the same parties where young men stood in line to dance with them. Abigail Adams, the vice president's wife, took a dim view of Philadelphia's cosmopolitan style, describing young women such as Sally and Dolley as "rouged up to the ears" and clad in gowns so revealing that they "literally look like nursing mothers."[2]

McKean lavished attention on Sally, who, like her mother, had an acerbic wit and a sharp tongue. She and Dolley especially enjoyed gossiping about the doyens and denizens of Philadelphia society. They pilloried the Spanish consul, José Ignacio de Viar, who, according to Dolley, had been discovered "in the middle of the day, in the act of fornication with the wife of a servant." They took particular pleasure in making fun of social climbers and the wives of powerful men. Sally mocked Abigail Adams as "that old what shall I call her—with her hawk eyes."[3]

Among the other guests at President Washington's home that summer evening were the painter Gilbert Stuart and the British ambassador Sir Robert Liston and his wife, Henrietta. Not long after the McKeans arrived, Carlos Martinez de Yrujo, the new Spanish ambassador to the United States, was announced at the front door.

Yrujo had only recently arrived in Philadelphia. Earlier in the summer he had visited the president at his Mount Vernon home. Washington described him as "a young man, very free and easy in his manners . . . appears to be well informed."[4] Yrujo, who often donned a red satin sash around his waist, was handsome and dashing, with reddish-brown hair and dark brown eyebrows. He charmed the other guests, including Henrietta Liston, the British ambassador's wife, who characterized him as a "lively, good-humored young man."[5]

Sally McKean immediately caught Yrujo's eye. She looked especially beautiful that evening, wearing a blue satin dress trimmed with white crepe and flowers, and a white, richly embroidered petticoat, and across the front "a festoon of rose color caught up with flowers." They sat next to each other at dinner and afterward spent most of the evening talking together.[6]

Not long after the dinner at the president's house, Sally and Yrujo began a courtship. Sally described her beau to one friend as "handsomer than ever" and "charming." Yrujo played the guitar, and Sally reported that he had given her a few lessons and that "I am serenaded every night with divine music."[7] Yrujo was Catholic and Sally was Presbyterian. But the Spaniard was descended from nobility and extremely wealthy, and the chief justice approved of the relationship. Months later, Sally and Yrujo became engaged. A year later Sally converted to Catholicism, and only two days after her baptism, the young couple was married in an elaborate ceremony at St. Mary's, Philadelphia's largest Catholic Church.

THE PRESIDENTIUAL CAMPAIGN BETWEEN ADAMS AND JEFFERSON INTENSIFIED during the fall of 1796. In Pennsylvania it was especially hard fought, and just days before the election, the French ambassador to the United States unexpectedly announced his support for the Republicans. With the legacy of Washington's presidency looming over the campaign, and the first president's advice to avoid "entangling alliances," the French ambassador's comments led to charges of unwanted foreign intervention. Despite Washington's warning, McKean and other prominent Republicans remained loyal to Thomas Jefferson. On November 8, Thomas McKean joined several other party members in publishing a letter endorsing the Jefferson candidacy. The letter described the former secretary of state as a man "of such enlightened views, such pure patriotism, such unsullied integrity, and such zeal for human happiness" and declared "only such a man could make America flourishing, tranquil and happy." The letter also took direct aim at Vice President Adams as someone "who has proclaimed to the world his hostility to republican government" and accused him of being "the enthusiastic friend of hereditary power."[8] This not only was an unfair caricature of Adams but also represented a breach of their friendship, marking the first time that McKean had so openly identified himself with the Republican Party.

The endorsement by McKean and the other Republicans may have helped Jefferson win a slim victory over Adams in Pennsylvania. But when the final results for all states were tallied and announced on December 7, Adams had won enough states to eke out a narrow victory over Jefferson, with 71 electoral votes to 69. The next day, after Congress had proclaimed him the second president of the United States, Adams wrote a bittersweet letter to his wife, Abigail, acknowledging the pride he felt in his victory but expressing deep sadness at the political betrayal of old friends. "Nothing effects me so much," he wrote Abigail, "as to see McKean . . . even Sam Adams and such men in opposition to me." Adams confessed that he found their behavior "very disgusting, very shocking."[9] During the months of debate and political jockeying leading up to passage of the Declaration of Independence, Adams and McKean had stood shoulder to shoulder and supported one another. But now, in the wake of a hard-fought presidential election, they were barely on speaking terms, and there would be no correspondence between them for many years.

The only question lingering from the election of 1796 was who would be Adams's vice president. Under the Constitution, which did not take into consideration the emergence of political parties, the candidate who received the second most votes would be vice president. Jefferson had lost by only three electoral votes, but the campaign had been contentious and no one actually expected him to serve. He had, after all, walked away from his job as secretary of state in the administration of President Washington, and it was assumed he had no interest in being relegated by Adams to presiding over the Senate. But Jefferson surprised friends and foes alike by announcing that he was both "humbled and envious" to accept the vice presidency. Adams wrote Abigail on December 27, reporting sardonically that "Jefferson will be Daddy Vice" and that he expected "more ample provision made for him, that he may live in style." Adams continued to vent about his old friends as exhibiting "despicable and detestable Phenomena for Governors, Judges, and Heads of colleges." He seemed especially upset by McKean, whom he dismissed sarcastically as "charged with a little too much Madeira and Infidelity to friendship and political principle."[10]

As the March date for his inaugural approached, Adams got down to business. He made an important decision to ask Washington's cabinet to stay on and serve his presidency. As he explained later, "Washington had appointed them and I knew it would turn the world upside down if I removed any one of them."[11] The four cabinet secretaries were all Federalists, foremost among them was Timothy Pickering, the secretary of state, who was anti-French and passionately pro-British. Adams may have hoped that Pickering would counter Jefferson, whom he described to one friend as having "too many French about him to flatter him." Still, Adams hoped to improve relations with France, which had interpreted the Jay Treaty as signaling a American-British alliance and which now viewed the United States warily.

⊷┼┼⊷

PRESIDENT WASHINGTON LEFT OFFICE IN MARCH 1797 WITH A RECORD OF substantial accomplishment. He helped to establish the institutions of American government, most notably symbolized by his role in the decision to locate the permanent national capital in the District of Columbia and by passage of the Judiciary Act of 1789, which established a six-member Supreme Court. That same year, Washington signed a bill into law establishing an executive Department of Foreign Affairs to be called the Department of State. In foreign policy, Washington opted for neutrality in the wars between France, an ally, and Britain, America's leading trading partner. The Jay Treaty, although extremely controversial, averted war with Great Britain and solved many contentious issues left over from the Revolution. Finally, Pinckney's Treaty in 1795 established sound relations between the United States and Spain by clearly defining boundaries with Spanish colonies and guaranteeing navigation rights on the Mississippi River. Because his presidency was marked as much by the restraint, respect, and dignity he brought to the office as by his accomplishments, he helped Americans to develop a sense of inclusive nationalism.

Washington had also hoped to leave office without a legacy of domestic political factionalism. But as the country had witnessed in the race between Adams and Jefferson that just ended, on that score he was not entirely successful. In fact, as far back as 1793, following his first term, Federalists and Republicans had begun to organize into political parties reflecting their sectional and ideological differences. The political differences had only intensified during his second term and were both trumpeted and amplified in the press as newspapers picked sides. To his dismay, political division reached its apex in the election of 1796.

Alexander Hamilton accurately described the widening chasm in American politics, writing to Washington that the Republicans believed in "a serious plot to overturn the state Governments and substitute monarchy to the present republican government. The other side firmly believes that there is a serious plot to overturn the General government and elevate the separate power of the states upon its ruin." Hamilton concluded, "Both sides may be equally wrong and their mutual jealousies may be material causes of the appearances which mutually disturb them, and sharpen them against each other." Still, he favored a standing army, a national bank, and, overall, a strong central government. He had once referred to the British style of government as "the best system in the world."[12]

McKean found himself in agreement with James Madison, who characterized the Federalists' approach to governing, personified by Hamilton, as "narrowed into fewer hands, and approximated to hereditary form."[13] In sharp contrast to Hamilton, Madison declared hereditary power "an insult to the reason and an outrage to the rights of man."[14] This view resonated with McKean, who had no problem with a powerful chief executive but didn't want another king. The distinction was far from a settled issue at the time, but McKean and other liked-minded leaders set the tone for the evolution of the American presidency that continues to this day.

# 20

## The Rise of Republicanism

OELLER'S HOTEL, IN THE SHADOW OF THE STATE HOUSE, WAS ONE OF Colonial Philadelphia's most popular social destinations for politicians and the city's elite. Opened in 1791 at the corner of Sixth and Chestnut on the site of the former Episcopal Academy, the hotel was the first place in the city to offer guests an ice cube in their drink. But, on the night of August 1, 1797, the mood was decidedly heated. Thomas McKean stood in front of a gathering of like-minded men to honor James Monroe, who months earlier had been ordered by President Washington to return from his post as ambassador to France shortly before Washington left office.

"We have heard nothing, for which an American Republican ought to blush," said McKean, raising a glass of wine in honor of Monroe. The former senator from Virginia, thirty-nine years old, had been relieved of his post because Washington, egged on by Hamilton and others, concluded that Monroe had shown himself too agreeable in negotiations with the French and had exhibited too great an affinity for his hosts. McKean shook his head slowly and inveighed against an administration that had failed to protect Monroe's "honor from obloquy and reproach."[1] It was, in his view, only the latest in a series of Federalist mistakes. Jay's Treaty had appalled him, as had Hamilton's British bias. Now the recall of one of America's great patriots as minister to one of its most steadfast allies convinced him that those around Washington—and now Adams—had forsaken the leadership that had saved the country from British domination.

As Monroe looked on, McKean raised his glass and told an audience that included Vice President Thomas Jefferson, Robert Livingston, Albert Gallatin, and fifty or so members of the House and Senate, "You have uniformly endeavored to fulfill the objects of your mission; to render yourself and your country agreeable to the Republic of France."[2]

No issue dominated the political debate more during the Adams presidency than relations with France. The French had come to America's aid during the Revolution, but now their country was undergoing a political transformation and stirring controversy in the United States. The Bourbons, the ruling family descended from Louis I, had controlled France through the ancien régime, a system of government that favored a narrow segment of the country's aristocracy. However, by the 1780s their hold on the country had frayed as the economy teetered on the edge of ruin. When King Louis XVI was finally forced to call a national assembly in 1789 to deal with the country's deteriorating financial situation, the long-smoldering conflict among the many socioeconomic groups burst into the open with a revolutionary ferocity. In an effort to impose order and to protect the throne, the king proclaimed a constitutional monarchy.[3]

During this period, McKean developed a friendship with the French ambassador to the United States, Edward Genet. "Citizen" Genet, as he was known, had been sent to America by the new French government to whip up support for the French Revolution. He had abundant energy and charm and managed to stimulate a large following in Philadelphia, including the publisher of the General Advertiser, Benjamin Franklin Bache—Benjamin Franklin's grandson—who wrote "upon the establishment or overthrow of liberty in France probably will depend the permanency of the Republic in the new world."[4] McKean and Genet saw each other often at parties and occasionally dined together. Like Bache, McKean saw parallels between France and the United States; he believed that in America, as in France, an educated elite should govern through established institutions in order to restrain the passion of the masses and thereby protect the freedom of all citizens.

Ultimately, the radicals in France gained the upper hand, and on July 14, 1789, a mob overran the Bastille in Paris and later executed King Louis XVI by guillotine. They declared a republic with universal suffrage and a commitment to a broad range of civil and political rights. But Europe's first modern democracy descended quickly into what came to be called the Reign of Terror, in which thousands of French men and women were executed for alleged counterrevolutionary activities.[5] For some American observers such as Alexander Hamilton, it only proved that democracy carried to the extreme resulted in mob rule.

Many years later, McKean would write John Adams that the killing of the French king so shocked him that over time he revised his view of France as a model for America.[6] Although he appreciated that French money, ships, and tactics had been at least partially responsible for the great victory at Yorktown, McKean's Republican views were driven more by his abiding fear and long-standing contempt for the British than by love of France. He feared that Federalists wanted hereditary government in America and perhaps even a return to monarchy. And like many Republicans, he worried that the Federalists might precipitate a war with France. He wanted to avoid another conflict at all costs, and in this regard he was very much aligned with a group he had embraced twenty years earlier: the radicals in Pennsylvania.

One of those radicals was a wealthy Quaker named Dr. George Logan, who served in the state assembly. Logan believed that the nation's increasing engagement with Britain and growing estrangement from France meant that its hard-won gains might ultimately be reversed. He made it his mission to rectify what he perceived as a serious imbalance in American foreign policy and decided to travel to France and personally implore its government to mend relations with the United States. He sold some of his property to raise money for the expedition, but he worried that his entire estate would be confiscated if federal authorities caught wind of his plans.

Logan was friendly with McKean. He knew the chief justice was sympathetic to his views, so he assigned him a power of attorney and asked him to keep watch over his property while he was abroad. Because travelers in those days didn't have passports issued by the government, Logan asked for letters of introduction from McKean and from Vice President Thomas Jefferson. Notwithstanding support from such prominent officials, and even though France responded to Logan's entreaties by lifting the trade embargo and freeing American seamen who had been jailed, his mission had not been officially authorized, and he was roundly criticized, as were to a lesser extent Jefferson and McKean. Congress worried about the precedent that Logan was setting, and it passed legislation that was signed into law by President Adams on January 30, 1799. Known today as the Logan Act, it prohibits individual American citizens from conducting foreign policy by engaging in negotiations without the knowledge and consent of the government. The criticism didn't hurt Logan—at least in Pennsylvania—where he was subsequently elected to the senate and remained a steadfast friend and ally of McKean.

McKean also supported John Dickinson, who, though not a radical, hoped in 1797 to publish some writings—titled "Letters of Fabius"—in France. Dickinson first published a series of "Fabius" letters nine years earlier in the *Delaware Gazette* to rally support for the ratification of the new United States Constitution. Now, in this second collection of letters, Dickinson sought to raise public awareness over the danger of America's deteriorating relations with France. In a letter to McKean, Dickinson declared, "Never was the happiness of a people more wantonly exposed to hazard" than in "the impending break of relations with France." He committed himself to fight the "ignorance, passion, selfishness and the frenzy of political speculation" that in his view so often fueled war. When Dickinson's letters were published, Federalists pounced and called him naive and even traitorous, but McKean leapt to his defense.[7]

Logan's mission and Dickinson's letters were indicative of the degree to which foreign policy now dominated national politics and defined the battle lines between Federalists and Republicans. Growing out of this divide, an especially controversial and noxious piece of legislation cemented the rift between President Adams and Chief Justice McKean.

In 1797, Federalists introduced legislation known as the Alien Act. The act targeted individuals who were not American citizens by granting broad authority to the president to detain or deport any noncitizen deemed dangerous to the United States. After President Adams signed the Alien Act into law, many French and Irish immigrants promptly fled the country.

The Sedition Act was even more draconian and sweeping in its application and potential impact: it criminalized all "false, scandalous and malicious" comments about the United States. Adopted overwhelmingly by the Federalist Congress only seven years after the First Amendment had guaranteed freedom of speech and association, and signed into law by President Adams in July 1798, the Alien and Sedition Acts appeared to violate the very spirit of America's independence.

Federalists, the majority party in Congress, justified the laws by asserting that the Republic was fragile and that war might break out at any point. In the name of "national security," they argued, the government needed the preemptive power to quash dissent. As a result, criticism of the president became tantamount to subversion. One legal historian, Geoffrey Stone, has called it "perhaps the most grievous assault on free speech in the history of the United States."[8]

The Alien and Sedition Acts had a profound impact on the politics of the country. Republicans believed that the acts represented nothing more than an attempt by the Federalists to eviscerate them as a fledging party, so they changed their tactics and redoubled their efforts. They continued to focus on national issues but increasingly emphasized states' rights and local issues, often on a sectional basis. As Thomas Jefferson explained years later, "leading Republicans in Congress who found themselves of no use there" decided "to retire from that field, take a stand in their state legislatures, and to endeavor there to arrest" the rise of the Federalists.[9]

Republicans like McKean considered the right of citizens to voice their opposition to the government to be one of the hallmarks of the young Republic and one of the features that separated America from European nations. Although the Alien Act was never enforced, a circuit court convicted Matthew Lyon, a Republican congressman from Vermont, under the Sedition Act for libeling President Adams. He paid a $1,000 fine and served four months in jail. Over the next two years, there were fifteen indictments and ten convictions stemming from the Sedition Act.

McKean strongly supported the right of individuals to criticize one's government, but he had less patience for speech that maliciously impugned one's character—especially his own. In the summer of 1798, two incidents highlighted the important distinction that he drew between speech that libeled an individual and speech that criticized the government.

Writing under the pseudonym "Peter Porcupine," the editor of the *Philadelphia Gazette*, William Cobbett, picked a fight with McKean's son-in-law, Carlos Martinez de Yrujo, the Spanish ambassador to the United States, who was a frequent and vociferous critic of British foreign policy. Cobbett thought Yrujo was trying to drive a wedge between the United States and Britain, and he accused the ambassador of "foreign interference," which was somewhat ironic given that Cobbett had recently immigrated to America from England and was not yet an American citizen. Cobbett wrote that the Spanish king had been "disgraced" by Yrujo's repudiation of America and that Spain had been "manipulated by the crooked politics of France." He called Yrujo "frivolous," "a political puppet," and "a half don, half *sans coulotte*."[10]

Initially, McKean wrote to Secretary of State Timothy Pickering to complain about Cobbett. McKean asked that Cobbett, who had never renounced his English citizenship, be thrown out of the country—presumably under authority of the Alien Act. It was another example of how McKean, who opposed application of the Alien Act to political speech, made a distinction when the speech was directed at him or members of his family. When the Department of State failed to take action, McKean adopted another approach. He issued a warrant on behalf of the state charging Cobbett with "tending to defame the . . . King, envoy and minister [of Spain], and the subjects of the King to alienate their affection and regard from the Government and citizens of the United States of America . . . and to incite them to hatred, hostilities and war against the United States." Next, McKean convened an oyer and terminer court to determine whether to formally bring criminal charges against Cobbett.[11]

As the jury sat in stiff wooden chairs, McKean provided a long-winded history of libel law and declared, "Libeling has become a kind of national crime." Turning to the charges against Cobbett, he specifically alleged that Peter Porcupine's editorials about Yrujo were "licentious and virulent beyond all former examples." Cobbett later wrote that McKean's pleadings were those of "an advocate."[12]

However, McKean failed to convince the jury that there was enough evidence to indict Cobbett, and the case was dismissed. Cobbett later wondered how he could be dragged before McKean and accused of libel when James Callender, the editor of the *Philadelphia Aurora,* who had referred to Federalist congressmen as crooks and scoundrels "without any dashes, feigned names or circumlocution," was not subject to the same treatment. Ironically, Callender came to the defense of Cobbett, his journalistic competitor and political nemesis. He claimed McKean had attempted to overwhelm Cobbett "by the expense of litigation" because he had been "unable to meet" his "accuser on the fair ground of argument and detail."[13] But McKean, who had acted as prosecutor, judge, and witness in the Cobbett libel case, was clear that free speech had its limits, and he served notice that character assassination would not be tolerated in Pennsylvania.

That same year McKean gained national notoriety when he intervened in an altercation involving some of Philadelphia's most controversial public figures and their right to free speech. Members of the United Irish, a pro-Irish revolutionary group, including its leader, Dr. James Reynolds, and the radical publisher of the *Aurora* newspaper, William Duane, were soliciting signatures for a petition to Congress against the Alien Act in the courtyard of St. Mary's Roman Catholic Church on Fourth Street in Philadelphia during one Sunday service in October. They affixed a placard to the church wall soliciting "The natives of Ireland who worship at this Church . . . to remain in the yard after Divine service until they have affixed their names to a memorial for repeal of the Alien bill."[14] When elders of the church tore down the placard, Reynolds and Duane put it back up. As a mob formed, with men on both sides pushing and shoving each other, Reynolds pulled a gun from his jacket and waved it in the air. Moments later, the police arrived, disarmed Reynolds, and placed him, Duane, and two of the protesters in handcuffs. The police paraded the prisoners through the streets to the home of the Federalist mayor Robert Wharton, where the men were charged with disturbing the peace.

Wharton, a former city alderman appointed mayor by the city council in 1797, had earned the reputation of an enforcer by quelling a revolt in 1796 among sailors demanding higher wages, and again two years later, in 1798, by putting down a prison riot at the Walnut Street jail. As the hand-cuffed prisoners sat on wooden chairs in the waiting room of his house, Wharton stood and accused them of being "evilly disposed persons who willfully and maliciously stirred up a riot on an holy day and in an holy place."[15]

Suddenly, there was a loud knock at his door. At first, the constables ignored the rapping, but then they heard a voice demand, "Open the door immediately, I am the Chief Justice of the state!" When Wharton finally directed a policeman to open the door, a red-faced McKean burst inside. Duane, still handcuffed, must have been surprised to see him. They were not friends, and Duane had often criticized McKean's legal decisions in his newspaper. Moreover, Duane and McKean's oldest son, Robert, had once come to blows over an unflattering article Duane had written about the chief justice. But now McKean came to Duane's defense. Outraged by the mayor's support of what the chief justice considered mob justice, he demanded indignantly, "What is the reason, Mr. Mayor, of all his fuss, that you keep the city in an uproar with a mob marching these gentlemen up one street and down another, handcuffed and tied?" McKean ordered that the prisoners be freed immediately. "They have the right to take up their hats and go about their business." One observer described the chief justice as "in a delirium of rage." Wharton sputtered a somewhat incoherent defense of his actions. After a heated argument, the mayor relented and the protesters were released on bail—paid by McKean.[16]

Newspapers around the country reported the incident in great detail, prompting moderates in Republican Party circles to scratch their heads in puzzlement as to why the chief justice would come to the defense of some-one they considered an intemperate radical, not to mention someone who had so publicly criticized McKean in the past. Although McKean had his differences with Duane, the chief justice was president of the Hibernian Society, of which Duane was a member. Moreover, Reynolds was an elected official in the society. Most importantly, neither man, in McKean's view, had committed a crime. They were only exercising their right to free speech.

Meanwhile, in Federalist circles, McKean was derided for defending someone who had often viciously attacked President Adams in the press. Upon hearing of the fracas in Philadelphia, Abigail Adams wrote William Shaw, her husband's close aide, and sharply criticized McKean's handling of the incident: "As to the conduct of McKean, he should never sit upon the Bench as judge again."[17]

Notwithstanding the First Lady's poor opinion of McKean, the St. Mary's Church incident catapulted him into a more highly visible political role than he had previously enjoyed as chief justice. People began to talk about him as a possible candidate for governor of Pennsylvania. Duane wrote glowingly about him in the *Aurora*.

The governor at the time was Thomas Mifflin, who McKean had known for four decades. Mifflin had been an aide-de-camp to General Washington during the Revolutionary War and was elected Pennsylvania's first governor in 1790. Plagued by illness and financial problems, Mifflin's grip on power had begun to wane. A year before the St. Mary's Church incident, Secretary of the Treasury Oliver Wolcott had privately referred to Governor Mifflin as "a habitual drunkard" and observed "the efficient powers of the government are exercised by Judge McKean and [Alexander] Dallas."[18] If McKean was already de facto running the state, as Wolcott and many others believed, it was Alexander Dallas who encouraged the chief justice to be an official candidate for governor after the publicity surrounding the St. Mary's Church incident.

# 21

## Governor McKean

ALEXANDER DALLAS, THE CLERK OF PENNSYLVANIA'S COURTS, NOT only had an able legal mind but was also one of the shrewdest political operatives of his time. In 1791, Governor Thomas Mifflin named him secretary of the commonwealth, responsible for recording everything from pardons to deeds to fines. Politically adept and highly competent, Dallas played an even more powerful and influential role than his job description. Mifflin, a functioning alcoholic, largely turned over management of the state to Dallas.

During the 1790s, the population in Philadelphia had ballooned from 42,000 to 76,000, largely as a result of immigration. Dallas understood that in Pennsylvania a well-organized political campaign could stitch together the various constituencies of French American, German American, and especially Irish American voters. Now, in 1799, he calculated that his former boss, McKean, could be elected to replace Mifflin and become the first Republican governor in America.

McKean had been widely vilified in Federalist newspapers for his role in the St. Mary's Catholic Church incident, but after coming to the defense of William Duane, he had gained a strong supporter in the Republican press. Duane's closest political ally was thirty-eight-year-old Dr. Michael Leib, a member of the Pennsylvania Assembly and a protégé of Benjamin Franklin's. Leib, notwithstanding his populist politics, was something of a dandy. He wore tailored clothes, doused himself in perfume, and often appeared in a powdered wig even though it was no longer in style.[1] He was highly influential because he commanded much of the city's German vote.[2]

Neither Duane nor Leib particularly liked McKean or his politics. They did not consider him sufficiently progressive—he was, they felt, nothing more than a Federalist patrician masquerading as a Republican populist. McKean had opposed Pennsylvania's liberal state constitution in 1776, supported the federal Constitution of 1787, and long been an outspoken advocate for property qualifications for both voting and office holding. But Duane and Leib were practical men determined to transform the politics of Pennsylvania by electing a Republican governor. They agreed to support McKean if he ran.

In some respects, McKean was an unlikely candidate for elective office. At sixty-five, he was still tall and strong and carried himself erect; yet his weathered face showed the signs of age. He had served the public in one capacity or another for over three decades, but he had a reputation in some circles for being arrogant and overbearing. He was also well known throughout the state, widely respected for his intellect, and generally perceived as having been fair and moderate on the bench. He had done more than anyone to elevate the rule of law and stature of the courts in Pennsylvania. There is no evidence that McKean was contemplating a run for political office before being approached by Dallas. He had been a candidate for local office in Delaware four decades earlier, and had lost his first election. He never referred to his his defeat, and most of his close friends were unaware of it, but he knew the sting of public rejection.

Nevertheless, the challenge of running for governor appealed to McKean, who was growing somewhat weary of life on the bench. The federal courts, and especially the Supreme Court, now handled the vast majority of important and precedent-setting cases. McKean was likely persuaded to think about a new career in politics at age sixty-five by a combination of the confidence he had in his own abilities, the obligation he felt to the people of Pennsylvania, and the lifelong calling he felt to shape the governmental institutions of the state as well as the nation.

Other leaders in the Republican Party were mentioned as possible candidates. Peter Muhlenberg, George Logan, and Dallas were all popular figures, but none of them could compete with McKean's experience and reputation. On March 1, 1799, party leaders met and chose McKean as their standard-bearer; the chief justice accepted their nomination.

With the Federalists entrenched in Pennsylvania, Dallas and McKean knew the campaign for governor would be an uphill climb. His opponent was one of the most popular political figures in the state, US senator James Ross. The senator enjoyed a sterling reputation: one contemporary political pundit remarked on his "majestic countenance." Ross, a lawyer like McKean, was distantly related to Attorney General John Ross of Delaware, who had promoted McKean's career forty years earlier. At thirty-seven years old, Senator Ross was younger and wealthier than the chief justice. He also spoke fluent German, an important advantage in Pennsylvania with its sizable German population. Though he was a Federalist, he had deep support in the Republican stronghold of western Pennsylvania, where he had served as a commissioner during the Whiskey Rebellion and had taken a conciliatory approach toward the rebels. Perhaps most importantly, Ross enjoyed the support of William Cobbett, the English immigrant who published the widely read *Pennsylvania Gazette*, which tapped into a deep well of pro-British sentiment. Cobbett respected Ross and undoubtedly harbored continuing resentment against McKean for keeping alive Spanish Ambassador Marquis de Yrujo's lawsuit for libel.

Ross announced his candidacy in the *Pittsburgh Gazette* on March 23, and political pundits immediately anointed him the next governor. Although there was no doubt that Ross was personally well liked and widely respected, the politics of Pennsylvania were changing, and many of his Federalist, party-line views were increasingly controversial. He had been a staunch supporter of the Alien and Sedition Acts, was linked to the Federalist direct property tax, and was a consistent critic of France and promoter of Britain—all positions that had dwindling support in the state. Dallas, the de facto chief political strategist for McKean's campaign, sensed an opening.[3]

During the summer of 1799, as Philadelphia was once again gripped by an outbreak of yellow fever, the campaign for governor gained intensity and attracted significant national attention. Thomas Jefferson had narrowly won Pennsylvania in the presidential election three years earlier. No one felt assured of a repeat victory for the Republicans in the next election for president, but everyone assumed the McKean-Ross matchup would be a harbinger. The *Gazette of the United States* declared, "The effect then of the election for governor [in Pennsylvania] will be incalculable" on the presidential election of 1800.[4] Moreover, issues in the governor's race, such as property taxes and the Alien and Sedition Acts, were being debated on a national level. Even foreign policy, which in theory was not a state issue, played a role in the campaign. The *Federal Gazette* warned its readers that, if elected, McKean would turn "the whole state . . . into a filthy kennel of Jacobinical depravity."[5] A Federalist pamphlet charged, "McKean is a friend of France" and "desirous of a war with Great Britain." Writing in the *Philadelphia Aurora*, Duane consistently tied Senator Ross to the British and accused the editor William Cobbett of being a British agent engaged in "a most audacious foreign interference in our elections and attempt to sap our political principle."[6]

Unlike modern campaigns, the candidates made only occasional appearances in public. McKean spent most of the summer fulfilling his responsibilities as chief justice, a role that gave him the ability to travel widely and be seen and heard throughout the state. For the most part, campaigning was carried out in the press and in pamphlets that were written and distributed by like-minded activists. Duane and Cobbett battled almost daily in their respective papers, the *Aurora* and the *Philadelphia Gazette*, with less prominent country newspapers and pamphleteers chiming in as well. One diatribe published anonymously in a rural newspaper focused on McKean's role in the Stamp Act Congress: "His boasts of weight and influence and services are well known to all who have heard him for the last twenty years spout out his own praise."[7]

Some of the attacks were deeply personal. In perhaps the first incidence of "swiftboating," as it came to be known over two hundred years later, a soldier who served with McKean twenty-five years earlier, in 1776, wrote that the chief justice was not only a poor leader but also a coward. It was a lame attempt to revive the old charge that McKean was antimilitary. McKean countered with an endorsement from German American Revolutionary War hero Peter Muhlenberg, who pointed out that McKean had served in the military, while Ross had not.[8]

The ethnicity and religion of the candidates also emerged as issues. Federalist sympathizers spread rumors that McKean planned to send an "army of 50,000 United Irishmen" across the state to plunder and pillage the homes of law-abiding citizens.[9] The *Gazette* smeared McKean as "a man who had suffered his daughter to form a connection with a Spanish nobleman" and accused him of converting to Catholicism and subjugating himself to the pope.[10] McKean quietly seethed over the attacks leveled against him and his family but did not speak out publicly. His supporters fought back with equally scurrilous tactics, labeling Ross as an apostate, even though their own candidate rarely attended church.[11]

The newspaper war became so vitriolic that former president George Washington concluded that legal action needed to be taken. He wrote Charles Pinckney that the *Aurora*'s charges of foreign interference in the election were designed to "poison the minds of the people" and concluded "punishment ought to be inflicted."[12] US Secretary of State Timothy Pickering instructed the US attorney for Pennsylvania, William Rawle, to explore an indictment of the *Aurora*. Federalists in Norristown presented bills of indictment, under the Sedition Law, against Duane and the *Aurora*. Though the judge for the circuit was a nephew of President Washington, the bills languished.[13]

On Election Day many more voters than expected turned out, particularly in western Pennsylvania, where both candidates had run spirited campaigns. The voting went smoothly, although it took nearly a week to tally the ballots. While the ballots were being counted, Republicans charged the Federalists with election chicanery, alleging that as many as five hundred soldiers voted illegally in Pittsburgh. McKean had no doubt that Federalists had conspired to deny him his election victory, but in the end it didn't matter. On November 5, the results were announced: Ross had won one county more than McKean, but the chief justice had outpaced his opponent in the popular vote by 6,669 votes. Out of a record of nearly 70,000 votes cast, McKean garnered 37,255. He won Philadelphia and he nearly won Carlisle—the town where on two occasions he had been burned in effigy.

Against the odds, and in his first real run for public office, Thomas McKean was elected governor of Pennsylvania, the first Republican governor in the country. His improbable victory represented a rejection of the Federalist vision both in Pennsylvania and on a national level. The hopes of the Republican Party were summed up in an editorial in the *Aurora* that congratulated McKean on his victory and then anointed Thomas Jefferson as the future standard-bearer and "faithful guardian of our rights."[14] Massachusetts Federalist Fisher Ames, a fierce critic of McKean, had a somewhat ironic perspective: "It is all the better. Every good man will feel shocked and roused to action, by so scandalous an event. Had Ross been chosen, they would have gone to sleep, expecting him to keep all the wild Irish who voted for McKean in good order." Ames predicted, "The Feds will have a proper stimulus for the next three years."[15]

━╉╂━

ON THE COATTAILS OF MCKEAN'S ELECTION, THE REPUBLICANS IN PENN-sylvania also took control of the lower house of the assembly and cut the Federalist majority in the state senate to only one seat. Republicans throughout Pennsylvania were elated, hailing McKean as a "friend of freedom." The celebrations in Philadelphia were especially boisterous. His victory was celebrated with bonfires, ox roasts, and a display of fireworks. McKean was predictably delighted by the result, but having been previously scheduled to hear cases in western Pennsylvania, he briefly thanked his supporters before packing a satchel and heading west to hold court.[16]

Notwithstanding his impressive victory, the attacks on McKean in the press did not subside. William Cobbett derisively predicted that McKean "will consume more gin per annum than [departing Governor] Mifflin." He also gravely forecast that "the Election of my Democratic judge as governor of Pennsylvania, undeniably the most influential state in the nation, has, in my opinion, decided the fate of what has been called Federalism."[17] Cobbett announced that McKean's election had persuaded him to pack up and leave Philadelphia for New York, although the truth was that Cobbett had decided to relocate because he feared that an impending judicial action against him in Pennsylvania might bankrupt him.

If Cobbett's reaction to the election of the chief justice to the state's highest office reflected his mixed motives, others were genuinely alarmed by McKean's victory and the rise of republicanism. Congressman William Vans Murray described McKean in a letter to John Quincy Adams as a "vain, conceited, rusty old weathercock."[18] Abigail Adams, who for years had harbored resentment of McKean's betrayal of her husband, observed, "The state of Pennsylvania is a strange medley. Its late election has withered all the laurels it ever had."[19] Even the ordinarily phlegmatic former president, George Washington, was despondent over McKean's victory. Thomas Jefferson, on the other hand, characterized McKean's success as "a subject of real congratulations and hope."[20] And from Virginia, James Monroe wrote McKean that his victory signified "a change in our political system, which promised to restore our country to the state it formerly enjoyed." Monroe predicted McKean would revive "those liberties we acquired by our revolution, and which ought never to have been put in danger," and he thanked him for his commitment "to promote the sacred cause of our country."[21]

Thomas McKean was inaugurated second governor of Pennsylvania on December 17, 1799. He delivered his inaugural address in the State House chamber to both houses of the legislature. He spoke briefly, urging harmony and cooperation, and, seizing upon one of the themes of President Washington's Farewell Address, he advocated the abandonment of party politics and the exercise of "wisdom and fortitude . . . in the business of government."[22] Given that he had won a highly partisan and bitterly contested election, the irony of his remarks seems to have been lost on him. Perhaps he was signaling that even though he had won election as a Republican, he would not govern as a radical. The only concrete proposal he offered in his address was a call to strengthen the state's judiciary through the establishment of more courts and the appointment of more judges—a decidedly Federalist notion, but one he had advocated for years.

McKean's inauguration came only a few weeks after the announcement by President Adams that the federal government would be moved from Philadelphia to Washington, DC. Both events, however, were overshadowed by the death of George Washington.

━━┫┣━━

GEORGE WASHINGTON SUCCUMBED TO PNEUMONIA ON DECEMBER 14, 1799, at his home in Mount Vernon, Virginia. The entire country mourned the death, and on December 26, Philadelphia, the capital city, staged an impressive memorial service. Uniformed soldiers marched slowly from Congress Hall behind a riderless white horse with reversed boots in the stirrups. They wound six blocks through the city as thousands of citizens came to pay their respects to the man who had guided the nation through difficult times and who had warned against political factionalism in his Farewell Address. Accompanied by a slow and steady drumbeat and the chiming of church bells, the funeral procession moved solemnly to the German Lutheran Church at Fourth and Cherry Streets. Musketeers fired their rifles while a trumpeter played a baleful, final anthem.

Bishop William White of Christ Church led the religious service. Those in attendance included President John Adams and his wife, Abigail. Many other dignitaries—Federalists and Republicans, cabinet officials and military leaders—filled the pews as Henry "Light-Horse Harry" Lee eulogized President Washington as "first in war, first in peace, first in the hearts of his countrymen."[23]

Governor McKean, however, did not attend the funeral. He gave no reason—perhaps he was still angry that the first president had excluded him from his cabinet and had not offered him a position on the US Supreme Court. Perhaps, notwithstanding the Farewell Address, he faulted Washington for seeming to favor the Federalists over the Republicans. He may have heard that Washington disdained his election as governor. Whatever the reason, McKean was roundly criticized in the press for his absence. The only mitigating factor was that Thomas Jefferson, Washington's secretary of state, now the vice president, had not attended either, an absence that overshadowed that of McKean's. Jefferson claimed that he had been detained at Monticello. But others came from greater distances, and it seems clear that Jefferson could have been in Philadelphia had he chosen to do so. Certainly, McKean could have been there.

# 22

## Power and Politics

A S GOVERNOR, MCKEAN MOVED QUICKLY TO TAKE CONTROL OF THE
state government. The day after inauguration, he appointed Hugh
Henry Breckinridge to be an associate justice of the state supreme court.
Breckinridge had previously argued before McKean's court in George
Washington's lawsuit against the squatters who had settled on his land in
western Pennsylvania. During the gubernatorial campaign, Breckinridge
had served as a key leader of the Republican Party in the western counties
and had campaigned on behalf of McKean. His appointment was a reward
for his support and loyalty. Next, McKean announced Alexander Dallas,
clerk of courts during the time McKean served as chief justice and most
recently his campaign manager, would continue to serve as secretary of
state for Pennsylvania.

Dallas advised McKean to consolidate his gains quickly and install
Republicans to prominent positions in the state government. The governor, working with Dallas and Breckinridge, forced the resignation of dozens
of Federalist state employees, told them not to reapply for their positions,
and replaced them with loyal Republicans. McKean wrote to John Dickinson that, though he was no "Hercules," he had undertaken to "cleanse the
Augean stable."[1] Months after McKean's election, Federalist congressman
Uriah Tracy complained "the few remaining honest men and Federalists"

were now being evicted from office by "every scoundrel who can read and write." Tracy accused McKean of installing "Irishmen, and with very few exceptions, they are United Irishmen . . . the most God-provoking Democrats on this side of Hell."[2]

In Richmond, Virginia, James Callender, former editor of the *Philadelphia Aurora*, writing from a prison cell because he had been thrown in jail for his seditious editorials, applauded McKean's recasting of the Pennsylvania bureaucracy: "Nothing can be an act of more exquisite justice than that . . . these tyrants should feel the pangs they gave."[3] Because of his brazenly political approach to staffing the state government, many historians credit McKean with introducing the "spoils" system in America.

Practicing political patronage and nepotism on a grand scale, he handed out key positions in his administration to his sons and other members of his extended family. He arranged for his oldest son, Joseph, to be the register for probate of wills for the city of Philadelphia, and a month later, after the state's top law enforcement job opened up, Joseph was installed as attorney general. Robert was appointed to the lucrative post of auctioneer for Philadelphia, while Thomas Jr. served as his private secretary. In 1801, the governor's nephew, Thomas McKean Thompson, replaced Alexander Dallas as secretary of the commonwealth.

McKean, of course, was not the first public official to practice nepotism. When the British government appointed Benjamin Franklin as deputy postmaster for the colonies, he doled out post office jobs to friends and family across America.[4] And although McKean appointed many Republicans, he also appointed some Federalists, including Edward Shippen, the father-in-law of Benedict Arnold, as chief justice of the Pennsylvania Supreme Court. Newspapers had speculated that the governor might appoint a well-known Republican, Tench Cox, or even his son Joseph, but McKean felt that Shippen was most qualified for the job. And perhaps to counter charges of nepotism, McKean fired one of his relatives, Joseph Hopkinson, who had been a court clerk. Joseph was the son of Francis Hopkinson, who had died in 1791. In a letter to Vice President Jefferson, the newly elected governor noted that he was replacing "his graceless nephew." McKean must have taken delight in exacting postmortem revenge against his former brother-in-law, who had so often publicly denounced him.[5]

Governor McKean had an ambitious agenda to bring the citizens of Pennsylvania into the nineteenth century. He laid out plans to reform the land grant system and fired public officials who had been bribed by land speculators. He started construction on the first macadam road in the United States, the third turnpike of Pennsylvania. He proposed to reform public education by making it more accessible to more children, and he worked to strengthen and expand the University of Pennsylvania. Most significantly, he pledged to reform the state judiciary, complaining that "the extension of Commerce and Agriculture, the increase of population and the Multiplication of counties" had rendered the state's court system "no longer adequate to the regular and efficient administration of justice."[6]

Not all of McKean's constituents approved of his reform agenda. On February 24, the *Gazette of the United States* reported "his excellency Thomas McKean was knocked down with a brick-bat while walking the streets of Lancaster by one Moses Simons who is said to be insane. It was said his Excellency was taken up almost lifeless."[7] Two weeks later, the governor appeared fully recovered, writing to Vice President Jefferson, "I have had some boisterous gales, and have weathered the storm."[8] In that same letter, McKean also expressed his vision for change nationally. The governor knew his election in Pennsylvania had raised the hopes of Republicans throughout the country for the impending presidential election of 1800, and he encouraged Jefferson once again to be a candidate. Political wisdom of the day focused in on New York and Pennsylvania as the key battleground states, and McKean promised Jefferson that if the vice president ran, he would deliver Pennsylvania's Republicans.

Jefferson did not need a lot of convincing to make a second attempt for the presidency. Horrified by Adams's Alien and Sedition Acts, which he referred to as the "Reign of Witches," he had been working behind the scenes to undermine the legislation. He conspired with James Madison to write the Kentucky and Virginia resolutions condemning the acts. In the case of Kentucky, the resolution went so far as to embrace nullification, which meant the state would not have to comply with federal law.[9] Given that Jefferson was vice president at the time, his actions amounted to insubordination. Nevertheless, he was McKean's choice for president.

McKean's relationship with John Adams had deteriorated from bad to worse during the Adams presidency. Decades earlier, McKean had managed to separate policy differences from his personal friendship with John Dickinson; when they disagreed, they did so respectfully. But Adams was a more prickly personality than the low-key Quaker. He believed McKean had betrayed him. In truth, McKean only adhered to principles that had guided him for decades, and his drift to the Republican Party resulted from major differences with the Federalists, most especially over foreign policy. But it was also true that with the departure of Washington, politics in America had become somewhat nasty and personal.

As Republicans and Federalists around the country girded for battle in the election of 1800, everyone assumed the race would be very close. In March, ensconced at Monticello, Vice President Jefferson declared, "No mortal can foresee in which direction the election will go."[10] Meanwhile in Washington, DC, McKean's former opponent in the race for governor, James Ross, still a United States senator, introduced and secured enactment of legislation to rig the system in favor of the Federalists in the upcoming presidential election: Ross wanted to create a thirteen-member "Grand Committee" that would determine "the admissibility or inadmissibility of the votes given by the electors for President and Vice President." This would have given the Federalist-dominated Congress the power to nullify electoral votes, which in a close election, could have been pivotal.[11]

Ross likely targeted the legislation to his home state of Pennsylvania where Federalists, who controlled the state senate, wanted the electors chosen by districts, which they believed would result in more votes for Adams. On the other hand, Pennsylvania Republicans, led by McKean, were pushing to reenact the law providing for the election of presidential electors by a statewide general ticket. The governor understood that Republicans had the popular majority in Pennsylvania and the "winner-take-all" approach would deliver all fifteen electoral votes to Jefferson—as he had promised to the vice president. This alarmed Massachusetts congressman Fisher Ames, who worried, "If Gov. McKean and Dallas should effect their design . . . all Pennsylvania will be thrown into that scale." Treasury Secretary Oliver Wolcott predicted, "If this course should be pursued, and the choice of president should depend on the votes of Pennsylvania, a civil war will not be improbable."[12] The stalemate in Pennsylvania continued throughout the summer and into the fall, leading McKean to worry that Pennsylvania Federalists were content to have no solution, and thereby forgo the state's participation in the national election. McKean decided to broker a compromise and settle for a split slate of electors: eight Republicans and seven Federalists.[13]

⟡⟡⟡

FOUR YEARS EARLIER, VICE PRESIDENT ADAMS AND SECRETARY OF STATE Jefferson had competed for President Washington's attention and approval. The candidates in 1800 were the same, but they offered very different visions as to how they would govern. The personal friendship that Adams and Jefferson had once enjoyed was now in tatters. They disagreed with one another on virtually every important issue, including how to deal with the national debt, the appropriate size of the army, and the broader issue of the role of government itself. But no issue divided them more, or divided the country more, than America's relations with France and with England. President Adams, who had once vilified the monarchy but later served as ambassador to England in the 1780s, venerated British-styled democracy. Vice President Jefferson, ambassador to France from 1784 until 1789, had cheered the French overthrow of the aristocracy, though he was subsequently horrified by the execution of King Louis XVI. McKean, who had not visited either country, viewed international relations solely through a parochial political lens, and although his personal sensibilities were more English than French—the powdered wig he wore on the bench was the most obvious manifestation—he could never do what he believed President Adams had done: embrace his former English masters.

Besides Adams and Jefferson, the other candidates running for president were Charles Cotesworth Pinckney, Federalist of South Carolina, and Aaron Burr, Republican of New York. Jefferson had known he would need New York's electoral votes to defeat Adams, and Burr had promised to deliver them if he were on the ballot. He had run for president previously in 1796 and had been a former attorney general and senator from New York. A brilliant lawyer, he was not without controversy, and his nemesis Alexander Hamilton bluntly characterized him as "unprincipled."[14] No one gave Pinckney nor Burr any chance of winning. With the emergence of political parties, everyone assumed that electors would vote a party "ticket"; if Adams was reelected, Pinckney would serve as vice president, whereas if Jefferson won the election, Burr would serve as vice president.

⇥ ⇤

As in the Pennsylvania gubernatorial contest, the presidential campaign was largely waged in the press. The *Aurora* had been the most ardent supporter of McKean in 1799, and it played a similar role for Jefferson a year later. In editorial after editorial, William Duane used his poison pen to label Adams a closet monarchist. He attacked him personally as "blind, bald, crippled, toothless and querulous." However, the vast majority of newspapers in the country supported the president. The *Washington Federalist* praised Adams as "among the surviving, steady and tried patriots" and commended him for making "his sole object . . . the present freedom and independence of his country and its future glory."[15] An editorial in another federalist newspaper, the *Gazette of the United States*, lauded Adams for his support for the Sedition Act: "it is patriotism to write in favor of the government, it is sedition to write against it."[16] Most Federalist newspapers, however, spent less time extolling the presidency of John Adams than attacking the character of Thomas Jefferson. He was labeled a "radical."[17] He was accused of marital infidelity. And he was denounced as godless and immoral. The latter smear was one that McKean had used effectively against Ross the previous year.

By late summer, the election seemed to be trending toward Jefferson, prompting arch-Federalist Fisher Ames of Massachusetts to confide in Alexander Hamilton. "I see almost no chance of preventing the election of Mr. Jefferson. . . . The question is not, I fear, how we shall fight, but how we and all Federalists shall fall, like Antaeus, the stronger for our fall."[18]

The states cast their votes for electors at various times during the autumn of 1800. McKean was disheartened that he was not be able to deliver all of the electors to Jefferson, but in the end, the eight of fifteen votes of Pennsylvania proved critical to what turned out to be a far closer race than anyone had anticipated. Jefferson narrowly carried New York, and after Republicans won South Carolina in early December, everyone assumed that they had won the election. The Republican sweep continued when they captured the United States House of Representatives 69 to 36. But after all the electoral votes were tallied, it became clear that an anomaly had occurred in the race for president.

As it turned out, the two Republican candidates for president, Jefferson and Burr, tied with 73 votes each. President Adams had received only 65 votes, and his running mate, Charles Pinckney, had received 64 votes.

Because it was a tie vote, the Constitution stipulated that the House of Representatives should determine the outcome of election. For the good of the party—and the country—most Republicans assumed that Burr would step aside in favor of Jefferson. McKean wrote Jefferson in early January warning that Federalists might conspire to cause mischief, but "given the explicit and honorable conduct of Mr. Burr there will be no competition on his part."[19]

McKean, however, was wrong. On January 5, 1801, the *Philadelphia Gazette* reported that Burr "was heard to insinuate that he felt as competent to the exercise of the Presidential functions as Mr. Jefferson."[20] This was welcome news to the Federalists, who didn't much like Burr but still preferred him to Jefferson.

Vote after vote in the House of Representatives produced a tie and therefore stalemate. As deadlock dragged for several weeks, many in the Republican Party became increasingly concerned. Rumors began to circulate that Federalists had a secret plan to perpetuate the stalemate, to wait for the date of the planned presidential inauguration to pass, and then, in the name of saving the Republic, to install one of their own. The name of John Marshall, Adam's secretary of state who had been only recently elevated to chief justice, was floated as a possible compromise candidate.[21]

The threat of Federalist subterfuge elicited dramatic and potentially dangerous responses from some of Jefferson's supporters. For his part, Governor McKean was outraged by the possibility that someone other than Jefferson might become president. He believed the Federalists wanted to steal the election. He convened a small group of close advisers at his house in Lancaster, including his friend Senator George Logan. In constant contact with the supporters of Vice President Jefferson in Washington, McKean and his Philadelphia colleagues resolved to take whatever measures might be necessary to enforce the will of the people. First, McKean and his team drafted a proclamation that called upon the citizens of Pennsylvania to give their allegiance to Jefferson as president. Next, the governor took the extraordinary step of preparing orders to call up the state militia. McKean was ready to open the armories and distribute weapons, unused since the Revolutionary War, to twenty thousand men who would march on Washington under General Peter Muhlenberg, a Republican congressman from Pennsylvania who had commanded a brigade at the battle of Yorktown and had been a key validator for McKean in the gubernatorial contest.[22]

McKean was not the only governor prepared to take action. In Virginia, Governor James Monroe—a close friend of Jefferson's—ordered armed militia to guard the state arsenal at New London to prevent its store of four thousand weapons from falling into the hands of any potential mob of Federalists seeking to preserve their power. McKean and Monroe had served together in Congress. The Virginia governor was also ready to call his legislature back into session and, like McKean, to order the state militia to march on Washington.[23]

News of these developments created alarm in Washington, where the *National Intelligencer* warned that any such moves by Pennsylvania and Virginia might lead to civil war. Not surprisingly, more rumors took flight. On the second Sunday in February, during a hiatus in the voting, word spread in the capital that a huge, angry mob had stormed the armory in Philadelphia, had seized thousands of weapons, and were preparing to march on Washington to dislodge the Federalists once and for all. The report was untrue and was likely hatched in Richmond by Monroe, who was not above employing a disinformation campaign to help Thomas Jefferson.[24]

On February 17, House members cast their thirty-sixth ballot. To the surprise of everyone, a little known Federalist representative from McKean's home state of Delaware, James Bayard, broke the stalemate by submitting a blank ballot, thereby removing his state's vote from the Burr column and placing it in the "not-voting" category. There is no evidence that McKean played any role in Bayard's decision, but interestingly McKean had written Jefferson in early January assuring the vice president that Bayard would ultimately vote for him. In any event, after Bayard voted, Federalist congressmen from Maryland and Vermont who had previously supported Burr now abstained, allowing their Republican colleagues to cast their states' votes in support of Jefferson. Federalists in the South Carolina delegation, who had supported Burr as a bulwark against the election of Jefferson, also abstained. With Delaware and South Carolina no longer supporting Burr, the logjam had been broken: Jefferson also added Maryland and Vermont to his column and won decisively, ten votes.[25]

As news of the outcome spread around the country, Republicans gathered in taverns, meetinghouses, and parlors to toast the new president. The *Federalist Gazette* reported sardonically, "The bells have been ringing, guns firing, dogs barking, cats mewing, children crying, and Jacobins getting drunk."[26] In Philadelphia, however, the *Aurora* proclaimed, "The Revolution of 1776 is now, for the first time, arrived at its completion."[27]

Within the week, Governor McKean had sent the president-elect a congratulatory letter that echoed the newspaper reports. "The bells in this borough have been ringing ever since [your election]." McKean also revealed to Jefferson that he had been prepared to call out the militia. He euphemistically described the plan as "my intended operations in case of a certain unfortunate event in the decision of the House of Representatives." McKean had actually laid out the plan in great detail in a prospective letter to Jefferson, but upon receiving the "glorious" news of his election, he reported, "my long letter has been committed to the flames."[28]

Three weeks later, president‑elect Jefferson responded to McKean's letter. He blithely asserted that "had [the election] terminated in the elevation of Mr. Burr, every Republican would, I am sure, have acquiesced in a moment, for however it might have been variant from the intentions of the voters, yet it would have been agreeable to the constitution." Jefferson, however, profusely thanked McKean for his efforts and wrote, "I am sorry you committed to flames the communication of details you mention to have been preparing for me." He added, "They would have been highly acceptable."[29] This was an extraordinary admission because it not only contradicted his previous statement regarding respect for the constitutional legitimacy of a Burr presidency, but also could be viewed as an endorsement of military action. Whatever the case, in a final irony, Burr would himself one day plan a coup d'état—against Jefferson.

The president closed his letter to McKean by expressing satisfaction that because his presidency was now "shouldered on two such massive columns as Pennsylvania and Virginia, nothing is to be feared."[30] Historian Saul Cornell has since observed, "The actions of McKean, Monroe, and Jefferson took the states' rights theory of militia, first articulated by Antifederalists a decade earlier, and made it orthodoxy among Republicans."[31] It was true that Monroe was Antifederalist: he opposed the Constitution. Jefferson was representing the United States in Paris at the time of ratification, but his views were probably more in line with those of Madison, who favored the Constitution. McKean, however, was an unabashed supporter of the Constitution, elected by Pennsylvania Federalists to represent them at the convention for ratification. Now, more than a dozen years later, McKean worried that the federal government had grown too powerful and that in the election of 1800, Federalists had been willing to subvert the rule of law and to trample the rights of citizens. Cornell may be right that the events in Virginia and Pennsylvania surrounding the election presaged the rise of republicanism, but McKean's willingness to call out the militia, in his mind, was less about states' rights than it was about defense of the federal constitution.

⇒⇤+⇥⇐

Soon after his election, President Jefferson set in motion plans
to vastly expand the territory of the United States. The president sent a
letter to General James Wilkinson, commanding general of the US Army,
and included as well a sealed letter to "Lieut. Meriwether Lewis, not
knowing where he may be." President Jefferson gave Wilkinson two reasons for wanting to contact Lewis: first, Lewis's knowledge of the western
wilderness, and, second, "A personal acquaintance with him, owing from
his being of my neighborhood."[32] Lewis had been born and raised on his
family's farm, Locust Hill, located approximately ten miles from Jefferson's
home at Monticello. The president wanted Lewis to serve as his personal
secretary and to carry out his most delicate political tasks, including an
extraordinary and highly secret mission: an expedition across the continent
to document topography, vegetation, wildlife, and native peoples. Wilkinson eventually located Lewis, who enthusiastically accepted the offer to
serve the president.

In May 1801, only weeks after he had joined the president's inner circle, Lewis dined at the house of Governor McKean.[33] As President Jefferson's most trusted political operative, Lewis was compiling information
on the personnel and politics of the United States Army, which had seen
an influx of Federalists during the Adams presidency. He may have been
seeking advice from McKean on his experience in purging the Pennsylvania state government of Federalists. Lewis was also beginning to share
with a few important supporters the president's vision of a corps to explore
the vast wilderness west of the Mississippi and was undoubtedly aware
McKean was a member of the American Philosophical Society, which
ultimately sponsored the expedition.

It would take another three years before Lewis, joined by Second Lieutenant William Clark and thirty-one other explorers, launched the Corps
of Discovery on the Mississippi near St. Louis in May 1804. Their mission
would last two years and chart a route by river and over land across the
western half of the United States; along the way they would make over
140 maps and charts, encounter some 70 Indian tribes, and discover and

describe over 200 new plant and animal species. It would change the map of America and set the stage for manifest destiny, America's expansion from the Atlantic Coast to the Pacific Coast. But in those days, when the mission was secret and the vision still inchoate, McKean was one of the very first to know.

After listening to Lewis, he also may have been somewhat of two minds: on the one hand, his loyalty to Jefferson and commitment to his country would have convinced him of the soundness of the proposition; but, on the other, he would have understood the potential for conflict between the United States and one of its most stalwart allies, Spain, which claimed territory west of the Mississippi and contested areas of the southern United States as well. The Spanish ambassador, the Marquis de Yrujo, of course, was married to his beloved daughter Sally.

The marquis had been slated by his government to leave the United States for another position in 1801, but McKean had successfully appealed to Jefferson two months earlier to lobby the Spanish government to retain him, telling the president, "I love him as a child and never expect to see my daughter again after their departure to Europe."[34]

Several months later, President Jefferson began to broaden the circle of those who knew about the proposed expedition. The first outsider whom he apprised of the plan was the marquis. The president and Yrujo were friends; they both enjoyed good food and fine wine, and when Jefferson was first elected, the ambassador had even recommended a personal chef for the president.[35] The president was equally fond of Sally, and she and the marquis often dined with Jefferson at the president's house. More than anything, Jefferson knew that he needed Spain's assent to his plan for westward expansion, and he carefully cultivated a friendship with the young, vain ambassador.[36]

Yrujo was arrogant but not easily fooled. In a letter to his superior, the Spanish foreign minister, Yrujo later explained that the president had "asked him in a frank and confident tone if our court would take it badly that the congress decree the formation of a group of travellers who would form a small caravan and go and explore the course of the Missouri river with no other view than the advancement of the geography." Yrujo genuinely liked and respected Jefferson, but he had difficulty believing the president only envisioned a corps of discovery to simply complete the map of the unexplored territories. Rather, as Yrujo wrote to the foreign minister, "the President has been a man of letters all his life, very speculative and a lover of glory, and it would be possible he might attempt to perpetuate the fame of his administration . . . by discovering the way by which the Americans may someday extend their population and their influence up to the coasts of South America." He was, of course, exactly right.[37]

Weeks later, after receiving instructions from his foreign minister, Yrujo told the president very directly that the proposed expedition would cause "umbrage" to his government. Jefferson proceeded with the plans anyway.[38]

⟡

ON JULY 21, 1802, McKEAN SENT THOMAS JEFFERSON ANOTHER LETTER advising the president to purge the federal government of Federalists— just as he had done after being elected governor in Pennsylvania. McKean noted that he "received letters from several loyal friends," who "not having the honor of being personally known to you, I take the liberty of repairing some of the observations." He quoted a loyal Republican who opined "to overcome [the Federalists] they must be shorn of their fire—like Sampson's loss of hair—their disposition for mischief may remain, but the power of doing so will be gone." And he quoted another friend who wrote, "A dagger ought not to be put in the hands of an assassin."[39] McKean knew that the early days of the new republic when everyone in government worked for a common purpose had receded. Political parties had been institutionalized as a part of American democracy, and he feared that the Federalists were already working to undermine the new president and preparing for the next election.

Three days later, Jefferson responded. He acknowledged that the removal of Federalists from the government was "a subject most difficult of all." Whereas McKean viewed the issue in stark political terms, Jefferson, at least for the moment, took a broader, more idealistic, and more inclusive view: "My idea is that the mass of our countrymen, even those who call themselves Federalists, are Republican. . . . They were decoyed into the net of monarchists by XYZ contrivances."[40]

The "XYZ contrivances" involved a diplomatic commission consisting of Charles Cotesworth Pinckney, John Marshall, and Elbridge Gerry, who were sent to France in July 1797 to negotiate differences between the two countries that threatened to lead to war. However, agents of the French foreign minister Talleyrand approached the diplomats, demanding bribes and a loan before formal talks could begin. The Americans were offended and departed France without ever entering into negotiations. When details of the events in Paris were leaked to the American public, widespread outrage and anger were directed toward the French. Federalists, who controlled the government, took advantage of the national mood to build up the nation's military. They also used the incident for political advantage by attacking Jeffersonian Republicans for their pro-French stance.

Three years later the furor over the XYZ affair had faded, and Jefferson now communicated to McKean his belief that the Federalists "have come or are coming back." He then explained, "Between the monarchists and the Federalists, I draw a clear line. The latter is a sect of Republicanism, the former its implacable enemy." Jefferson therefore recoiled from the idea of a wholesale purge of Federalists from the government. Instead, he revealed to McKean his hope to "restore that harmony which our predecessors so wickedly made it their object to break up, to make us one nation."[41] Jefferson was, of course, referring to Adams and the Federalists, but in the election of 1800 he had done as much as anyone to promote political partisanship in America—going so far as to personally provide financial support for newspapers that attacked Adams.

The president then cautioned McKean: "There is a rock ahead, far more dangerous than monarchists. It is the discord showing itself among Republicans. It is no place more threatening as in Delaware. . . . Some threatening symptoms show themselves in Pennsylvania also." Although Jefferson's letter took direct aim at the state McKean had represented in Congress and the one he now served as governor, he concluded his missive by flattering McKean: "You may, my dear sir, be instrumental to their reconciliation, you will save the Republican cause in the state [Delaware] which otherwise is lost . . . your station enables you to take a broad view, and your communication is therefore of the first value."[42] Jefferson had lost Delaware in the election, and it remained a Federalist stronghold. Pennsylvania was deeply divided between the two parties, and even the Republicans weren't united. No one knew better than McKean of the discord among Republicans in both Delaware and Pennsylvania. He had regularly confronted factional infighting among Republicans, not to mention partisan sniping from the Federalists. And he long ago decided that trying to reconcile the different points of view yielded very few positive results. In the final analysis, affiliation with a political party was not that important to McKean, who believed in taking a position and sticking to it.

This became abundantly evident in the debate over naturalization. Governor McKean was reelected easily in November 1802, winning nearly 49,000 votes out of the 65,000 and 33 out of the 36 counties in the state.[43] He won the overwhelming majority of ethnic voters, and in early 1803 the Republican-dominated assembly in Pennsylvania voted that immigrants could participate in politics after living in the state for only two years. This was a major victory for the radical Irish, who had played a critical role in McKean's campaigns and hoped to lock in a Republican majority in the state for years to come. McKean, the founder and former president of the Hibernian Society, nevertheless vetoed the proposal on the theory that immigrants needed to be "weaned from the monarchical prejudices." Duane, the prickly editor, and Leib, the oily politician, were furious and vowed the governor would pay a political price for betraying "his best supporters and friends in the immigrant community."[44]

McKean was not easily intimidated. When President Jefferson completed the Louisiana Purchase in early 1804, it was celebrated at the Tammany festival in Philadelphia. During the ceremony, both Duane and Leib offered elaborate toasts. However, neither mentioned McKean—an omission noted by everyone in attendance. The governor had had enough of the radicals, who he knew had never liked him personally and were increasingly critical of his politics. McKean began to cozy up once again to the Federalists, as he had done around the time of ratification of the Constitution, going so far as to write former secretary of the treasury Timothy Pickering that "I have never been able to discover from any gentleman, under the name of Federalist, wherein he differs from me in the principles of government."[45]

# 23

## Pinnacle of Power

PRESIDENT JEFFERSON LOOKED UNBEATABLE IN 1804. HE HAD REDUCED federal taxes and spending and had cut down the size of both the army and navy. Notwithstanding US Navy skirmishes with Barbary pirates, America was at peace. On the political side of the ledger, Republicans in Congress outnumbered Federalists two to one. But Jefferson's greatest accomplishment was the purchase of the Louisiana territory from a cash-strapped Napoleon Bonaparte of France for only $15 million. The addition of such a vast territory led the *National Intelligencer* to proclaim "a proud day for the president" and an event of "widespread joy," which "history will record among the most splendid in our annals." The president's popularity, however, remained largely regional. He was still not liked in New England, where many disapproved of the Louisiana Purchase because they now feared it signaled an inevitable shift in power from east to west.[1]

Jefferson had originally planned to serve in the presidency for one term and then return to his beloved Monticello—at least that is what he told Governor McKean in late 1802.[2] Although the Louisiana Purchase remained somewhat controversial, he was confident that in the long run he had secured a favorable place in history. But the Federalists never let up in their attacks on Jefferson, including salacious allegations about a relationship with a slave at Monticello named Sally Hemings. Jefferson was not one to walk away from a challenge, and by 1803 he no longer viewed Federalists as one side of the Republican coin—as he had earlier written to McKean. Not only did he consider the criticisms directed to him to be petty and personal but also he concluded the Federalists did not share the same long-term goals for the nation. In March 1804, he declared that attacks on his policies and on him personally "have obliged me to throw myself on the verdict of my country for trial."[3] Convening in Philadelphia that summer, Republicans nominated Jefferson unanimously. The only drama occurred when his vice president, Aaron Burr, an object of scorn and ridicule, whom Jefferson had largely ignored during the first term, was unceremoniously dropped from the ticket.

Jefferson was also determined to make sure that there could be no more electoral ties between candidates for the presidency who represented either the same party or different parties. Legislation that would become the Twelfth Amendment, designed to prevent a repeat of the 1800 electoral tie, was working its way through the ratification process in the individual states. The president expressed his concerns to McKean in a letter in 1804 "that great opposition is and will be made by the Federalists to this amendment." As he explained it, "They know that if it prevails, neither a President or Vice President, can ever be made but by the fair vote of the majority of the nation, of which they are not."[4]

As pundits speculated about who would replace Aaron Burr on the Republican ticket, newspapers around the country mentioned McKean as a possibility. Some thought the McKean trial balloon might have been the work of Duane, the firebrand editor of the *Philadelphia Aurora* who had helped McKean become governor but now tired of what he perceived as the governor's intransigence and conservatism. Duane reckoned a McKean candidacy could have the dual benefit of helping to reelect Jefferson and opening up the governor's seat in Pennsylvania to a radical Republican. Others argued that Federalists, who would do anything to thwart the ambitions of Jefferson, had fueled the speculation about McKean. One British diplomat derisively predicted that if McKean were on the ticket, Federalists would cast their ballots for him, and with enough Republicans, he could actually be elected president. The diplomat declared that

Federalists were so thoroughly disgusted with Jefferson "they were willing to be governed for four years by an incomparably inferior man of headstrong and ungovernable passions, whose conduct would degrade the country and expose it to contempt."[5] Given McKean's views on Britain, the diplomat's derision was not especially surprising. In fact, a McKean vice-presidential candidacy made political sense. He was one of the most prominent Republican politicians in the country and the most popular politician in one of the most closely contested states. Jefferson, as his biographer Dumas Malone put it, "would have been comfortable with McKean."[6]

National Republican leaders recruited Alexander Dallas to sound out McKean about his willingness to serve as vice president, but Dallas, the governor's principal political adviser, averred that he did not believe "there exists another man in Pennsylvania, to whom, at this period the real interests of the state can be confided." McKean anticipated what future historians—and vice presidents—would conclude: the vice presidency had very limited power. He asked rhetorically, "What would be the probable result of the acceptance of my proposed post?" Answering his own question, McKean wrote somewhat self-servingly, "Little, very little benefit to the people of America, but at least a doubtful situation to my fellow citizens in Pennsylvania."[7] McKean told Dallas that he wasn't interested in seeking national office. The Republicans ultimately turned to George Clinton of New York as the most acceptable compromise candidate.

—~+~—

BY EARLY 1804, GOVERNOR MCKEAN WAS AT THE PINNACLE OF HIS political power and popularity. He had also grown increasingly intolerant of partisan politics and more than a little arrogant, frequently complaining to friends that someone with his experience, knowledge, and judgment should not be so consistently attacked in the press by the likes of the mercurial *Aurora* editor, Duane, on the one hand, and by Federalist smear mongers on the other. For instance, a young satirist named Benjamin Silliman, writing in the *Federalist Gazette*, wrote an apocryphal story about a Philadelphia tavern owned jointly by a Republican and a Federalist who could not agree

on the sign for the establishment. The Republican suggested hanging a portrait of Thomas McKean, who was the "patron saint" of all tavern goers.
The Federalist, according to Silliman, "consented, but gave the printer private orders to represent the Republican magistrate in the attitude in which
he generally appears at four o'clock p.m. The governor accordingly stands
forth, or rather staggers forth, on the sign, a solemn memento to the lovers
of brandy and Democracy."[8]

This kind of personal attack, directed at his character, was not a phenomenon limited to McKean: the president continuously absorbed his share
of slanderous barbs as well. Nevertheless, in the eyes of McKean the press
had become a national travesty, and he decided to confer with President
Jefferson to determine whether there was anything to be done. He wrote to
the president complaining about "infamous and seditious libels, published
almost daily in our newspapers." As the governor saw it, "This vice has
become a national one and calls aloud for redress." McKean had some ideas
about how to deal with the press's recklessness, but he told Jefferson that he
had "declined until now to obtain your advice and consent."[9]

Jefferson read McKean's letter with interest. He sensed a political
opening. The president's carefully worded reply revealed sympathy for
McKean's views. Once among the most vociferous opponents of the Alien
and Sedition Acts, Jefferson now agreed with McKean and complained
that the Federalists assaulted free speech by "pushing its licentiousness
and its lying to such a degree as to deprive it of all credit." Jefferson suggested that he had "long thought that a few prosecutions of the most
prominent offenders would have a wholesome effect in restoring the
integrity of the process." Ever the wily politician, Jefferson didn't want
to quash free speech—only to improve it and in the process presumably
curtail the attacks on his character. In his letter to McKean, Jefferson
noted that he didn't favor "a general prosecution, for that would look
like a persecution; but a selected one." And Jefferson enclosed with his
letter to McKean a newspaper article, likely an essay by Joseph Dennie,
the publisher of *Port Folio*, that he felt epitomized the kind of writing to
which they both objected. Jefferson was only too happy to encourage that
McKean, a like-minded elected official, test the limits of free speech.[10]

A few months later McKean arranged for a suit charging seditious libel to be brought against Dennie, based on a scathing attack the editor had penned under the pseudonym Oliver Oldschool, Esq., on the fragility and imperfections of Jeffersonian democracy. In the article, Dennie described "the institution of a scheme of policy so radically contemptible and vicious that it is a memorable example of what the villainy of some men can devise, the folly of others receive, and both establish in spite of reason, reflection, and sensation."[11]

Although Dennie was acquitted of libel charges, his trial had a temporary chilling effect on the exercise of free speech. Not surprisingly, this was especially true in the case of Dennie himself, who never again publicly criticized Jefferson and instead leveled his attacks on the "democracy" found in France under Robespierre and Napoleon.

⊷⊷

IN THE FALL OF 1804, CONGRESS PASSED THE MOBILE ACT DECLARING that the panhandle in western Florida, then a territory of Spain, had actually been part of the Louisiana Purchase. The act directed the president to extend federal jurisdiction over the area "whenever he shall deem it expedient." The legislation both surprised and infuriated McKean's son-in-law, Spanish ambassador Marquis de Yrujo, who argued that because Spain had never sold the territory to the French, the French had no legal authority to sell it to the Americans. A fierce defender of his country, Yrujo had tried to reconcile his government to Jefferson's Louisiana Purchase and had even tried to smooth over differences with the Americans concerning the fate of New Orleans. Now, however, he believed that the United States government had intentionally deceived him and was violating the sovereignty of Spain. Yrujo stormed into Secretary of State James Madison's office in Washington, DC.

The secretary had married Dolley Payne Todd, Sally McKean's best friend, and he and Yrujo had established a cordial relationship. But on this day the ambassador was visibly angry. He berated Madison for several minutes and demanded that the legislation be vetoed. Madison, who stood only five feet four inches and weighed no more than a hundred twenty pounds, was not easily intimidated. The secretary politely listened to the ambassador's rant for several minutes. Then, he showed him the door.

Yrujo would not be dissuaded. He decided to lobby the president directly and managed to arrange for an invitation to visit Jefferson at his home in Virginia, at Monticello. However, before he left Washington, Yrujo made a costly blunder. Having failed to persuade Madison and uncertain that he would have greater success with the president, Yrujo decided to take his case to the newspapers. This was not the first time that Yrujo had stealthily attempted to undermine the Jefferson administration through the press. Indeed, Madison suspected Yrujo's hand in any number of stories that had been critical of the administration's foreign policy.

In early October, Yrujo approached Major William Jackson, the editor of the *Philadelphia Gazette*, with an essay he had written about the Mobile Act. The ambassador and the editor had a private conversation, and Jackson later claimed that Yrujo had attempted to bribe him in exchange for anonymously publishing an editorial based on the essay criticizing the administration's policy toward Spain. It is more likely, however, that Jackson, an ardent Federalist, simply wanted to embarrass Governor McKean and, in the process, teach the arrogant Spaniard a lesson.

On October 13, Yrujo traveled to Monticello where President Jefferson greeted him warmly. The ambassador was enjoying his visit when unbeknownst to him the *Columbian Centinel* of Boston published his essay, with Jackson's affidavit stating, "The following letter communicated to the Secretary of State is published at the request of the Marquis for Casa de Yrujo." Major Jackson had quietly provided the ambassador's essay to the editors at a number of newspapers, including the *Columbian Centinel*. Supported by his own affidavit, he accused the Spaniard of treachery and attempting to undermine the government of the United States. Jefferson learned of Yrujo's letter from an aide, but said nothing to the ambassador, who had no access to the news at Monticello.

A few days later, Jefferson hosted a garden party for his Keswick County neighbors. As the president and the Spanish ambassador strolled the lawn together, the other guests sipped wine, and some may have gossiped about the Marquis's chicanery. Yrujo, ignorant of the growing furor in the press, may have flattered the president about his daughter, Martha Randolph, whom he often referred to as "fitted to grace any court in Europe."[12] He undoubtedly appealed to the president that he should veto the Mobile Act legislation and maintain the close relations that Spain and the United States had enjoyed. President Jefferson would have listened respectfully, never letting on that he knew of Yrujo's duplicity.

The following morning Jefferson was called back suddenly to Washington on business. The president insisted that Yrujo remain as his guest at Monticello and instructed his house staff to take good care of him. Only after returning to Washington several days later did Yrujo learn that his letter had been published and that he was the object of widespread vilification. Mortified, Yrujo wrote the president a heartfelt apology. But it was too late. Secretary of State Madison had been authorized to demand the Spanish government recall its ambassador. Sally was devastated, and Dolley Madison told her sister that she still felt a "tenderness" for her friend regardless of the circumstances.

Once again, Yrujo appealed directly to the president, suggesting that perhaps the humiliation of a formal recall might be avoided if he left of his own volition. He promised to leave early in the new year—as soon as the winter storms passed and calm seas prevailed. Jefferson, who was genuinely fond of both the marquis and Sally, graciously assented to the reprieve.[13]

Months passed, Yrujo not only remained in America but continued to work on behalf of his government and made plans to return to Washington from Philadelphia, where he and Sally had moved to avoid controversy. When Secretary of State Madison learned that Yrujo had resumed his official duties, he was outraged. Yrujo's actions undermined the authority of the president, and, notwithstanding his wife's friendship, Secretary Madison wrote the ambassador a sharp rebuke, forbidding him to set foot in the nation's capital. The marquis ignored Madison. Not only did he and his wife return to Washington but he sent the secretary of state a curt letter informing him that only his government could order him to leave the country. He sent copies of the letter to other members of the diplomatic corps as well as to the press. For the moment, at least, Yrujo successfully defied the United States government.[14]

Governor McKean must have been embarrassed by the arrogance and impudence of his son-in-law and worried that his daughter Sally would be forced to leave the country. Earlier in the year he had experienced the loss of his daughter Ann, who had died at the age of twenty-one. Ann had always held a special place in McKean's heart because his first wife, Mary, had died not long after giving birth to her. And only two years before Ann's death, the governor's oldest son, Robert, named after McKean's beloved older brother, had died as well. McKean rarely discussed his family, but, in an emotional letter to Ann's husband, Andrew, he rued the fact that "more than twenty-five years have passed, since I was without father or mother, sister or brother, Grandfather or Grandmother, Uncle or Aunt, and several of these connections departed this life from forty to sixty years ago."[15] Now, he feared, he might lose yet another loved family member.

# 24

## The Last Signer

THOMAS JEFFERSON WON REELECTION EASILY IN 1804, TROUNCING HIS opponent Charles Pinckney, a former Revolutionary War general and a signer of the Declaration of Independence, with more than 70 percent of the popular vote. Pinckney won 14 electoral votes out of 176, winning only Connecticut and Delaware and losing his own state of South Carolina.[1]

Although the Republican Party was successful on a national level, in Pennsylvania, the party was racked by internecine warfare. Duane and Leib had grown impatient with McKean. They wanted to revolutionize Pennsylvania state government, starting with a new constitution. Pennsylvania, at the urging of McKean and others, had adopted a bicameral legislature in 1790, but the radicals wanted to revert to a unicameral assembly. They also continued to press for the popular election of judges and for universal suffrage. More than anything, they rejected the common law as an anachronism of the English monarchical rule; they wanted the people to rule without constraints.

Duane and Leib turned their wrath on McKean. Duane referred to McKean and his supporters as "sickly royalists" and "black and barbarous traitors of the American Revolution."[2] This was not the same man, they argued, who two decades earlier had circumvented the state assembly to craft a new state constitution in support of American independence. He had changed. He had become what he had once railed against: an autocrat unwilling to put his trust in the people. After a contentious party caucus in Lancaster, the Republicans, led by Michael Leib, withdrew their support for McKean in the upcoming election and threw it behind Simon Snyder, an arch Jacobin and a farmer from the western part of the state.[3]

Governor McKean, undeterred by Duane, Leib, and the Republicans, decided to run for a third and final term. Early in 1805, a group of Democratic Constitutional Republicans, known as "Quids," held a dinner at the White Horse Tavern in Philadelphia to celebrate the second inauguration of Thomas Jefferson. Senator George Logan was there and was greatly encouraged by the support for a new party that identified itself as pro-Jefferson in national politics and anti-Duane in Pennsylvania. The Quids also counted among their members many Federalists whom Logan and McKean had battled in the past. If it meant the Quids could now mount a serious challenge to Duane's lock on the Republican Party, Logan and McKean warmly accepted the support of their former adversaries.[4] They would wage an unconventional campaign and fight for reelection at the polls every bit as fiercely as they had in McKean's first gubernatorial campaign in 1799.

President Jefferson abhorred the split in the Republican Party in Pennsylvania and distanced himself from both the Quids and McKean. Jefferson's close friend Thomas Leiper, a Philadelphia businessman, who wrote the president, "Our governor is a wicked man and all his officers are obliged to fall in with him or be turned out of office," was keeping him abreast of political developments in Pennsylvania.[5] In December, Duane wrote Jefferson and hyperbolically claimed that the state's militia would not support McKean in the event of a domestic or international crisis.[6] The president privately groused about McKean's abandonment of the Republican Party, but he was also critical of Duane, faulting his "passions" as being "stronger than his prudence" and criticizing him for being "intolerant."[7] In truth, the constantly shifting sands of politics in Pennsylvania reflected nothing more than the youth and volatility of the Republic.

McKean's closest political ally, the operative Alexander Dallas, had defended Duane after his arrest in the St. Mary's Church incident seven years earlier. Now, Dallas worked to discredit the editor and to parry his attacks on the governor. Allowing McKean to stay above the fray, Dallas orchestrated a campaign based on scare tactics. He accused Snyder and his supporters of being malcontents who wanted to deprive the people of an independent judiciary and replace it with mob justice. He claimed they would repeal the right to free and fair elections. Pamphleteers likened the Republicans to anarchists. Dallas caricatured Snyder as an inexperienced, lower-class simpleton even though Snyder had served in the Pennsylvania House of Representatives for a decade.

Once again, McKean did not actively campaign, but during the election season a group of legislators led by Snyder met with him about reforming the courts. They chastised the governor and accused him of having failed to honor his promises. One legislator threatened to do "his utmost at elections to prevent . . . all lawyers and rich men, from being elected." McKean interpreted the statement as a criticism of his administration and him personally. He asked angrily, "Why are not lawyers and rich men to be trusted in the administration of legal affairs as any others?" The exchange grew heated, and the next day the *Philadelphia Aurora* reported that the governor had lost his temper, yelled expletives at the delegation, and called them a "set of clodhoppers who had no more understanding than geese." The incident only deepened the political divide and the appearance of class warfare in Pennsylvania.[8]

Over the summer Dallas worked once again to stitch together a winning coalition, as he had done in McKean's previous two campaigns for governor. One of the most effective campaign tools was a long address that he wrote in defense of McKean that was distributed throughout the state, including five thousand copies printed in German. In the end, McKean pulled off the narrowest victory of his political career, winning an unprecedented third term. Both McKean and Snyder each won seventeen counties, but McKean carried his adopted hometown of Philadelphia, which gave him a razor-thin majority of five thousand votes out of more than eighty thousand. As Dallas had envisioned, McKean won by fashioning a broad coalition of conservative Republicans and moderate Federalists—men such as Horace Binney, who observed, "We did our duty . . . not from love for McKean, but from scorn of his former politics."[9]

President Jefferson, who years earlier warned McKean about the deepening rift among Republicans in Pennsylvania, was unhappy and angry that in gaining victory on the Quid ticket McKean had ruptured the already divided state Republican Party. He wrote George Logan of the "infinite pain" with which he viewed the political dysfunction in Pennsylvania. Jefferson had shown on many occasions that he could be extremely partisan and highly political when it suited his purposes, but now he adopted a somewhat aloof attitude, commenting to Logan on "the duty of an upright administration . . . to pursue its course steadily, to know nothing of these family dissensions, and to cherish good principle of both parties."[10] At this point in his career, McKean, age seventy-two, was not particularly interested in healing political divisions, and his once close friendship with Thomas Jefferson was now fraying.

President Jefferson was also concerned about McKean's son-in-law, the Marquis de Yrujo, who was still in the country and spreading rumors in Washington about former Vice President Aaron Burr. Yrujo claimed that Burr, aided by General James Wilkinson, Jefferson's appointed governor for the Louisiana Territory, was encouraging western state leaders to secede by promising them Mexican treasure and land. Burr, in fact, had approached the ambassador to obtain a visa to travel to Mexico, which Yrujo had denied him. And the marquis was aware that Wilkinson was a sometime spy for the Spanish government who played both sides when it suited him.[11]

The Marquis de Yrujo published anonymous articles under the heading "Queries" in the *United States Gazette,* later reprinted in several major newspapers across the country, alleging that Burr planned to convene the leaders of the Mississippi and Ohio River states, urge them to secede from the Union, and then join forces with Britain to invade Mexico. Yrujo thought Burr foolhardy, and he informed the Spanish foreign minister, "The supposed expedition against Mexico is ridiculous and chimerical in the present state of things."[12] The marquis instructed Spanish authorities to arrest Burr if he entered Mexico.

Months later, the egomaniacal Burr had a new plan. Working through an intermediary, Burr relayed to Yrujo that he had given up on the idea of invading Mexico and instead intended to overthrow the US government by capturing Washington, DC. According to the intermediary, Burr planned to enlist a band of heavily armed men and to travel to the nation's capital, where he would occupy the banks, arsenal, and Navy Yard. Then, he would take President Jefferson as his prisoner and seize control of the US government. Once in command, the intermediary explained to Yrujo, Burr would liberate New Orleans and ensure Spain's interests in a New World empire.[13]

At the time, Spain was negotiating with the Jefferson administration over the sale of Florida. Yrujo was convinced that Jefferson wanted to annex not only Florida but all of Spain's holdings in America. He wrote his superiors in Madrid advising them to advance Burr $1 million to carry out his plan. But the Spanish foreign minister was highly dubious of such a wild-eyed, fantastic scheme and agreed to allow Yrujo to advance Burr only a few thousand dollars. Yrujo's actions on behalf of Spain, even if viewed in the context of loyalty to his king, were supportive of Burr's plan for a coup d'état. Had he known of Yrujo's support for such a nefarious plot, McKean would assuredly have been furious.

⊷ ⊷

IN HIS THIRD-TERM INAUGURAL ADDRESS DELIVERED TO THE STATE assembly on December 17, 1805, Governor McKean returned to one of his shibboleths, continuing his assault on what he viewed as an inflammatory press. He asked the legislature to "curb the political incendiaries," singling out the editors and publishers whom he contended were attempting "to acquire for sinister purposes the mastery of the passions and prejudices of the people." The former chief justice also asked for a revision of the trial system and recommended a new system for selecting juries, which would comprise more qualified jurors and which in his view meant more highly educated and economically advantaged citizens.[14]

McKean started what he knew was his last term as governor on an optimistic and hopeful note. He wrote John Dickinson that he had "two cardinal rules to guide him: one, not to govern too much; and the other never to use compulsion when reason and persuasion will effect the purpose. I pray for moderation and conciliation of parties."[15]

But the radical Republicans in Pennsylvania were in no mood to compromise with the governor. They recognized that McKean was a lame duck, constitutionally prohibited from seeking office again, having served three consecutive terms. Still smarting from the defeat of Snyder, Dr. Leib wrote a scathing rebuttal to McKean's address that was published in a number of Republican newspapers. And the attacks in the press continued. By mid-January 1806, rumors were circulating that Leib was contemplating drawing up impeachment charges against the governor.

Political partisans increasingly used impeachment as a tool to punish or silence their adversaries. The most egregious example occurred two years earlier in 1804, when the US House of Representatives, dominated by Republicans, impeached Associate Justice Samuel Chase, a Federalist. Some congressmen, unhappy with the decision in *Marbury v. Madison*, wanted to send a message to the court. As Congressman William Branch Giles put it, if "the judges of the Supreme Court should dare . . . to declare an act of Congress unconstitutional," as they had done, then "it was the undoubted right of the House of Representatives to impeach them and of the Senate to remove them."[16] Though he had killed Alexander Hamilton in a duel only months earlier, Vice President Aaron Burr presided over the trial, and the Senate ultimately acquitted Chase by a wide margin.

McKean had not violated any laws, but the political divisions in Pennsylvania were so deep that the likelihood of his impeachment increasingly gained currency in newspapers around the state. McKean tried to ignore his critics and get on with the business of running the state, but the ongoing controversy dogged him. He complained that "God had permitted . . . [to] disturb the sociability and tranquility of their species, sometimes from a prospect of advantage to themselves, but generally from envy and propensity to mischief; their happiness seems to consist in making others miserable; demons in human shapes."[17] Undoubtedly referring to Duane and Leib, he told Dickinson on another occasion that he feared Duane "frustrated and beaten, might now recommend an appeal to arms." But McKean, who never shied away from a fight, was unbowed, declaring, "such wretches must be controlled by fear and force."[18]

—+——+—

IN EARLY 1806 EDWARD SHIPPEN RESIGNED AS CHIEF JUSTICE OF PENN-
sylvania. Now, early in his third term, McKean had the opportunity to
appoint a new chief justice. Many coveted the position, including, somewhat surprisingly, former vice president Aaron Burr. Burr visited Philadelphia to discuss his ambition with his close friend Charles Biddle, a former
Pennsylvania state senator. Biddle, aware that Burr was planning a trip
to the West but unaware that the former vice president had also secretly
hatched a plan to subvert the national government, would later speculate,
"Burr would have given up his expedition if he could have procured an
appointment that would have made him independent."[19] Biddle knew that
Governor McKean would never appoint Burr, a disgraced politician, to such
a prestigious position, but he agreed to float Burr's name with McKean's son
Joseph, then the state attorney general. Joseph McKean met with Biddle but
discouraged the idea of Burr as a potential chief justice. Joseph, of course,
could not have predicted that a year later Burr would be placed under arrest
for treason. Rather, Joseph, unbeknownst to Biddle, desperately wanted the
position himself.

Not surprisingly, the governor's family and close friends fervently supported the appointment of Joseph. McKean equivocated, perhaps because
he had been so harshly criticized for previous acts of nepotism. The *Aurora*,
which had broken with McKean by this time, sarcastically referred to
McKean and his children as "the royal family" and called the governor's
son Joseph "the heir apparent." The governor also had close friends and
associates who either had their own candidates or wanted the job themselves. Finally, McKean may have hesitated to appoint Joseph because he
was aware of the increasing calls for his own impeachment.[20]

In the end, McKean settled on William Tilghman, brother of Tench
Tilghman, who two decades earlier had brought McKean word of Cornwallis's defeat at Yorktown. Tilghman was originally from Maryland, where
he had served briefly in the state assembly and state senate; in early 1801,
as part of the midnight appointments, President John Adams nominated

him to be a federal judge on the Third Circuit. Republicans vociferously objected to McKean's choice of Tilghman, but McKean knew that Federalists had been at least partly responsible for his reelection. No longer feeling any allegiance to the Republican Party, in the summer of 1806 he moved the appointment.

After Tilghman's appointment, Republicans in Pennsylvania turned against McKean with a vengeance. In anticipation of the fall elections for assembly, an anonymously published pamphlet entitled *Quid Mirror* gained a growing audience with its acerbic and biting stories about McKean and his cronies, describing the governor as "one of fortune's frolics," a man who handed out political offices to "every whelp and cub of his own," and deriding Alexander Dallas as a "sycophant, a hypocrite, a coward and a traitor."[21]

The negative campaign garnered results for the Republicans, who gained seats in both houses in the off-year elections that fall. Frustrated, McKean wrote Senator George Logan, "It appears to me that the faction would set the church on fire if only to roast eggs on it." McKean believed, probably accurately, that Leib was behind the attacks: "It appears to me, that one wicked man can effect more political, if not personal mischief, that a hundred well disposed persons in the good."[22]

Notwithstanding the ad hominem and often deeply personal attacks on him in the newspapers, Governor McKean had a remarkably successful first year in his third term. Reverting to his earlier years during the fight for independence, he used his powers of persuasion and built ad hoc coalitions with members of the state assembly to pass numerous laws: to improve the efficiency of the judiciary, to broaden access to education, and to expand Pennsylvania's infrastructure of roads and bridges. The *Lancaster Journal* hailed it as "the best legislature in 5 or 6 years in Pennsylvania." But the achievements were not enough for the radicals, who continued to press for a more progressive agenda and who bristled when McKean vetoed what they viewed as far-reaching judicial reform passed by the legislature.[23]

On January 30, 1807, Leib introduced a motion to create a committee of inquiry for the purpose of determining whether to bring impeachment charges against the governor. The vote was a tie, and the motion failed. But Leib would not relent, and two months later his committee presented a report to the legislature containing six charges against the governor. They ranged from the seemingly trivial accusation that McKean had allowed his name to be stamped on official papers instead of personally signing the documents to the more serious charges of unlawfully removing officials from office and tampering with the results in a local election. Leib's committee recommended that the impeachment resolution come up for debate before the entire legislature, and over the next several months, members debated it.

Angered by what he viewed as unfair and unseemly attacks on his father, the governor's son Thomas McKean Jr. entered the fray in July by challenging William Leib to a duel. Leib accepted the challenge but then had second thoughts and instead secured the indictment of young Thomas on the grounds that sending an invitation to duel was illegal under Pennsylvania law. McKean Jr. responded by having Leib indicted for receiving the challenge, which was also illegal. The case was later dropped by mutual consent, but McKean Jr. had scored something of a public relations victory because Leib appeared somewhat cowardly by opting to file a lawsuit.[24]

Meanwhile Governor McKean submitted an official reply to the articles of impeachment. He claimed that his defense rested "neither upon an arrogant claim of infallibility" nor "a humiliating appeal for compassion." McKean returned, as he always had in the past, to the foundation of law. He argued that for an act to be impeachable under the law, it must have been "willfully committed, either corrupt in its motive, or unequivocally unlawful in its perpetration." He vehemently denied any wrongful behavior and meticulously answered the charges one by one. His most impassioned defense focused on the charge of nepotism: "By the law of God and nature," McKean declared, "man is taught to love and protect his offspring, his family and his friends," but by the law of society he is "forbidden to indulge the predilection, arising from the former, at the expense of the public welfare." The governor asserted that the public had benefited from the quality of his appointments, including from his own family.[25]

Even those who disliked McKean recognized that the charges against him were trumped-up political attacks. The governor's only crime was that he had parted ways with Duane, Leib, and the radicals. The reaction in many newspapers was typified by the *Huntington Gazette*, which asked its readers: "Are we to see our representatives employed at our expense prosecuting the Executive, and attacking one after another all the branches of our government, for what we know about nothing?"[26]

In early 1808, the legislature was in session, but because of poor weather, several Republicans from the western part of the state had stayed home. The Quids, seeking to take advantage of a temporary majority, called for a final vote on the articles of impeachment. The vote to impeach failed by a vote of 44 to 41. By cobbling together liberal Federalists, Philadelphia Republicans, and Quids—just as he had done in the last campaign—McKean triumphed.

But the trial had weakened him politically and physically. Just weeks before the final vote, he became seriously ill. He suffered from a severe case of gout in his hands and in his right leg and foot. His condition worsened, and after losing the use of his hands, he briefly appeared close to death. Over the course of several weeks, Sarah nursed him back to health, and once recovered, he served out the last months of his tenure as governor without controversy. The newspapers attacks ceased for the most part.[27]

On his last day in office, the *Aurora*, which had played such a prominent role in launching McKean's successful political career, and then played an equally noteworthy role in attempting to undermine him, proclaimed somewhat feebly, "The unhappy reign of Thomas McKean is over."[28] The truth was McKean left office in much the same way he had entered it: having successfully navigated the political shoals of Pennsylvania fractious politics in three elections, he could not really be categorized as either a Federalist or a Republican. He disdained the radicals, who had gained control of Pennsylvania's Republican Party. He still retained the same independent streak—some would say "chip on the shoulder"—that made him skeptical of Federalists, Republicans, and any other group or individual whom he felt did not have the best interests of the nation in mind.

He was undeterred by his enemies and greatly admired by his friends; McKean's steadfastness had not changed over the years. However, during his tenure as governor, Pennsylvania had become a very different place from what it had been only a decade earlier. The state had nearly tripled in population and it boasted one of strongest economies in the country. Philadelphia continued to be one of the leading cities in America, having opened the first art academy and museum of fine arts in the country and the first academy of natural sciences. It was emblematic of a larger national phenomenon.

The United States was increasingly a confident nation. Although still preoccupied by relations with France and Britain, the country had an abundance of land and natural resources that had given its citizens a sense that the future would be bright. The economic middle class envisioned by Benjamin Franklin had emerged, and trade between the states brought them closer together. However, there was still no national currency and the health of individual state economies varied widely.

Political parties had been institutionalized. Although President Washington had warned against their development, they actually had strengthened American democracy. They encouraged participation in elections and helped create a sense of national identity. Moreover, after six presidential elections, the peaceful transfer of power from one individual to another and from one party to the other now seemed like the natural course of events.

Likewise, that America was now a nation of laws seemed undisputed. Chief Justice John Marshall's decision in *Marbury v. Madison* had greatly strengthened the Supreme Court, and the government now had three more or less coequal branches, which created the kind of stability envisioned by Madison and Hamilton in the Constitution.

The greatest unresolved counterweight to national harmony, dividing north and south—not just in terms of economics but in moral and political terms as well—was slavery, which would exact its terrible price on the country as a whole in the war that would break out a half century later.

But for the moment the United States was in many ways the shining example of benevolent government that Francis Alison had once idealized for young Thomas McKean.

# Epilogue

AFTER LEAVING OFFICE, McKEAN SPENT HIS RETIREMENT YEARS between his house in Philadelphia and his estate in the country, Penllyn. He and Sarah continued to enjoy their children, now grown: three from his first marriage and four of their own as well as over thirty grandchildren. Four of his children had died, and he missed his beloved daughter Sally, who finally left the United States in 1808 with the Marquis de Yrujo. Not long after the acquittal of Aaron Burr in his trial for treason, the Spanish government appointed Yrujo as ambassador to Rio de Janeiro. The marquis was later appointed ambassador to France and served on three separate occasions as Spain's foreign secretary. Yrujo and Sally provided Thomas with three grandsons, one who became a prime minister of Spain.

In his later years, McKean seemed largely content to withdraw from public life. Of his fellow signers of the Declaration of Independence, only a few remained alive, including former presidents John Adams and Thomas Jefferson. The rest had died, many under hard circumstances, having paid a high price for the ideal to which they had affixed their names. Robert Morris, who had been so critical to financing the Revolutionary War, saw his financial empire collapse and wound up serving time in debtors' prison. Richard Spaight of North Carolina died from gunshots wounds received in a duel. McKean's colleague, former Supreme Court justice James Wilson, who served with him on the Pennsylvania Supreme Court and cochaired the state constitutional convention, died destitute and on the run from the law for his debts. Gouverneur Morris, who signed the Declaration from New York and later served as a United States senator and as ambassador to France, was still alive but died in 1816. McKean's Delaware colleague Caesar Rodney had passed away more than thirty years earlier in 1784 from the cancer that had afflicted him for years.

John Dickinson, with whom McKean shared the distinction of having served as chief executive of both Delaware and Pennsylvania, died in 1808, just months before McKean retired from public life. President Jefferson responded to news of Dickinson's death with a heartfelt tribute: "A more estimable man, or truer patriot, could not have left us. Among the first of the advocates for the rights of his country when assailed by Great Britain, he continued to the last the orthodox advocate of the true principles of our new government and his name will be consecrated in history as one of the great worthies of the revolution."[1] Notwithstanding their disagreement over independence, McKean and Dickinson had remained close friends for fifty years. It was undoubtedly the most enduring friendship in McKean's life.

—◆—

ON JUNE 2, 1812, JOHN ADAMS SENT MCKEAN A LETTER FROM HIS HOME in Braintree, Massachusetts—the first correspondence or contact between the two men in nearly fifteen years. Adams wrote, "I am determined no longer to neglect to write to you, lest I should glide away, where there is no pen and ink." The former president recalled, "Nearly thirty-eight years ago our friendship commenced. It has never been interrupted, to my knowledge but by one event. Among all gentlemen with whom I have acted and lived in the world, I know not any two who have more uniformly agreed on sentiment upon political sentiments, forms of government, and national policy, than you and I have done except upon one great subject—a most important and momentous one to be sure. That subject was the French revolution." Nearly twenty-five years later, Adams sought to bury the hatchet: "There can be no question of honors or profits, or rank or fame, between you and me at present. Personal friendship and private feelings are all that remain." Adams was also concerned that there was no definitive history of the American Revolution, and he encouraged McKean to write down his recollections.[2]

McKean was delighted to hear from his old friend and one-time political ally. The same day he received Adam's letter, he wrote back. He began by observing, "I remain the only surviving member of the first American Congress, held in the city of New York in October, 1765; and but three more, of whom you are one remain alive of the second congress, held in this city in September, 1774." And in keeping with the fiction that he and Adams had been always politically aligned, McKean concluded, "I embraced the political sentiments of none with more satisfaction than ours, nor do I recollect a single question in which we differed."[3]

In 1814, McKean turned eighty years old. Although he confessed to Adams that he was suffering the "symptoms of old age," he continued to closely follow national events.[4] America had grown from the thirteen colonies when he had signed the Declaration of Independence to eighteen states. The country had greatly expanded and so had trade with other countries, especially in the West Indies. When Britain interfered with American commerce on the high seas, Madison, president since 1809, had declared war. At the time the British had been preoccupied with Napoleon Bonaparte's conquests in Europe, but after the abdication of Napoleon in April 1814 Parliament focused increasingly on the war against the United States. By August 1814, Britain threatened the United States from Canada to New Orleans, and on August 24, British troops burned to the ground the White House and Capitol in Washington. Two days later, McKean was elected to chair a large meeting at the State House yard—the same place where four decades earlier he had joined radicals to dissolve the state constitution. Now, he vowed to defend the federal constitution and to consider measures in case Philadelphia was attacked next. He communicated to John Adams his view that "every preparation should be made for the continuance of the war. . . . When the British arms have been successful, I have never found their rulers or ministers otherwise than haughty, rude imperious, nay insolent."[5]

It was McKean's last public office and, in the end, the British did not move against Philadelphia. After the War of 1812 ended in 1814 with Andrew Jackson's victory in the Battle of New Orleans and the subsequent Treaty of Ghent, McKean retreated altogether from public view. His health continued to deteriorate: both his eyesight and his hearing were failing. Nevertheless, he decided that while he still had his mental faculties, he would do what President Adams had encouraged him to do—write down his recollections of the American Revolution. He chose to provide what he called "biographical sketches" and began, without a scintilla of humility, by noting that "the lives of most men pass away unobserved, unheralded and unknown, the whole that is reported of them is the day their birth and the day of their death. Those who emerge out of the general obscurity and are distinguished for their talents and virtues are characters which are suitable for the delineation of the historic pencil, as their example may be useful to others." Having completely abandoned all pretense of modesty, McKean described himself as

> a man that has waded through many difficulties, lived in turbulent and tempestuous times that tried men's souls, and constantly retained his integrity and fortitude, and the confidence of his fellow citizens for fifty years in public stations of government, tho often assailed by the ambition, envy and malice of powerful individuals, and the flattery, or hatred of different factions and parties, as his conduct chanced to correspond with their views; a man who placed his dependence upon God, and who by divine grace was crowned with victory over every opposition, and with the smiles of approving Heaven.[6]

━┼┝━

THREE MONTHS AFTER HIS INAUGURATION IN 1817 AS THE FIFTH PRESIDENT of the United States, James Monroe arrived at Gray's Ferry in Philadelphia aboard a naval barge. Plainly dressed in short, old-fashioned pantaloons and white-topped boots, Monroe was greeted at the dock by his old friend, former senator George Logan. After exchanging pleasantries, Logan informed the president that Thomas McKean was gravely ill. The president asked to be taken immediately to McKean's home.[7]

Monroe and McKean had never been especially close, but they had known each other for nearly four decades and had shared a strong commitment to independence. McKean had been there to toast Monroe when he had returned from France in 1797 deeply embittered and angered by his experience as the American ambassador. And in one of the most stirring episodes of the young republic, they had conspired to ensure the installation of Thomas Jefferson as the third president of the United States. Monroe visited his old colleague, whom he referred to as "Judge McKean," and the two men reminisced about the long struggle for independence they had witnessed and helped shape.

Two days after the president's visit, McKean died peacefully in his sleep. No grand parades of the kind he had so much enjoyed during his lifetime would celebrate him. His will stipulated that his burial be "decent but not expensive," and he was laid to rest in the cemetery of the First Presbyterian Church on Market Street with only his immediate family in attendance. He willed land and money to his wife and each of his children, but certain family members received more than others. He left the country house that he and Sarah had purchased together entirely to her. He bequeathed "eight tracts of land" to Sally. To his oldest son, Joseph, he willed the house in Philadelphia as well as his gold-tipped cane. And to Thomas Jr., he bequeathed the working farm and "the silver gilded small sword" that he had carried at Perth Amboy.[8]

On June 25, 1817, the *Aurora*, still published by McKean's nemesis William Duane, printed an obituary of Thomas McKean. Largely a tribute, it nonetheless contained commentary by Duane that McKean "had been better adapted to the bench, than to the executive chair." The editor praised McKean's "severity" combined with "probity" on the bench and declared that he "gave the laws dignity by enforcing them." Duane excused McKean's "small sins of passion and pride" during the time he was governor. He called McKean "one of the earliest and most trusted friends of American independence" and praised him as "one who never wavered."[9]

IN ONE OF HIS LAST LETTERS TO JOHN ADAMS, MCKEAN WROTE: "WE have been spectators within the last fifty years of our lives as perhaps were never seen before in the same space of time. Tempests, convulsions, wars and revolutions have succeeded each other with such rapidity & violence as to cause the utmost astonishment of the human mind."[10] It was true that McKean was witness to an extraordinary number of events during the creation of the Republic. More than a passive observer, he was a participant who often joined with those leading the way, notably when it was not popular or fashionable. He joined the constitutionalists when the balance of power was not clear and before the new constitution was completed; joined the Federalists when skepticism of central government was most acute; and not only joined but actually led the Republicans when city, state, and national politics were still firmly controlled by the Federalists.

The truth was he allied with anyone who shared the core principles that he abided by throughout his public life. As one of the few Founding Fathers who served in the legislative, judicial, and executive branches of government, he favored a balance of power between the branches. After independence, he quickly came to the conclusion that it was only the rule of law that stood between democracy and social anarchy. Though he hated British imperialism, he used British law as the foundation for law in Pennsylvania. During his decade as governor of Pennsylvania, he became much more political in his application of power, punishing political opponents and the press.

McKean remains somewhat enigmatic in terms of his personal life. His critics over the years claimed he drank too much—an aspersion that was often directed at Irish Americans during the era. His opponents criticized him for being vain and overbearing, but he won three statewide elections and showed leadership qualities in a number of public arenas. They accused him of appearing cold and calculating, but he was sentimental enough to value his family above all else, often closing his letters to his wife with a request "to kiss the children for me."[11]

McKean was in many ways a heroic, if often flawed, character from a quintessential American novel—someone who rose from a modest background, who through education and hard work achieved success, rising to the highest echelons of political leadership during the uncertain and often turbulent early years of the American Republic to help shape its institutions. He was a pragmatist who nonetheless worked for and believed in the idea of right and wrong and was most at sea when events put that conviction to the test. He confided to John Adams late in life that he enjoyed reading novels because, as he put it, they "universally make vice detested and punished, and virtue triumphant, which is not the case of history and real life."[12] The course of McKean's long, revolutionary life, however, would have left little doubt in his mind that his core conviction—that the side of right would endure and that as a man of means and good character he was on it—had prevailed.

# Acknowledgments

I T'S A CHALLENGE TO PUBLISH A BOOK ABOUT SOMEONE WHO VERY FEW people have ever heard of, so I am enormously grateful to Susan Weinberg and Clive Priddle of PublicAffairs for recognizing that a biography of Thomas McKean not only could tell something about a largely forgotten, but nevertheless important, figure of the Revolutionary era but also might shed new light on the times in which he lived.

I began writing this book while serving as a fellow at the Woodrow Wilson International Center. I owe a debt of gratitude to Jane Harman, Wilson's dynamic president, and Mike Van Dusen, Jane's former deputy, for bringing me on board and supporting my work. While at Wilson, I also had a wonderful research assistant, Avram Billig, who did some of the early research for the book.

I wrote this book over a period of six years: at night, on weekends, and during vacations, but I could not have completed it without the encouragement and insights from a number of people who read the manuscript at various stages. Larry Gurwin and John Zentay, friends for many years, edited several drafts. Douglas Frantz, who coauthored my first book, provided invaluable advice. Likewise, Cliff Sloan, coauthor of my third book, helped frame the narrative.

Four fellow historians read the manuscript: Walter Stahr, the author of two highly regarded biographies on John Jay and William Seward; Charles

Edel, the author of a biography of John Quincy Adams; John Alter, the acclaimed author of biographies on Franklin Roosevelt and Barack Obama; and Steve Randolph, one of the nation's finest diplomatic historians; all were helpful. I'm deeply grateful for their expertise and assistance.

Clive Priddle and Maria Goldverg of PublicAffairs expertly guided the book during the entire process of research and writing. A good editor knows the right questions to ask, and both Clive and Maria asked lots of questions. I also want to thank Sandra Beris, my project manager, and Christina Yeager, my copyeditor, for their superb work.

Finally, this book became something of a family endeavor. My cousin Jim Cooke did some of the initial research. My brother Robert read early drafts. My son Christian proved to be a fine editor, and his brother, Shaw, and sister, Kaye, worked on the bibliography. Finally, my wife, Kathleen, endured my bringing along Thomas McKean—at least a literary facsimile of the signer—on every family vacation for five years. Kathleen read the manuscript many, many times and always offered patient encouragement, helpful advice, and unwavering support. I'm a lucky man.

# Notes

**Introduction**

1. McCullough, *John Adams*, 395.
2. Rush quoted in Hopkinson, *Miscellaneous Essays*, 349–422.
3. Rowe, *Embattled Bench*, 194.

## PART I

### One

1. Buchanan, *Genealogy of the McKean Family*, 3, 4.

2. Schlesinger, *Birth of a Nation*, 8, 9.

3. Coleman, *Thomas McKean*, 17.

4. Ibid.

5. Schlesinger, *Birth of a Nation*, 203–205.

6. Coleman, *Thomas McKean*, 19; Munroe, *History of Delaware*, Chapter 1.

7. Ibid., 25.

8. Rowe, *Thomas McKean*, 45nn19–20.

9. Coleman, *Thomas McKean*, 49.

10. Rowe, *Thomas McKean*, 16–18.

11. Coleman, *Thomas McKean*, 32.

12. Burnaby, *Travels Through North America*, 178.

13. Ibid.

14. Baltzell, *Puritan Boston and Quaker Philadelphia*, 163.

15. Flower, *John Dickinson*, 26.

16. Lunt, *Tales of Delaware Bench and Bar*, 77, 78.

17. Rowe, *Thomas McKean*, 413n27.

18. JD to TM, 6/8/1762, Thomas McKean Papers, HSP.

19. Coleman, *Thomas McKean*, 36.

## Two

1. Rowe, *Thomas McKean*, 414.

2. Unger, *Lion of Liberty*, 30–32.

3. Ibid.

4. Morgan and Morgan, *Stamp Act Crisis*, 83.

5. Ibid., 40–45.

6. Stockdale and Holland, *Middle Temple Lawyers*, 89.

7. Morgan and Morgan, *Stamp Act Crisis*, 180.

8. Unger, *Lion of Liberty*, 45.

9. Burnett, *Continental Congress*, 28.

10. Rowe, *Thomas McKean*, 26.

11. Coleman, *Thomas McKean*, 52.

12. Schlesinger, *Birth of the Nation*, 40.

13. Coleman, *Thomas McKean*, 53.

14. Stockdale and Holland, *Middle Temple Lawyers*, 12.

15. Raphael, *First American Revolution*, 26.

16. FH to TM, 1772, letter held in private collection.

17. Unger, *Lion of Liberty*, 49–50.

18. Coleman, *Thomas McKean*, 72.

19. Ibid., 74, 75.

## Three

1. Coleman, *Thomas McKean*, 103, 104.

2. Schlesinger, *Birth of the Nation*, 139.

3. Coleman, *Thomas McKean*, 104, 110.

4. Hogeland, *Declaration*, 22.

5. Weigley, *Philadelphia*, 118.

6. Rowe, *Thomas McKean*, 56.

7. Ibid., 55.

8. Coleman, *Thomas McKean*, 105. McKean traveled from Delaware to Philadelphia in late August, then returned briefly to New Castle to be married in early September, before attending the opening of Congress on September 5 back in Philadelphia.

9. Hogeland, *Declaration*, 6.

10. Miller, *Origins of the American Revolution*, 379.

11. Beeman, *Our Lives, Our Fortunes*, 49.

12. Ellis, *Passionate Sage*, 40.

13. JA to AA, 7/1/1774, John Adams Papers, MHS.

14. Ibid.

15. Ibid.

16. Bowen, *John Adams*, 499.

17. Hogeland, *Declaration*, 70.

18. Randall, *Benedict Arnold*, 75.

19. Hogeland, *Declaration*, 74.

## Four

1. Hogeland, *Declaration*, 74.

2. *New York Journal*, 5/25/1775, quoted in Schlesinger, *Prelude to Independence*, 232, 233.

3. Rowe, "A Valuable Acquisition," 239.

4. Flower, *John Dickinson*, 131.

5. Sinclair and McArthur, *They Signed for Us*, 7.

6. Chernow, *Washington*, 409.

7. Hogeland, *Declaration*, see, generally, 57–62.

8. Coleman, *Thomas McKean*, 138.

9. Rowe, *Valuable Acquisition*, 240.

## Five

1. McCullough, *1776*, 117–119.

2. Hogeland, *Declaration*, 4, 5.

3. Ibid., see, generally, 35–38. Rowe, *Thomas McKean*, 62.

4. Peeling, "Public Life of Thomas McKean," 263.

5. Hogeland, *Declaration*, 24, 25.

6. Ibid.

7. Ibid., 31, 32.

8. Ibid., 45.
9. Ibid., 147.
10. Ibid., 93.
11. Ibid., 193.
12. Smith, *John Adams*, 256.
13. Beeman, *Our Lives, Our Fortunes*, 348.
14. Flower, *John Dickinson*, 151.
15. Raphael, *Founders*, 246.

## Six

1. Ferling, *John Adams*, 147. See also Brodsky, *Benjamin Rush*, 147.
2. Maier, *American Scripture*, 257n33.
3. Brodsky, *Benjamin Rush*, 147.
4. Fleming, *1776: Year of Illusions*, 276.
5. Hogeland, *Declaration*, 169.
6. Bowers, *Jefferson in Power*, 597.
7. Hogeland, *Declaration*, 172.
8. Bowen, *John Adams*, 577, 578.
9. Ibid., 173.
10. Sinclair and McArthur, *They Signed for Us*, see, generally, 8–10.
11. Beeman, *Our Lives, Our Fortunes*, 378.
12. McCullough, *John Adams*, 138.

## Seven

1. JA to AA, 7/3/1776, John Adams Papers, quoted in McCullough, *John Adams*, 130.
2. Chernow, *Washington*, 237.
3. McGuire, *Stop the Revolution*, 59.
4. De Bolla, *Fourth of July*, 12.
5. Ibid.
6. Rowe, *Thomas McKean*, 85.
7. TM to SM, 8/1/1776, Thomas McKean Papers, HSP.
8. McCullough, *1776*, 140.
9. TM to SM, 8/1/1776, Thomas McKean Papers, HSP.
10. Ibid., 193.
11. Ibid.
12. Isaacson, *Benjamin Franklin*, 313.
13. Brodsky, *Benjamin Rush*, 150.
14. Hogeland, *Declaration*, 176.
15. De Bolla, *Fourth of July*, 25.
16. Ibid., 26, 27.

17. Coleman, *Thomas McKean*, 180. John Dickinson served in the military and eventually signed the Declaration of Independence, but he was not present in Congress on July 4, 1776, and he did not support independence at that time. Oliver Wolcott also signed the Declaration of Independence and served in the military. However, Wolcott was not a member of Congress on July 4, 1776.
18. Ibid., 93.
19. McCullough, *1776*, 146, 147.
20. Coleman, *Thomas McKean*, 192, 193.
21. McCullough, *1776*, 151.
22. Rowe, *Thomas McKean*, 86.
23. Holland, *Delaware State Constitution*, 31.
24. Flower, *John Dickinson*, 127.
25. Hogeland, *Declaration*, 180, 181.
26. Flower, *John Dickinson*, 179.

## PART II

### Eight

1. Rowe, *Thomas McKean*, 101
2. Treese, *Storm Gathering*, 172.
3. Rowe, *Thomas McKean*, 95.
4. Ibid.
5. Ibid., 99.
6. Ibid.
7. Rowe, *Embattled Bench*, 237.
8. Ibid., 139
9. Ibid., 161.
10. Lunt, *Tales of the Delaware Bench*, 90.
11. Rowe, *Embattled Bench*, 139.
12. Rowe, *Thomas McKean*, 105.

### Nine

1. Jackson, *With the British Army in Philadelphia*, 11.
2. Johnston, *History of Cecil County*, 329.
3. Rowe, *Thomas McKean*, 146.
4. Ibid., 107.
5. Bodle, "Ghost of Clow," 21.
6. Flower, *John Dickinson*, 186.
7. Jackson, *With the British Army in Philadelphia*, 16.
8. Randall, *Benedict Arnold*, 371.

9. William Penn Association, Philadelphia, 204.

10. Flower, *John Dickinson*, 187.

11. TM to JA, Letters of the Delegates to Congress, vol. 14, UVA.

12. Lockhart, *Drillmaster of Valley Forge*, 65, 66.

13. Rowe, *Thomas McKean*, 107.

14. GW to TM, 10/10/1777, George Washington Papers, LOC.

## Ten

1. JA to AA, 9/29/1777, John Adams Papers, MHS.

2. Deconde, *History of American Foreign Policy*, 27.

3. TM to SM, 5/11/1778, Thomas McKean Papers, vol. VI, HSP.

4. Jackson, *With the British Army in Philadelphia*, 265.

5. Isaacson, *Benjamin Franklin*, 342.

6. Ibid., 267.

7. Randall, *Benedict Arnold*, 409.

8. Jackson, *With the British Army in Philadelphia*, see, generally, 265–279.

9. Adams, *Gouverneur Morris*, 120

10. Rowe, *Thomas McKean*, 157.

11. Smith, *John Adams*, 439.

12. TM to JA, 11/20/1779, Letters of the Delegates to Congress, vol. 14, UVA.

13. TM to RHL, 3/25/1780, Letters of the Delegates to Congress, vol. 14, UVA. Thomas Jefferson held a similar view during this period: "The members of Congress are no longer, generally speaking, men of worth or distinction." Quoted in Ellis, *The Quartet*, 81.

## Eleven

1. Rowe, *Embattled Bench*, 150, 151.

2. Granger, *Political Satire*, 134, 135.

3. Rowe, *Embattled Bench*, 162.

4. Burrows, *Forgotten Patriots*, 152.

5. Rowe, *Thomas McKean*, 148.

6. Burnett, *Continental Congress*, 369.

7. Rowe, *Thomas McKean*, 156.

## Twelve

1. Randall, *Benedict Arnold*, 454.

2. Ellis, *His Excellency*, 128.

3. TM to SM, 7/20/1779, Thomas McKean Papers, PHS.

4. TM to RHL, 3/25/1780, Letters of the Delegates to Congress, UVA.

5. Stinchcomb, *American Revolution*, 140.

6. Ellis, *His Excellency*, 128.

7. Ibid., 126.

8. Granger, *Political Satire*, 134, 135.

9. TM to JD, 12/25/1780, Letters of the Delegates to Congress, vol. 66, UVA.

10. Stahr, *John Jay*, 92, 93.

11. TM to SA, 7/8/81, Letters of the Delegates to Congress, vol. 17, UVA.

12. Ibid.

13. Burnett, *Continental Congress*, 503.

14. TB to TM, 8/29/1781, Thomas McKean Papers, HSP.

15. BF to TM, 11/5/1781, Benjamin Franklin Papers, vol. 13, Yale University.

16. JE to TM, 7/23/1781, Thomas McKean Papers, HSP.

17. Rowe, *Thomas McKean*, 164, 165.

18. Ibid., 166.

19. Burnett, *Continental Congress*, 514, 515.

## Thirteen

1. TM to GW, 7/14/1781, Thomas McKean Papers, HSP.

2. GW to TM, 7/21/1781, Thomas McKean Papers, HSP.

3. Ellis, *His Excellency*, 130.

4. GW to TM, 7/21/1781, Thomas McKean Papers, HSP.

5. General Arthur St. Clair to TM, 9/12/1781, Thomas McKean Papers, HSP.

6. TM to AL, 8/23/1781, Thomas McKean Papers, HSP.

7. Chernow, *Washington*, 416.

8. TM to GW, 7/28/1781, Thomas McKean Papers, HSP.

9. JJ to TM, 9/20/1881, reprinted in Commager and Morris, *Spirit of 'Seventy-Six*, 1252.

10. GW to TM, 7/21/1781, Thomas McKean Papers, HSP.

11. TM to GW, 7/26/1781, Thomas McKean Papers, HPS.

12. TM to GW, 8/3/1781, Thomas McKean Papers, HSP.

13. TM to GW, 8/3/1781, Thomas McKean Papers, HSP.

14. Ellis, *His Excellency*, 133.

15. Rappleye, *Robert Morris*, 257, 258.

16. Ibid.

17. Davis, *George Washington*, 396.

18. Ibid., 397.

19. Chernow, *Washington*, 410

20. Davis, *George Washington*, 396.

21. BF to TM, 11/5/1781, Benjamin Franklin Papers, vol. 23, Yale University.

22. Fleming, *Man Who Dared Lightning*, 427.

23. Rappleye, *Robert Morris*, 259.

24. Burnett, *Continental Congress*, 522, 523.

25. Chernow, *Washington*, 409.

26. TM to JR, 9/11/1781, Thomas McKean Papers, Box 2, PHS.

27. TM to GW, 8/15/1781, Letters of the Delegates to Congress, vol. 18, UVA.

28. GW to TM, 9/15/1781, George Washington Papers, no. 113, LOC.
29. Ibid.
30. Chernow, *Washington*, 413.
31. GW to TM, 10/6/1781, George Washington Papers, no. 125, LOC.
32. Chernow, *Washington*, 419, 420.
33. TM to GW, 10/18/1781, George Washington Papers, LOC.
34. Davis, *George Washington*, 440.
35. Ferling, *Leap in the Dark*, 240. Also, Fleming, *Perils of Peace*, see, generally, 20–29.
36. Davis, *George Washington*, 440.
37. TM to GW, 10/31/1781, reprinted in Lang, *Letters in American History*, 30.
38. Ibid.
39. GW to TM, 11/15/1781, George Washington Papers, no. 138, LOC.
40. TM to SA, 8/6/1782, Letters of the Delegates to Congress, vol. 19, UVA.
41. Ibid.
42. Ibid.
43. Levy, *Emergence of a Free Press*, 209.

## Fourteen

1. TM to JA, 11/18/1782, Letters of the Delegates to Congress, vol. 19, LOC.
2. Ellis, *The Quartet*, 60.
3. Stockdale and Holland, *Middle Temple Lawyers*, 135.
4. Rowe, *Embattled Bench*, 242.
5. *Republica v. de Longchamps*, 1 Dallas (PA) 111–113, 1784.
6. Rowe, *Embattled Bench*, 177, 178.
7. Flower, *John Dickinson*, 292.
8. Ibid.

## Fifteen

1. Treese, *Storm Gathering*, 189.
2. Ibid., 199.
3. Rowe, *Embattled Bench*, 168.
4. Coleman, *Thomas McKean*, 265.
5. Rowe, *Thomas McKean*, 414.
6. McKean and Sloan, *Great Decision*, xiv.
7. Rowe, *Embattled Bench*, 186.
8. TM to GW, 10/18/1781, George Washington Papers, LOC.
9. Handlin and Handlin, *Liberty in Expansion*, 14.
10. Rowe, *Thomas McKean*, 191–193.
11. Ibid., 190.
12. Ibid., 56.

13. GW to RM, 4/12/1788, George Washington Papers, LOC.

14. Rowe, *Thomas McKean*, 233.

15. Lightner, *Slavery and the Commerce Power*, 240.

16. McLaughlin, *To His Excellency Thomas Jefferson*, 134.

17. TM to SM, 7/12/1779, Letters of the Delegates to Congress, vol. 13, LOC.

18. TM to SM, 7/29/1779, Letters of the Delegates to Congress, vol. 13, LOC.

19. Norton, *Liberty's Daughters*, 181.

## Sixteen

1. TM to JA, 4/30/1787, Thomas McKean Papers, HSP.

2. McCullough, *John Adams*, 373–377.

3. TM to JA, 4/30/1787, Thomas McKean Papers, HSP.

4. Ibid.

5. Rowe, *Embattled Bench*, 268.

6. McCullough, *John Adams*, 379.

7. Ellis, *The Quartet*, 105.

8. Beeman, *Plain, Honest Men*, 20.

9. Meacham, *Thomas Jefferson*, 211.

10. Beeman, *Plain, Honest Men*, 68, 69.

11. *Pennsylvania Herald*, 7/5/1787, quoted in Stewart, *Summer of 1787*, 113.

12. Beeman, *Plain, Honest Men*, see, generally, 181–187 and 223–225.

13. Unger, *Mr. President*, 47.

14. Beeman, *Plain, Honest Men*, 376.

15. Ibid.

16. Ibid., 381.

17. Ibid., 373, 374.

18. Rowe, *Thomas McKean*, 244.

19. Rutland, *Ordeal of the Constitution*, 52, 53.

20. Stewart, *Summer of 1787*, 167.

21. Maier, *Ratification*, 278.

22. Rutland, *Ordeal of the Constitution*, 55.

23. Maier, *Ratification*, 205.

24. Hasking and Johnson, *History of the Supreme Court*, 328–329.

25. Ibid., 104, 105.

26. Beeman, *Plain Honest Men*, 383.

27. St. John, *Child of Fortune*, 86; Maier, *Ratification*, 274.

28. St. John, *Child of Fortune*, 86; Bowen, *Miracle at Philadelphia*, 276, 277.

29. St. John, *Child of Fortune*, 96.

30. Ibid.

31. Publicola, *Boston Gazette*, 11/28/1787, quoted in St. John, *Child of Fortune*, 96.

32. Ridner, *Town In-Between*, 151.

33. Ibid., 173
34. Hindle, *David Rittenhouse*, 8.
35. Cornell, *Other Founders*, 128.
36. Rutland, *Ordeal of the Constitution*, 267.
37. Cornell, *Other Founders*, 128–133; Levy, *Emergence of a Free Press*, 209–214.
38. Ibid.

## Seventeen

1. Ketchum, *James Madison*, 278.
2. TM to GW, 4/27/1789, Thomas McKean Papers, HSP.
3. Achenbach, *Grand Idea*, 102.
4. Ibid., 146–150.
5. McKean and Sloan, *Great Decision*, xv.
6. Wood, *Idea of America*, 290.
7. McKean and Sloan, *Great Decision*, xv.
8. Rowe, *Embattled Bench*, 292.
9. TM to William Murray, Earl of Mansfield, 10/30/1790, Thomas McKean Papers, HSP.
10. Rowe, *Thomas McKean*, 363.
11. Bradburn, *Citizenship Revolution*, 183.
12. Baltzell, *Puritan Boston*, 192.
13. Ibid.
14. Rowe, *Embattled Bench*, 234.

## PART III

## Eighteen

1. Wood, *Idea of America*, 252.
2. McCullough, *John Adams*, 397.
3. Ibid.
4. Meacham, *Thomas Jefferson*, 285.
5. Buel, *Securing the Revolution*, see, generally, 60–63.
6. Smith, *John Adams*, 875.
7. Malone, *Ordeal of Liberty*, 248.
8. Sharp, *American Politics in the Early Republic*, 122.

## Nineteen

1. TJ to Phillip Mazzai, 5/30/1795, Thomas Jefferson Papers, UVA. See also *The Papers of Thomas Jefferson*, vol. 28, 1 January 1794–29 February 1796, ed. John Catanzariti. Princeton: Princeton University Press, 2000: 368–371.

2. JA to AA, 12/27/1796, John Adams Papers, MHS.

3. Fleming, *Intimate Lives*, 371.

4. Washington, *Diary*, 265. George Washington to Timothy Pickering, 7/4/1796, George Washington Papers, LOC.

5. Rowe, *Thomas McKean*, 460n15.

6. Wharton, *Salons*, 154.

7. SM to Anne Payne, 6/6/1796, quoted in Ketchum, *James Madison*, 386.

8. Smith, *John Adams*, 901.

9. Ibid., 95, 96.

10. JA to AA, 12/27/1796, reprinted in Hogan and Taylor, *My Dearest Friend*, 422.

11. McCullough, *John Adams*, 471.

12. Sharp, *American Politics in the Early Republic*, 33.

13. Ibid.

14. Ferling, *Adams vs. Jefferson*, 55.

## Twenty

1. Cobbett, *Porcupine's Works*, 94.

2. Malone, *Ordeal of Liberty*, 324.

3. Winik, *Great Upheaval*, 242.

4. Sharp, *American Politics in the Early Republic*, 73.

5. Winik, *Great Upheaval*, 404.

6. TM to JA, 6/21/1812, Thomas McKean Papers, HSP.

7. Flower, *John Dickinson*, 279.

8. McKean and Sloan, *Great Decision*, 24.

9. TJ to Joseph Cabel Breckinridge, 12/11/1821, Thomas Jefferson Papers, UVA.

10. Cobbett, *Porcupine's Works*, 7/17/1797, 348.

11. Rowe, *Embattled Bench*, 227–229.

12. Ibid.

13. Durey, *With the Hammer of Truth*, 108.

14. Rosenfeld, *American Aurora*, 587, 588.

15. Ibid.

16. Wilson, *United Irishmen*, 52, 53.

17. Rosenfeld, *American Aurora*, 592.

18. Arbuckle, *Pennsylvania Speculator and Patriot*, 34.

## Twenty-One

1. Tolles, *George Logan*, 233, 234.

2. Wilson, *United Irishmen*, 263.

3. Ferguson, *Early Western Pennsylvania Politics*, 150, 151.

4. Larson, *Magnificent Catastrophe*, 57.

5. Ibid., 59.

6. Rosenfeld, *American Aurora*, 619.

7. Rowe, *Thomas McKean*, 310

8. Newman, *Fries's Rebellion*, 193.

9. Bradburn, *Citizenship Revolution*, 231.

10. Ferguson, *Early Western Pennsylvania Politics*, 149.

11. Rosenfeld, *American Aurora*, 682.

12. Ibid., 678.

13. Ibid., 709.

14. Larson, *Magnificent Catastrophe*, 61.

15. Allen, *Works of Fisher Ames*, Vol. II, 1320.

16. Larson, *Magnificent Catastrophe*, 61.

17. Rosenfeld, *American Aurora*, 722

18. Peeling, "Public Life of Thomas McKean," 320.

19. AA to William Shaw, quoted in Rosenfeld, *American Aurora*, 711n1872.

20. Larson, *Magnificent Catastrophe*, 62.

21. JM to TM, in Hamilton, *Writings of James Monroe*, vol. 3.

22. Governor's Papers, Pennsylvania Archives, Series 4, IV, 441, quoted in Peeling, *Public Life of Thomas McKean*, 523.

23. McKean and Sloan, *Great Decision*, 10.

## Twenty-Two

1. TM to JD, 6/23/1800, Thomas McKean Papers, vol. 3, HSP; Peeling, "Public Life of Thomas McKean," 324.

2. Wilson, *United Irishmen*, 1.

3. Durey, *With the Hammer of Truth*, 143.

4. Isaacson, *Benjamin Franklin*, 157.

5. TM to TJ, 3/7/1800, Thomas McKean Papers, HSP.

6. Ferguson, *Early Western Pennsylvania Politics*, 363.

7. Rosenfeld, *American Aurora*, 745.

8. TM to TJ, 3/7/1800, Thomas McKean Papers, HSP.

9. See Meacham, *Thomas Jefferson*, generally, 217–222; Burstein and Isenberg, *Jefferson and Madison*, 337–341.

10. Meacham, *Thomas Jefferson*, 367.

11. Ibid., 79.

12. Allen, *Works of Fisher Ames*, Vol. II, 1379.

13. Rowe, *Thomas McKean*, 316.

14. Isenberg, *Fallen Founder*, 120.

15. McKean and Sloan, *Great Decision*, 21.

16. Ibid.

17. Ibid.

18. Allen, *Works of Fisher Ames*, Vol. II, 1378.

19. TM to TJ, Thomas Jefferson Papers, vol. 32, Princeton University Press, 432–436.

20. Meacham, *Thomas Jefferson*, 332.

21. Dos Passos, *Men Who Made the Nation*, 434.

22. Tolles, *George Logan*, 217, 218.

23. Ferling, *Adams vs. Jefferson*, 188, 189.

24. Knudson, *Jefferson and the Press*, 48

25. Tolles, *George Logan*, 218.

26. Smith, *John Adams*, 1062.

27. Ackerman, *Failure of the Founding Fathers*, 107.

28. TM to TJ, 2/20/1801, Thomas Jefferson Papers, Princeton University Press.

29. TJ to TM, 3/9/1801, Thomas Jefferson Papers, Princeton University Press.

30. Ibid.

31. Cornell, *Well-Regulated Militia*, 100, 101.

32. Ambrose, *Undaunted Courage*, 60.

33. Ibid., 64.

34. Rowe, *Thomas McKean*, 321.

35. Malone, *Jefferson the President*, 97.

36. Ambrose, *Undaunted Courage*, 77.

37. Ibid.

38. Ibid.

39. TM to TJ, 7/21/1801, Thomas Jefferson Papers, quoted in Peeling, "Public Life of Thomas McKean," 327.

40. TJ to TM, in Thomas Jefferson Papers, vol. 8, Princeton University Press, 79, 80.

41. Ibid.

42. Ibid.

43. Peeling, "Public Life of Thomas McKean," 328.

44. Wilson, *United Irishmen*, 63.

45. Rowe, *Thomas McKean*, 346.

## Twenty-Three

1. Brandt, *James Madison*, 230, 231.

2. Ambrose and Brinkley, *Making of the Mississippi*, 14.

3. TJ to TM, 2/27/1804, Thomas Jefferson Papers, vol. 8, quoted in Malone, *Jefferson the President*, 72.

4. Malone, *Jefferson the President*, 357.

5. Brandt, *James Madison*, 231.

6. Malone, *Jefferson the President*, 71.

7. Peeling, "Public Life of Thomas McKean," 333.

8. Brown, *Benjamin Silliman*, 111.

9. Cunningham, *In Pursuit of Reason*, 270.

10. Ibid.

11. Ibid.

12. Ibid.

13. Brandt, *James Madison*, 312–320.

14. Ibid., 324, 325.

15. TM to Andrew Buchanan, 6/2/1804, quoted in Coleman, *Thomas McKean*, 3.

## Twenty-Four

1. Meacham, *Thomas Jefferson*, 406.

2. Bushey, "William Duane," 154.

3. Tolles, *George Logan*, 253–255.

4. Ibid.

5. Rowe, *Thomas McKean*, 383.

6. Ibid., 384.

7. Bushey, "William Duane," 143.

8. Peeling, "Public Life of Thomas McKean," 338, 339.

9. Ibid., 449.

10. Tolles, *George Logan*, 253–255.

11. Linklater, *Artist in Treason*, 231.

12. Tolles, *George Logan*, 246.

13. Linklater, *Artist in Treason*, 241.

14. Peeling, "Public Life of Thomas McKean," 342–343.

15. Ibid.

16. Anderson, *William Branch Giles*, 96.

17. Peeling, "Public Life of Thomas McKean," 342, 343.

18. Ibid.

19. Lomask, *Aaron Burr*, 106.

20. Peeling, "Public Life of Thomas McKean," 324.

21. Ibid., 345.

22. Rowe, *Thomas McKean*, 376.

23. Ibid., 447.

24. Ibid., 344.

25. Ibid., 350

26. Ibid., 352.

27. Ibid., 349, 350.

28. Ibid., 353.

## Epilogue

1. TJ to Joseph Binghurst, 2/24/1808, Writings, 249, Thomas Jefferson Papers, Princeton University Press.

2. JA to TM, 6/2/1812, Thomas McKean Papers, HSP.

3. TM to JA, 6/21/1812, Thomas McKean Papers, vol. X, HSP.
4. TM to JA 6/13/1812, Thomas McKean Papers, HSP.
5. TM to JA, 8/20/1813, Thomas McKean Papers, HSP.
6. TM to JA, 1/7/1814, Thomas McKean Papers, HSP.
7. Tolles, *George Logan*, 313.
8. Buchanan, *Genealogy of the McKean Family*, 111.
9. Ibid., 114.
10. TM to JA, 7/1/1815, Thomas McKean Papers, HSP.
11. Coleman, *Thomas McKean*, viii, 105.
12. TM to JA, 11/15/1813, Thomas McKean Papers, HSP.

# Bibliography

## Collections

Thomas McKean Papers, Historical Society of Pennsylvania, Philadelphia, Pennsylvania.

John Adams Papers, Massachusetts Historical Society, Boston, Massachusetts.

Letters of the Delegates to Congress, University of Virginia, Charlottesville, Virginia.

George Washington Papers, Library of Congress, Washington, DC.

Benjamin Franklin Papers, Yale University, New Haven, Connecticut.

Thomas Jefferson Papers, University of Virginia, Charlottesville, Virginia.

Thomas Jefferson Papers, Princeton University Press, Princeton, New Jersey.

## Articles and Legal Opinions

Bushey, Glenn L. "William Duane, Crusader for Judicial Reform." *Pennsylvania History* 5 (July 1938): 141–156.

Dallas' Reports, 1 Dallas (PA) 113–115 and *Respublica v. De Longchamps*, 1 US 111 (1784).

Futhey, J. Smith, and Gilbert Cope. *History of Chester County, Pennsylvania, with Genealogical and Biographical Sketches*. Philadelphia: Louis H. Everts, 1881.

Rowe, Gail S. "A Valuable Acquisition in Congress: Thomas McKean, Delegate from Delaware to the Continental Congress, 1774–1783." *Pennsylvania History: Quarterly Journal of the Pennsylvania Historical Society* 28 (July 7, 1971): 225–265.

## Books

Achenbach, Joel. *The Grand Idea: George Washington's Potomac and the Race to the West*. New York: Simon & Schuster, 2004.

Ackerman, Bruce. *The Failure of the Founding Fathers: Jefferson, Marshall, and the Rise of Presidential Democracy.* Cambridge, MA: Belknap Press of Harvard University, 2005.

Adams, Percy G., ed. *Crevecoeur's Eighteenth Century Travels in Pennsylvania and New York.* Lexington: University of Kentucky Press, 1961.

Adams, William H. *Gouverneur Morris: An Independent Life.* New Haven, CT: Yale University Press, 2003.

Allen, Thomas B. *Tories: Fighting for the King in America's First Civil War.* New York: HarperCollins, 2010, 2011.

Allen, W. B., ed. *Works of Fisher Ames.* Vol. I. Indianapolis: Liberty Classics, 1983.

———, ed. *Works of Fisher Ames.* Vol. II. Indianapolis: Liberty Classics, 1983.

Ambrose, Stephen E. *Undaunted Courage: Meriwether Lewis, Thomas Jefferson, and the Opening of the American West.* New York: Simon & Schuster, 1996.

Ambrose, Stephen, and Douglas Brinkley. *The Making of the Mississippi and the Making of a Nation.* Washington, DC: National Geographic, 2002.

Anderson, Dice R. *William Branch Giles.* Menasha, WI: George Banta Publishing, 1915.

Arbuckle, Robert D. *Pennsylvania Speculator and Patriot—the Entrepreneurial John Nicholson, 1757–1800.* University Park: Pennsylvania State University Press, 1975.

Baltzell, E. Digby. *Puritan Boston and Quaker Philadelphia.* New York: The Free Press, 1979.

Beeman, Richard R. *Our Lives, Our Fortunes and Sacred Honor: The Forging of American Independence 1774–1776.* New York: Basic Books, 2013.

———. *Plain, Honest Men: The Making of the American Constitution.* New York: Random House, 2010.

Berstein, R. B. *Thomas Jefferson.* New York: Oxford University Press, 2004.

Bobrick, Benson. *Angel in the Whirlwind: The Triumph of the American Revolution.* New York: Simon & Schuster, 1997.

Bodle, Wayne. "'The Ghost of Clow': Loyalist Insurgency in the Delmarva Peninsula." In *The Other Loyalists: Ordinary People, Royalism, and the Revolution in the Middle Colonies, 1763–1787,* ed. Joseph S. Tiedemann, Eugene R Fingerhut, and Robert W. Venables, 19–44. Albany: State University of New York Press, 2009.

Bordewich, Fergus M. *Washington: The Makings of the American Capital.* New York: Amistad, 2008.

Bowen, Catherine Drinker. *John Adams and the American Revolution.* New York: Grosset and Dunlap, 1949.

———. *Miracle at Philadelphia: The Story of the Constitutional Convention May to September 1787.* Boston: Little, Brown, 1966.

———. *The Most Dangerous Man in America: Scenes from the Life of Benjamin Franklin.* Boston: Little, Brown, 1974.

Bowers, Claude G. *Jefferson in Power*. Boston: Houghton Mifflin, 1967.

Bradburn, Douglas. *The Citizenship Revolution: Politics and the Creation of the American Union 1774–1804*. Charlottesville: University of Virginia Press, 2009.

Brands, H. W. *The First American: The Life and Times of Benjamin Franklin*. New York: Doubleday, 2000.

Brandt, Irving. *James Madison: Secretary of State, 1800–1809*. Indianapolis: Bobbs-Merrill, 1953.

Brodsky, Alyn. *Benjamin Rush: Patriot and Physician*. New York: St. Martin's Press, 2004.

Brookhiser, Richard. *Alexander Hamilton, American*. New York: Simon & Schuster, 1999.

Brown, Chandos Michael. *Benjamin Silliman: A Life in the Young Republic*. Princeton, NJ: Princeton University Press, 1989.

Buchanan, Roberdeau. *Genealogy of the McKean Family of Pennsylvania*. Lancaster, PA: Inquire Printing Company, 1890.

Buel, Richard, Jr. *Securing the Revolution: Ideology in American Politics, 1789–1815*. Ithaca, NY: Cornell University Press, 1972.

Burnaby, Andrew. *Travels Through North America*. New York: A. Wessels Company, 1904.

Burnett, Edmund Cody. *The Continental Congress*. New York: Macmillan, 1941.

Burrows, Edwin G. *Forgotten Patriots: The Untold Story of American Prisoners During the Revolutionary War*. New York: Basic Books, 2008.

Burstein, Andrew. *Jefferson's Secrets: Death and Desire at Monticello*. New York: Basic Books, 2005.

Burstein, Andrew, and Nancy Isenberg. *Madison and Jefferson*. New York: Random House, 2010.

Burt, Nathaniel. *The Perennial Philadelphians: The Anatomy of American Aristocracy*. Boston: Little, Brown, 1963.

Butler, Jon. *Becoming America: The Revolution Before 1776*. Cambridge, MA: Harvard University Press, 2000.

Cerami, Charles: *Young Patriots: The Remarkable Story of Two Men, Their Impossible Plan and the Revolution That Created the Constitution*. Naperville, IL: Sourcebooks, 2005.

Chernow, Ron. *Alexander Hamilton*. New York: Penguin Press, 2004.

———. *Washington: A Life*. New York: Penguin Press, 2010.

Clarfield, Gerard H. *Timothy Pickering and American Diplomacy, 1795–1800*. Columbia: University of Missouri, 1969.

Cobbett, William. *Porcupine's Works: Selections from Porcupine's Gazette*. 12 volumes. London: Crown and Mitre, 1801.

Coleman, John M. *Thomas McKean: Forgotten Leader of the Revolution*. Rockaway, NJ: American Faculty Press, 1975.

Commager, Henry Steele, and Richard B. Morris. *The Spirit of 'Seventy-Six: The Story of the American Revolution as Told by Participants*. New York: Harper and Row, 1958.

Cornell, Saul. *The Other Founders: Anti-Federalism and the Dissenting Tradition in America, 1788–1828*. Chapel Hill: University of North Carolina Press, 1999.

———. *A Well-Regulated Militia: The Founding Fathers and the Origins of Gun Control in America*. New York: Oxford University Press, 2006.

Cresson, W. P. *James Monroe*. Chapel Hill: University of North Carolina Press, 1946.

Cunningham, Noble E., Jr. *In Pursuit of Reason: The Life of Thomas Jefferson*. New York: Ballantine Books, 1988.

D'Agnese, Joseph, and Denise Kiernan. *Signing Their Rights Away: The Fame and Misfortune of the Men Who Signed the United States Constitution*. Philadelphia: Quirk Books, 2011.

Davis, Burke. *The Campaign That Won America: The Story of Yorktown*. New York: Dial Press, 1970.

———. *George Washington and the American Revolution*. New York: Random House, 1975.

De Bolla, Peter. *The Fourth of July—and the Founding of America*. New York: MJF Books, 2007.

De Conde, Alexander. *A History of American Foreign Policy: Growth to World Power, 1700–1914*. New York: Charles Scribner's Sons, 1963.

Dos Passos, John. *The Men Who Made the Nation*. Garden City, NY: Doubleday, 1957.

Dunaway, Wayland F. *History of Pennsylvania*. New York: Prentice Hall, 1944.

Durey, Michael. *With the Hammer of Truth: James Thomson Callender and America's Early National Heroes*. Charlottesville: University of Virginia Press, 1990.

Ellis, Joseph J. *Founding Brothers: The Revolutionary Generation*. New York: Alfred A. Knopf, 2000.

———. *His Excellency: George Washington*. New York: Alfred A. Knopf, 2004.

———. *Passionate Sage: The Character and Legacy of John Adams*. New York: W. W. Norton, 1993.

———. *The Quartet: Orchestrating the Second American Revolution, 1783–1789*. New York: Alfred A. Knopf, 2015.

Emerson, Everett. *American Literature, 1764–1789 The Revolutionary Years*. Madison: University of Wisconsin Press, 1976*lvania Politics*. Pittsburgh, PA: University of Pittsburgh Press, 1938.

Ferling, John. *Adams vs. Jefferson: The Tumultuous Election of 1800*. New York: Oxford University Press, 2004.

———. *Independence: The Struggle to Set America Free*. New York: Bloomsbury Press, 2011.

———. *John Adams: A Life*. New York: Oxford University Press, 2010.

————. *A Leap in the Dark: The Struggle to Create the American Republic*. New York: Oxford University Press, 2003.

Fleming, Thomas. *Duel: Alexander Hamilton, Aaron Burr, and the Future of America*. New York: Basic Books, 1999.

————. *The Intimate Lives of the Founding Fathers*. New York: HarperCollins, 2009.

————. *The Man from Monticello: An Intimate Life of Thomas Jefferson*. New York: William Morrow, 1969.

————. *The Man Who Dared Lightning: A New Look at Benjamin Franklin*. New York: William Morrow, 1971.

————. *The Perils of Peace: America's Struggle for Survival After Yorktown*. New York: HarperCollins, 2007.

————. *1776: Year of Illusions*. New York: W. W. Norton, 1975.

————. *Washington's Secret War: The Hidden History of Valley Forge*. New York: HarperCollins, 2005.

Flower, Milton E. *John Dickinson: Conservative Revolutionary*. Charlottesville: University of Virginia Press, 1983.

Fowler, William M., Jr. *American Crisis: George Washington and the Dangerous Two Years After Yorktown*. New York: Walker and Company, 2011.

Freeman, Douglas Southall (abridgment by Richard Harwell). *Washington*. New York: Charles Scribner's Sons, 1968.

Gordon-Reed, Annette. *The Hemingses of Monticello: An American Family*. New York: W. W. Norton, 2008.

Granger, Bruce Ingham. *Political Satire in the American Revolution, 1763–1783*. Ithaca, NY: Cornell University Press, 1960.

Hamilton, Stanislaus M. *The Writings of James Monroe: Including a Collection of Public and Private Papers and Correspondence*. Vols. I–VII. New York: G. P. Putnam, 1898.

Handlin, Oscar, and Lilian Handlin. *Liberty in Expansion, 1760–1850*. New York: Harper & Row, 1989.

Harley, Lewis R. *The Life of Charles Thomson*. Philadelphia: George W. Jacobs, 1900.

Haskins, George L., and Herbert A. Johnson. *History of the Supreme Court of the United States*. Cambridge: Cambridge University Press, 2002.

Hazelton, John H. *The Declaration of Independence: Its History*. Cambridge, MA: Dodd, Mead, 1906.

Herman, Arthur. *How the Scots Invented the Modern World*. New York: MJF Books, 2001.

Hindle, Brooke. *David Rittenhouse*. Princeton, NJ: Princeton University Press, 1964.

Hofstadter, Richard. *America at 1750: A Social Portrait*. New York: Random House, 1971.

Hogan, Margaret A., and James C. Taylor, eds. *My Dearest Friend: Letters of John and Abigail Adams*. Cambridge, MA: Belknap Press of Harvard University Press, 2007.

Hogeland. William. *Declaration: The Nine Tumultuous Weeks When America Became Independent May 1–July 4, 1776.* New York: Simon & Schuster, 2010.

Holland, Randy J. *The Delaware State Constitution.* New York: Oxford University Press, 2011.

Hopkinson, Francis. *The Miscellaneous Essays and Occasional Writings of Francis Hopkinson, Esq: Judgments in the Admiralty of Pennsylvania.* Charleston, SC: Nabu Press, 2014.

Ireland, Owen S. *Religion, Ethnicity, and Politics: Ratifying the Constitution in Pennsylvania.* University Park: Pennsylvania State University Press, 1995.

Isaacson, Walter. *Benjamin Franklin: An American Life.* New York: Simon & Schuster, 2003.

Isenberg, Nancy. *Fallen Founder: The Life of Aaron Burr.* New York: Viking, 2007.

Jackson, John W. *With the British Army in Philadelphia 1777–1778.* San Rafael, CA: Presidio Press, 1979.

Jay, John. *The Making of a Revolutionary: Unpublished Papers, 1745–1780.* New York: Harper & Row, 1975.

Jenkinson, Clay S. *The Character of Meriwether Lewis: Explorer in Wilderness.* Washburn, ND: Dakota Institute Press, 2011.

Johnston, George. *History of Cecil County, Maryland.* Elkton, MD: George Johnston, 1881.

Johnston, Henry R. *The Campaign of 1776 Around New York and Brooklyn.* Cranbury, NJ: Scholar's Bookshelf, 2005.

Kelley, Joseph J., Jr. *Pennsylvania: The Colonial Years 1681–1776.* Garden City, NY: Doubleday, 1980.

Ketchum, Ralph. *James Madison.* Charlottesville: University of Virginia Press, 1990.

Ketchum, Richard M. *Divided Loyalties: How the American Revolution Came to New York.* New York: Henry Holt, 2002.

Knudson, Jerry W. *Jefferson and the Press.* Columbia: University of South Carolina Press, 2006.

Kukla, Jon. *Mr. Jefferson's Women.* New York: Alfred A. Knopf, 2007.

Lang, H. Jack, ed. *Letters in American History: Words to Remember.* New York: Harmony Books, 1982.

Langguth, A. J. *Patriots: The Men Who Started the American Revolution.* New York: Simon & Schuster, 1988.

Larson, Edward J. *A Magnificent Catastrophe.* New York: Free Press, 2007.

Levy, Leonard W. *Emergence of a Free Press.* New York: Oxford University Press, 1985.

———. *Original Intent and the Framers' Constitution.* New York: Macmillan, 1988.

Lightner, David L. *Slavery and the Commerce Power: How the Struggle Against the Interstate Slave Trade Led to the Civil War.* New Haven, CT: Yale University Press, 2006.

Linklater, Andro. *An Artist in Treason: The Extraordinary Double Life of General James Wilkinson*. New York: Walker, 2009.

Lockhart, Paul. *The Drillmaster of Valley Forge: The Baron de Steuben and the Making of the American Army*. New York: HarperCollins, 2008.

Lomask, Milton. *Aaron Burr: The Conspiracy and Years of Exile, 1805–1836*. New York: Farrar, Straus and Giroux, 1982.

Lunt, Dudley C. *Tales of the Delaware Bench and Bar*. Wilmington: University of Delaware Press, 1963.

Maier, Pauline. *American Scripture: Making the Declaration of Independence*. New York: Alfred A. Knopf, 1997.

———. *Ratification: The People Debate the Constitution, 1787–1788*. New York: Simon & Schuster, 2010.

Malone, Dumas. *Jefferson and the Ordeal of Liberty*. Boston: Little, Brown, 1962.

———. *Jefferson the President: First Term, 1801–1805*. Boston: Little, Brown, 1970.

Mapp, Alf J., Jr. *Thomas Jefferson: Passionate Pilgrim*. Lanham, MD: Madison Books, 1991.

Mayo, Bernard, ed. *Jefferson Himself*. Charlottesville: University of Virginia Press, 1942.

McCullough, David. *John Adams*. New York: Simon & Schuster, 2001.

———. *1776*. New York: Simon & Schuster, 2005.

McDonald, Forest, ed. *Empire and Nation: Letters, John Dickinson and Richard Henry Lee*. Englewood Cliffs, NJ: Prentice Hall, 1962.

McGuire, Thomas J. *Stop the Revolution: America in the Summer of Independence and the Conference for Peace*. Mechanicsburg, PA: Stackpole Press, 2011.

McKean, David, and Cliff Sloan. *The Great Decision: Jefferson, Adams, Marshall, and the Battle for the Supreme Court*. New York: PublicAffairs, 2009.

McLaughlin, Jack. *To His Excellency Thomas Jefferson: Letters to a President*. New York: W. W. Norton, 1991.

Meacham, Jon. *Thomas Jefferson: The Art of Power*. New York: Random House, 2012.

Melton, Buckner F., Jr. *Aaron Burr: Conspiracy to Treason*. New York: John Wiley, 2002.

Miller, John C. *Origins of the American Revolution*. Boston: Little, Brown, 1943.

Morgan, Edmund S., and Helen M. Morgan. *The Stamp Act Crisis: Prologue to Revolution*. Chapel Hill: University of North Carolina Press, 1953.

Munroe, John A. *History of Delaware*. Newark: University of Delaware Press, 1979.

Murchison, William. *The Cost of Liberty: The Life of John Dickinson*. Wilmington, DE: ISI Books, 2013.

Newman, Paul Douglas. *Fries's Rebellion: The Enduring Struggle for the American Revolution*. Philadelphia: University of Pennsylvania Press, 2004.

Norton, Mary Beth. *Liberty's Daughters*. Ithaca, NY: Cornell University Press, 1996.

Peeling, James Hedley. "The Public Life of Thomas McKean." PhD diss., University of Chicago, 1929.

Philbrick, Nathanial. *Bunker Hill: A City, a Siege, a Revolution*. New York: Viking, 2013.

Phillips, Kevin. *1775: A Good Year for Revolution*. New York: Viking, 2012.

Rakove, Jack N. *Original Meanings: Politics and Ideas in the Making of the Constitution*. New York: Alfred A. Knopf, 1996.

Randall, Willard Sterne. *Benedict Arnold: Patriot and Traitor*. New York: William Morrow, 1990.

———. *Thomas Jefferson: A Life*. New York: Henry Holt, 1993.

Raphael, Ray. *Mr. President: How and Why the Founders Chose a President*. New York: Alfred A. Knopf, 2012.

———. *The First American Revolution: Before Lexington and Concord*. New York: New Press, 2002.

———. *Founders: The People Who Brought You a Nation*. New York: New Press, 2009.

Rappleye, Charles. *Robert Morris: Financier of the American Revolution*. New York: Simon & Schuster, 2010.

Ridner, Judith. *A Town In-Between: Carlisle, Pennsylvania and the Early Mid-Atlantic Interior*. Philadelphia: University of Pennsylvania Press, 2010.

Roberts, Cokie. *Ladies of Liberty: The Women Who Shaped Our Nation*. New York: HarperCollins, 2008.

Rosenfeld, Richard N. *American Aurora: A Democratic-Republican Returns*. New York: St. Martin's Press, 1997.

Rossiter, Clinton. *1787: The Grand Convention*. New York: MacMillan, 1966.

Rowe, Gail S. *Embattled Bench*. Newark: University of Delaware Press, 1994.

———. *Thomas McKean: The Shaping of an American Republicanism*. Boulder: Colorado Associated University Press, 1978.

Rutland, Robert Allen. *The Ordeal of the Constitution: The Antifederalists and the Ratification Struggle of 1787–1788*. Boston: Northeastern University Press, 1983.

Ryden, George Herbert, ed. *Letters to and from Caesar Rodney, 1756–1784*. Philadelphia: Historical Society of Delaware, 1933.

Schlesinger, Arthur M. *The Birth of the Nation: A Portrait of the American People on the Eve of Independence*. New York: Alfred A. Knopf, 1976.

———. *Prelude to Independence: The Newspaper War on Britain, 1764–1776*. New York: Alfred A. Knopf, 1958.

Schouler, James. *Americans of 1776: Daily Life in Revolutionary America*. Bowie, MD: Heritage Press, 1990.

Sehat, David. *The Jefferson Rule: How the Founding Fathers Became Infallible and Our Politics Inflexible*. New York: Simon & Schuster, 2015.

Shankman, Andrew. *Crucible of American Democracy: The Struggle to Fuse Egalitarianism and Capitalism in Jeffersonian Pennsylvania*. Lawrence: University of Kansas Press, 2004.

Sharp, James Roger. *American Politics in the Early Republic: The New Nation in Crisis*. New Haven, CT: Yale University Press, 1993.

Simmons, R. C. *The American Colonies: From Settlement to Independence*. New York: W. W. Norton, 1976.

Sinclair, Merle, and Annabel MacArthur. *They Signed for Us*. New York: Duell, Sloan and Pearce, 1957.

Smith, Page. *John Adams*. Vols. I and II. Garden City, NY: Doubleday, 1962.

Smith, Robert W. *Amid a Warring World: American Foreign Relations, 1775–1815*. Washington, DC: Potomac Books, 2012.

Stahr, Walter. *John Jay*. New York: Hambledon and London, 2005.

Stewart, David O. *The Summer of 1787: The Men Who Invented the Constitution*. New York: Simon & Schuster, 2007.

Stinchcombe, William C. *The American Revolution and the French Alliance*. Syracuse, NY: Syracuse University Press, 1969.

St. John, Jeffery. *A Child of Fortune: A Correspondent's Report on the Ratification of the US Constitution and the Battle for a Bill of Rights*. Ottawa, IL: Jameson Books, 1990.

Stockdale, Eric, and Randy J. Holland. *Middle Temple Lawyers and the American Revolution*. Eagan, MN: Thomson West, 2007.

Tiedemann, Joseph S., Eugene R. Fingerhut, and Robert W. Venables, eds. *The Other Loyalists: Ordinary People, Royalism, and the Revolution in the Middle Colonies, 1763–1787*. Albany: State University of New York Press, 2009.

Tolles, Frederick B. *George Logan of Philadelphia*. New York: Oxford University Press, 1953.

Treese, Lorett. *The Storm Gathering: The Penn Family and the American Revolution*. Mechanicsburg, PA: Stackpole Books, 2002.

Unger, Harlow Giles. *Lion of Liberty: Patrick Henry and the Call to a New Nation*. Boston: De Capo Press, 2010.

———. *Mr. President: George Washington and the Making of the Nation's Highest Office*. Cambridge, MA: Da Capo Press, 2013.

Weigley, Russell F., ed. *Philadelphia: A 300-Year History*. New York: W. W. Norton, 1982.

Weisberger, Bernard A. *America Afire: Jefferson, Adams and the Revolutionary Election of 1800*. New York: William Morrow, 2000.

Wharton, Ann Hollingsworth. *Salons, Colonial and Republican*. New York: J. P. Lippincott, 1900.

Wheelan, Joseph. *Jefferson's Vendetta: The Pursuit of Aaron Burr and the Judiciary*. New York: Carroll & Graff, 2005.

Wills, Gary. *Explaining America: The Federalist*. Garden City, NY: Doubleday, 1981.
———. *Inventing America: Jefferson's Declaration of Independence*. Garden City, NY: Doubleday, 1978.
Wilson, David A. *United Irishmen, United States: Immigrant Radicals in the Early Republic*. Ithaca, NY: Cornell University Press, 1998.
Winik, Jay. *The Great Upheaval: America and the Birth of the Modern World, 1788–1800*. New York: HarperCollins, 2007.
Wood, Gordon S. *The Americanization of Benjamin Franklin*. New York: Penguin Press, 2004.
———. *Empire of Liberty: A History of the Early Republic, 1789–1815*. New York: Oxford University Press, 2009.
———. *The Idea of America: Reflections in the Birth of the United States*. New York: Penguin, 2011.

# Index

KAYE MCKEAN

DAVID McKEAN is a senior official at the US Department of State. He is the author of three previous books on American political history and is a direct descendant of Thomas McKean.

PublicAffairs is a publishing house founded in 1997. It is a tribute to the standards, values, and flair of three persons who have served as mentors to countless reporters, writers, editors, and book people of all kinds, including me.

I. F. Stone, proprietor of *I. F. Stone's Weekly*, combined a commitment to the First Amendment with entrepreneurial zeal and reporting skill and became one of the great independent journalists in American history. At the age of eighty, Izzy published *The Trial of Socrates*, which was a national bestseller. He wrote the book after he taught himself ancient Greek.

Benjamin C. Bradlee was for nearly thirty years the charismatic editorial leader of *The Washington Post*. It was Ben who gave the *Post* the range and courage to pursue such historic issues as Watergate. He supported his reporters with a tenacity that made them fearless and it is no accident that so many became authors of influential, best-selling books.

Robert L. Bernstein, the chief executive of Random House for more than a quarter century, guided one of the nation's premier publishing houses. Bob was personally responsible for many books of political dissent and argument that challenged tyranny around the globe. He is also the founder and longtime chair of Human Rights Watch, one of the most respected human rights organizations in the world.

·     ·     ·

For fifty years, the banner of Public Affairs Press was carried by its owner Morris B. Schnapper, who published Gandhi, Nasser, Toynbee, Truman, and about 1,500 other authors. In 1983, Schnapper was described by *The Washington Post* as "a redoubtable gadfly." His legacy will endure in the books to come.

Peter Osnos, *Founder and Editor-at-Large*